Current Issues in U.S. Environmental Policy

Current Issues in U.S. Environmental Policy

Paul R. Portney, Editor

A. Myrick Freeman III

Robert H. Haveman

Henry M. Peskin

Eugene P. Seskin

V. Kerry Smith

57342

Published for Resources for the Future
By The Johns Hopkins University Press
Baltimore and London

Library of Congress Card Number 78-4328
ISBN 0-8018-2118-5
ISBN 8018-2119-3 paper

Library of Congress Cataloging in Publication Data
will be found on the last printed page of this book

Contents

Tables

Contents

Figures

Foreword

A significant social development of the past decade has been the general realization that important damage may be done to the environment if the economy is permitted to operate in an unfettered way. While certain environmental insults may be corrected automatically over time, other damaging effects will never be avoided in the absence of specific policies and programs for this purpose. This certainty of "market failure" has long been known in principle by economists, yet modern technology and mass consumption have made many of these undesirable side effects visible or otherwise known to many people in direct and often dramatic fashion.

The political system has reflected this general realization by the passage of much environmental legislation, especially since 1970. Most of this legislation has been designed to regulate or constrain the economy so that production and consumption will fall within certain environmentally acceptable limits. We have been generally unwilling or unable to build into the incentive system rewards and penalties which would have the economy automatically "produce" the kind of environment desired.

It is appropriate that economists concern themselves with this general group of problems. Just as the awareness of environmental problems becomes more general, it is now also becoming known more generally that environmental improvement requires more resources and greater sacrifices. Thus an economic problem exists whether lawmakers decide to protect the environment through direct regulation or whether they choose to modify the economic incentives that affect the behavior of millions of decision makers in the economic system.

Resources for the Future pioneered research on problems of the environment. Many specific and technical investigations have been undertaken, and RFF publications have reported the results of these studies. This procedure has resulted in a substantial literature, and there are several persons at RFF with extensive knowledge about many facets of environmental policy.

This book breaks somewhat with that tradition. It is a frank and direct statement on a wide range of environmental and pollution policy issues. It is not primarily a report of research results from specific projects, although some original research results are presented. Rather, it is an attempt to interpret existing research and apply knowledge to contemporary policy problems. While we intend to continue RFF's tradition of excellence in basic research, we also wish to emphasize the usefulness of such research and apply it wherever possible. As Paul R. Portney notes in chapter 1, this book is directed at legislators, other policy makers, students, and informed citizens.

The origin of the book was with the authors themselves. They developed the concept of the book, prepared an outline, and proposed the effort to the RFF administration. We are pleased that the Rockefeller and Mellon foundations were willing to share with the Ford Foundation the financial cost of this undertaking at RFF.

Emery N. Castle
Vice President
Resources for the Future

March 1978

Acknowledgments

In all cases the authors benefited from the criticisms of the other contributors to this volume. In addition, the following members of the RFF administrative and research staff gave helpful suggestions and assistance: Daniel J. Basta, Emery N. Castle, James A. Embersit, Leonard Gianessi, Raymond Kopp, Herbert C. Morton, Talbot Page, Clifford S. Russell, and Glen Weinberg. The authors would also like to thank the following for helpful comments and discussion on earlier drafts: Edward Berger, J. Clarence Davies III, David Donniger, Herbert Kaufman, John Mendeloff, Robert Miki, William Schulze, Joseph Seneca, Jon Sonstelie, and William Sullivan. The computer programming assistance of Louanne Sawyer and the competent typing of Linda Perrotta and Diana Tasciotti are gratefully acknowledged. Chapter 5 is based largely on research conducted for the National Bureau of Economic Research by its author, and Leonard Gianessi, and Edward Wolff under National Science Foundation grant SOC 74-21391.

Authors

Paul R. Portney is a Senior Research Associate in the Quality of the Environment Division of RFF and Visiting Professor at the Graduate School of Public Policy, University of California, Berkeley. He is the editor of *Economic Issues in Metropolitan Growth* (Baltimore, Md., Johns Hopkins University Press for Resources for the Future, 1976).

A. Myrick Freeman is a Fellow in the Quality of the Environment Division of RFF and Professor of Economics at Bowdoin College. He co-edited *Pollution, Resources, and the Environment* (New York, W. W. Norton, 1973).

Robert H. Haveman, formerly a Research Associate at RFF, is Professor of Economics and a Fellow of the Institute for Research on Poverty at the University of Wisconsin. He is coauthor of *Economics of Environmental Policy* (New York, Wiley, 1973).

Henry M. Peskin is a Fellow in the Quality of the Environment Division of RFF and coauthor of *Cost–Benefit Analysis and Water Pollution Policy* (Washington, D.C., The Urban Institute, 1975).

Eugene P. Seskin is a Senior Research Associate in the Quality of the Environment Division of RFF and coauthor of *Air Pollution and Human Health* (Baltimore, Md., Johns Hopkins University Press for Resources for the Future, 1977).

V. Kerry Smith, a Fellow in the Quality of the Environment Division of RFF, is the author of *Economic Consequences of Air Pollution* (Cambridge, Mass., Ballinger, 1976).

xv

CHAPTER 1

Introduction

PAUL R. PORTNEY

IN SPITE OF the volume and scope of environmental legislation passed in the 1970s, certain environmental problems seem to persist or even grow worse while new ones continue to appear. This is the source of considerable dissatisfaction with existing environmental legislation. Equally perplexing is the slow pace at which certain improvements occur. And most serious, perhaps, is the recognition that both our successes and our failures in the area of environmental quality improvement are extremely expensive—perhaps excessively so. For example, in the 1976 report of the Council on Environmental Quality, it is estimated that the nation will spend more than $250 billion between 1975 and 1984 to meet the requirements of the major federal environmental laws. By 1977, voters were more aware than ever before that these costs mean higher taxes and product prices or perhaps lower wages than would be the case in the absence of environmental protection.

Because improvements to environmental quality have proved to be elusive, slow to occur, or much more expensive to achieve than we would prefer, and because the environment will continue to loom large as a national concern, this is an appropriate time to review the status of major environmental legislation, to discuss several key issues surrounding it, and to suggest ways in which the legislation might be improved.

This review of U.S. environmental policy is appropriate for another reason. During the campaign that preceded President Jimmy Carter's election in 1976, he repeatedly emphasized his desire to reorganize the government and deregulate the private sector where at all possible. These words gained some force when he chose as the chairman of his Council of Economic Advisors, Charles Schultze, whose Godkin Lectures at Harvard

1

University had centered around the use of government-created economic incentives to guide the private sector in serving the public interest.[1] In these lectures, as in his book with Allen Kneese,[2] Schultze frequently used the environment to exemplify areas where economic incentives might supplant the more familiar regulation-and-enforcement approach. If this administration does prove to be more sympathetic to the economic incentives approach to environmental quality improvement, there is good reason to review past and current thinking in this area.

Moreover, the very nature of our environmental problems seems to be changing. This is evidenced by the Environmental Protection Agency's (EPA's) recent and somewhat dramatic shift in emphasis. At a news briefing on its fiscal year 1979 budget, EPA made it clear that it will begin to focus much more on the protection of public health and less on water resources, conservation, and land management.[3] In fact, there is some speculation that a possible result of the Carter administration's governmental reorganization will be a Department of Environment and Public Health, thus elevating EPA to cabinet level and formalizing its shift in emphasis.

In addition, the energy "crisis" is upon us. This will necessitate hard thinking about the costs—both financial and environmental—of such strategies as switching from oil and gas back to coal or onward to nuclear and solar energy. A review of current environmental policy should provide us with a list of "do's and don'ts" to be adhered to when making new policy in anticipation of increased energy development.

This book provides such a review. It is written by economists; for that reason it views in a special way our air and water pollution policies and those regulating exposures to toxic substances. But since this book is directed at legislators and other policy makers, at students and informed citizens, it is important to understand that the economist's view is not necessarily idiosyncratic but rather commonsensical. When we talk of benefit–cost analysis in the following chapters, for example, we mean no more than that society ought to weigh the good and bad effects of various environmental policies against one another before settling on one. When we urge that resources be allocated efficiently, we are only suggesting that

---

[1] See Charles L. Schultze, *The Public Use of Private Interest* (Washington, D.C., Brookings Institution, 1977).

[2] Allen V. Kneese and Charles L. Schultze, *Pollution, Prices, and Public Policy* (Washington, D.C., Brookings Institution, 1975) p. 2.

[3] Dick Kirschten, "EPA: A Winner in the Annual Budget Battles," *National Journal*, January 28, 1978, pp. 140–141.

society spend its dollars in such a way that it obtains the most for those dollars.

We try always to keep in mind that the choice of policies will, and indeed should, be guided as much by the *distribution* of benefits and costs as by their respective totals. In fact, two of the chapters address almost exclusively the distributional consequences of alternative environmental policies—that is, their "fairness" or lack of same. We also engage in occasional speculation about the possible political reasons that certain policies have gained favor while other, ostensibly more attractive policies, have foundered. In short, we have strived to shed the blinders that have often prevented economists from doing good policy analysis.

The book may be thought of as in two parts. The first consists of chapters 2 through 4, in which are discussed and analyzed existing federal policies regulating air and water pollution and exposures to toxic substances. Chapters 5 and 6 are conceptually distinct from their predecessors; they deal with (1) the distribution of benefits and costs and (2) with environmental policies and the level and composition of macroeconomic activity.

In chapter 2, A. Myrick Freeman discusses what many consider to be the backbone of U.S. environmental policy—the Federal Water Pollution Control Act Amendments of 1972 and those portions of the Clean Air Act of 1970 that deal with air pollution from stationary sources.[4] The recent amendments to the Clean Air Act, as well as the recommendation of the National Commission on Water Quality that our federal water pollution policy be rethought, make such a review both timely and important.

Freeman begins by reviewing the current status of legislation and the way in which it evolved. After discussing the need for goals against which to judge various policies, as well as the general approaches that can be taken to achieve specific goals, he points out one problem in the design of government regulatory policies which has received little attention. That is the potential conflict between the desirability of having clear and specific statements of objectives from Congress and the need of the administrative agencies for flexibility and discretion in dealing with individual cases and changing circumstances.

Freeman then carefully discusses the major components of our air and water pollution policies. He is critical of the congressionally mandated

---

[4] This is in contrast to air pollution from mobile sources such as the automobile (see chapter 3).

basis for setting primary air quality standards for two reasons. First, Congress has precluded any weighing of the costs of achieving standards against the anticipated favorable effects in whatever form. Second, the primary standards are based on the assumption that a threshold level of pollution exists, below which there are no adverse effects on human health. Air quality standards are to be set on the basis of this threshold. But scientific evidence has cast considerable doubt on the validity of the threshold concept. There may be significant benefits to be realized in some instances by reducing pollution levels below the present standards.

Next, Freeman discusses several relatively "new" issues in air pollution policy: noncompliance charges, nonattainment areas and the controversial "tradeoff" policy, the nondegradation policy, and the scrubber controversy. In each of these areas he shows how economic reasoning applied to an environmental issue could lead, or has led, to a less expensive way of accomplishing a specific goal. Incidentally, both the noncompliance charge and the gradual evolution of EPA's tradeoff policy give some credence to the view that economic tools need not be politically impossible.

In his discussion of the Federal Water Pollution Control Amendments, Freeman begins by arguing that the stated goal of the legislation, "zero discharges," may be neither achievable nor desirable in all cases. He then points out how the legislation confuses goals and means and the way in which this confusion could be simply eliminated. Specifically, mandating the installation of certain technologies without first considering how much they will cost and how we will benefit from them does not make economic sense. Moreover, mandating such technology-based standards weakens the incentive for firms to make innovations in pollution control technology.

Freeman also takes to task the program through which municipal waste treatment plants are federally subsidized. Although well meaning, Congress has created in the subsidy program an incentive for communities to choose treatment facilities that have high capital or construction costs relative to operating and maintenance costs. This is because the former are subsidized to the extent of 75 percent by the federal government, while the latter are borne entirely by local governments. In addition, Freeman shows that the municipal waste treatment subsidy program encourages local governments to build plants that will have greater than the proper amount of excess capacity. Finally, he points to the tendency for grant funds to be doled out on a first-come, first-served basis that ignores the need for the facility.

Freeman concludes his chapter by reiterating the necessity for examining both the bad as well as the good effects that would follow the implementation of any proposed environmental policy. He points out that such examination would lead to a reformulation of the goals of our major environmental legislation as well as a rethinking of the tools we have selected to accomplish those goals. In certain cases, Freeman argues, we might relax the regulations currently in effect—those controlling suspended solids and degradable organic compounds, for example. In other areas, however, a careful balancing of benefits and costs would probably lead to more stringent regulations, toxic air and water pollutants being prime candidates. Finally, he concludes, a reliance on market-like incentives for pollution abatement would speed the attainment of whatever goals we choose. In addition, such incentive mechanisms, be they effluent charges or whatever, would usually have the effect of reducing the costs of achieving our goals. Considering the Council on Environmental Quality's (CEQ's) estimates of the likely cost of the current approach, any savings would be most welcome. Savings on the order of those Freeman discusses would be nothing short of a blessing.

In chapter 3 Eugene Seskin shifts our attention to the automobile and our attempts to control its pollution emissions. We treat automotive air pollution separately because of the unique role of the automobile in our society and because of the controversy surrounding automobile emissions standards. Seskin begins by describing current trends in the levels of several of the automobile-related air pollutants with which we are concerned. Fortunately, concentrations of certain of these air pollutants have declined and this appears to be due to emissions control policy as mandated by the 1970 Amendments to the Clean Air Act. He then describes the long and sometimes inglorious history of automotive emissions control in this country, a history filled with unmet deadlines, subsequent postponement of those deadlines, and textbook examples of confrontation politics.

Seskin then carefully lays out the reasons for control of automobile emissions. These take the form of improved human and animal health, better vegetation and forestation, and lessened damage to materials and structures. These benefits come at a cost, of course, and Seskin discusses the quantitative nature of these costs as well. He then reviews the way these benefits and costs can be valued to be made commensurate. In so doing, he discusses the results of studies that have attempted to compare the benefits and costs of mobile-source emissions control. These studies indicate that we may be paying more for the benefits than they are worth.

Seskin then points out how the forced adoption of certain emissions control technologies has diminished the incentives of automakers to innovate.

After reviewing the problems of implementation and enforcement that attend present policy, Seskin turns his attention to alternative regulatory policies, ones that might improve upon the current approach. One such approach, the "two-car strategy," seems to have much to recommend it. This policy would require cars registered in large metropolitan areas with air pollution problems to meet stricter emissions standards than those registered, and presumably driven, elsewhere. Seskin argues that this would reduce the costs of mobile-source emissions control significantly without reducing the benefits appreciably since the benefits foregone under such an approach would be those in rural areas which comprise a small percentage of total benefits.

Seskin then weighs the desirability and feasibility of effluent charges on mobile-source emissions. While such a system might at first seem difficult to administer, if coupled with the annual vehicle inspection program that many states now have, such charges might indeed be feasible. In addition, they would allow car owners to reduce their smog tax in any one of a number of ways and would also provide an incentive to reduce total driving. Moreover, such charges would provide for some continuity in the response of automobile manufacturers if they could be assured that a given set of charges would remain in effect for several years. Seskin is careful to point out a number of potentially serious drawbacks to the use of charges. Despite the difficulties, he concludes that such a program of charges should be experimented with in some area of the country.

In chapter 4, I discuss the already large and growing body of legislation regulating what have come to be known as toxic or hazardous substances. These substances may occur naturally but they are more often synthetically produced chemicals to which we are exposed through the food chain, in the work place, or through the water supply, for example. While these substances are associated with a number of serious illnesses, toxic chemicals and other substances have come to the forefront of public attention because of their link to cancer, the second leading cause of death in the United States.

Before discussing the actual form of federal toxic substance control policy, I consider two alternatives. First, I examine how likely it is that the market for labor, land, or consumer products might "internalize the risk" of exposure to toxic substances. If these risks are internalized—that is, if they are reflected in higher wages for risky occupations, and lower prices for properties or products that carry with them higher risks than those accompanying other, similar products—government intervention might be superfluous. Not surprisingly, perhaps, I find that the nature of occupational *health* risks, as distinct from accident risks, say, is such that a clear and important role for government is indicated. I also consider the approach in which *all* exposures to toxic substances are prohibited. Here, I suggest that the benefits from allowing exposure to such substances may indeed occasionally outweigh the costs; in these instances the strict prohibition would be unwise.

The federal government predictably has chosen an approach somewhere between what I call the market solution and the zero-exposure policy. I next review the legislation that together comprises the main part of the federal effort. This ranges from the long-standing Food, Drug and Cosmetic Act to the Resource Conservation and Recovery Act of 1977. The most striking feature of the various pieces of legislation is the extent to which they differ from one another, in ways that are sometimes subtle and other times radical. These differences involve the definition of a toxic substance, the extent to which individuals should be protected from such substances, the role of economic analysis in establishing standards, and the assignment of the burden of proof for establishing the safety or danger of a substance.

I next consider the problems that this inconsistency creates as well as other problems that arise in the regulation of toxic substances. These include ethical dilemmas as well as economic ones. Why, for example, should we permit cigarette smoking but prohibit the use of saccharin in diet sodas when smoking is clearly so much more harmful to human health than saccharin is thought to be? Can we justify apparent paternalism on the grounds that everyone's health insurance costs are affected by the behavior of a few, perhaps foolhardy, individuals?

I also consider the problems inherent in the definition of and testing for toxicity. These problems are ones of expense (a single test could cost as much as $500,000), delay, statistical validity, possible manipulation or falsificaton and, finally, extrapolation. Nowhere have animal tests been more controversial than those that led to the Food and Drug Administration's (FDA's) proposed ban on the artificial sweetener, saccharin. This ban, an eighteen-month postponement of which was rushed through both houses of Congress, was mandatory for the FDA under the provisions of the "Delaney clause" in the Food Additives Amendments. Accordingly, I also consider the strengths and weaknesses of that clause and the conditions under which we might want to modify it to allow for a balancing of benefits and risks.

Finally, I discuss the suitability of various kinds of economic incentives in toxic substance policy. While no such incentives seem feasible for the purpose of limiting occupational exposures, a tax on consumer products containing toxic substances is considered. Such a tax would discourage the consumption of the products in question but would allow individuals so disposed to continue consuming them if they want to. Occupational exposures, I suggest, would be sensitive to the assignment of liability for the adverse effects of these exposures. There is, however, little reason to believe that jury awards will induce the right amount of protective expenditures on the part of employers.

In chapter 5 Henry Peskin takes a somewhat different tack than that of Freeman or Seskin. In a study based on the Clean Air Amendments of 1970, he gives an illustration of one type of methodology that can be used to analyze the distribution of benefits and costs of an environmental policy. Specifically, he examines not the magnitudes of such benefits and costs, but the way in which they are distributed across regions of the country, among the individuals in different income groups, and along racial lines as well. The methodology he uses is clearly applicable to any of the federal environmental policies. Needless to say, the distributional effects of any policy, environmental or otherwise, will have every bit as much to do with its acceptability as its benefit–cost ratio.

Peskin begins by pointing out how difficult it is to know who are the true beneficiaries of air quality improvements. Are they, for example, only those whose immediate air quality is improved? Or do they also include citizens many hundreds of miles away who benefit from the knowledge that air quality elsewhere is improving? The distribution of the benefits of air pollution abatement looks very different depending on the notion of benefits one adopts, Peskin shows.

The method he uses to distribute benefits and costs geographically depends on three things: first, data on total benefits and costs on an industry-by-industry basis; second, a strong but necessary set of assumptions about the way air pollution is distributed; and third, the way its reduction will be financed.

His results are quite surprising. Over 30 percent of the total national benefits of complying with the Clean Air Act go to the residents of the five dirtiest metropolitan areas, which contain but 8 percent of the population of the United States. The costs of air pollution control, on the other hand, are much more evenly distributed across the nation. This is because people all over the country help pay, through higher product prices and automobile costs, for pollution reductions that occur primarily in the East and Midwest. The net effects of the Clean Air Act, Peskin shows, are such that only 28 percent of the population "come out ahead" as a result of the act. Hence, a minority of the population can be said to gain from the act at the expense of the more numerous net losers.

Peskin then directs our attention to the way that individuals in different racial and income groups are affected by full compliance with the Clean Air Act. These estimates he derives using data on the spending characteristics of individuals in various income groups, the ownership of automobiles by different income and racial groups, as well as the geographic distribution of families by race and income. Several of these conclusions are also surprising. First, although all racial and income groups appear to benefit on a net basis from the control of stationary source, or industrial air pollution, no group benefits on net from the control of automobile emissions. In fact, when the effects of both stationary and mobile-source air pollution control are combined, only non-whites are net beneficiaries.

Using Peskin's methodology and considering the effects of the Clean Air Act *in toto,* the net benefits of the program are found to be neither progressively nor regressively distributed. That is, the poor do not appear to enjoy a consistently larger or smaller percentage of their income in net benefits than wealthier families. However, if the net benefits of industrial air pollution control are considered in isolation, the poor enjoy positive net benefits along with other income groups. In addition, these net benefits are progressively distributed throughout the range of incomes.

Peskin concludes by discussing the likely distributional consequences of alternative strategies for improving air quality. He offers, for example, some speculative thoughts on the distributional effects of the two-car strategy and of effluent charges to control automobile emissions. Finally, in speculating about the political support that the Clean Air Act has attracted, Peskin suggests that it may be due to the redistribution of income which the act has effected. That is, this act and others like it may derive their support not because of their efficiency or effectiveness but rather because they are consistent with a national goal of reducing income inequality.

In the sixth and final chapter, Robert Haveman and V. Kerry Smith redirect our attention away from specific acts and industries and toward the national economy, for it is their purpose to evaluate the many assertions we hear about the effects which the whole of U.S. environmental policy will have on unemployment, inflation, capital investment, and international trade. Such a chapter, *all* the authors felt, was essential to this book because of the importance of macroeconomic effects in choosing among ways to protect our environment.

Haveman and Smith begin by discussing the two types of models of the economy that have been used to predict the overall effects of environmental policy. Their discussion is somewhat more technical in parts than that of other chapters. This is by necessity, however; we cannot evaluate the legitimacy of various claims unless we understand the framework from whence they came. The models Haveman and Smith consider are microsimulation ones (focused on the behavior of individual households or firms) and macroeconomic models (based on the behavior of economic aggregates like overall investment, consumption, saving, and the like). After describing these two kinds of models as simply and carefully as they can, the authors discuss their relative strengths and weaknesses. The microsimulation models offer a more detailed view of the economy than the macroeconomic models but they have not, to date, been able to portray the sequence in which the adjustments to a new environmental policy would occur. The macroeconomic models seem to be superior on this latter count but inferior on the former. Both kinds of models, the authors point out, are only as good as the data on which they are based.

After this introduction to the models, Haveman and Smith analyze recent projections of the likely economic impacts of environmental policy. For example, they point out that the pollution control expenditures necessitated by federal legislation will have mixed effects on the unemployment rate. Until about 1981, it appears, the models predict there will be slightly *less* unemployment than would have existed in the absence of current environmental legislation. This is due, presumably, to the creation of jobs in the pollution control equipment industry. Beyond 1981, however, the unemployment rate exceeds that predicted for the no-legislation case; this is due to productivity losses and the general economic slowdown that accompanies higher product prices. Haveman and Smith also examine the effect of pollution control on housing starts, investment, and the general price level. Moreover, they compare these results with those obtained from several other countries to see if environmental policies are affecting our international trading partners in the same way. The direction of the changes is almost always the same across countries, they find, although the magnitudes vary.

After discussing the limitations of these projection methods, Haveman and Smith turn their attention to several current controversies surrounding environmental legislation. They examine the effects of the legislation on capital spending to see if environmental protection may be responsible for the alleged "capital shortage"; they look again at the effects of environmental policy on employment to see if a clean environment means fewer jobs; and they discuss the regional impacts of our national commitment to a cleaner environment. In each case Haveman and Smith shed light on issues often discussed loudly but naively.

Finally, the authors draw some implications for improved policy making. They suggest that environmental measures be coordinated with overall economic stabilization so that environmental protection does not frustrate other macroeconomic objectives. They point out the necessity of understanding the regional impacts of various policies so that these policies may be combined with ameliorative measures. And finally, they make a plea, common to all the chapters, that better information be collected so that the macroeconomic effects of environmental policy (and the microeconomic effects as well) may be determined more easily in the years to come.

CHAPTER 2

Air and Water Pollution Policy

A. MYRICK FREEMAN III

BETWEEN 1970 and 1972 Congress passed the two major pieces of legislation that established air and water pollution control strategies for the 1970s. The new laws were the Clean Air Amendments of 1970 (CAA-70) and the Federal Water Pollution Control Amendments of 1972 (FWPCA-72). They established new goals and standards for air and water quality, set deadlines for clean-up actions, and created new procedures and mechanisms for regulation and enforcement.

(At the time of their passage these laws were viewed by many as landmarks in the battle for environmental protection. Yet the two sets of amendments have not been immune to major pressures for changes to deal with problems that have emerged since 1972. Congress has seen fit to postpone the deadlines for meeting auto emission standards, and at least in part in response to the recommendations of the National Commission on Water Quality, to modify or postpone the deadlines for meeting some of the requirements of the 1972 amendments.)

The purpose of this chapter is to examine our experience with the Water Pollution Control Amendments and those portions of the Clean Air Amendments dealing with stationary sources, in the hope that such an examination might prove helpful in assessing recent and proposed changes in our basic air and water pollution control laws. We do not attempt a full-fledged evaluation of existing policies or a definitive judgment concerning their effectiveness. That would require a major research effort well beyond the scope of this chapter. Rather, we identify some of the major problems that have emerged during the Environmental Protection Agency's

(EPA's) efforts to implement the Clean Air Amendments and the Water Pollution Amendments. We also attempt to combine the lessons provided by this experience with the analytical perspective of economics to evaluate some of the proposed changes in policy.

⌠Pollution control policy is a dynamic, ongoing process. Past policy decisions and their consequences help to create the conditions under which present proposals must be evaluated. Any proposed change in policy must be examined in the context of past events and existing conditions. This point is sometimes forgotten, or at least ignored, by those who advocate sweeping reform of our pollution control laws. For example, it may be useful to discuss heuristically such major changes in policy as the adoption of a pure effluent or emissions charge system. Such an exercise might help us better understand how different policy approaches are meant to work. But it is probably not useful to propose seriously the adoption of a pure effluent charge system, at least at this time. There has already been a substantial commitment of resources to the implementation of the present regulatory approach to pollution control. Sweeping reform would require tearing down and rebuilding much of the existing administrative and bureaucratic machinery. In addition, major changes in policy are likely to create substantial uncertainties and delay as new laws are challenged and tested in the courts. It is doubtful that the political climate is right for sweeping reform in the absence of a major crisis or breakdown in the regulatory system. However, it is possible to modify our current regulatory approach to capture some of the incentive effects of effluent charges. In fact some proposals for grafting charge-like policies onto the existing regulatory structure have already gained substantial support in the Congress. We will discuss such schemes in later sections of this chapter.

The following section of this chapter contains a brief summary of the major provisions of the Federal Water Pollution Control Amendments of 1972 and those sections of the 1970 Clean Air Amendments governing stationary sources of air pollution. (Automotive air pollution is the subject of chapter 3.) We then turn to a discussion of selected issues raised by our policies toward stationary source air pollution and water pollution. The emphasis there is on the objectives of pollution control policy and the means that might be chosen to achieve these objectives.

The Present Laws

⌠In order to understand the issues and choices currently confronting Congress, it is necessary to have some familiarity with the basic structure and major elements of the existing laws governing air and water pollution.[1] In this section we briefly outline the major provisions of federal law governing stationary source air pollution and water pollution.

The Clean Air Amendments of 1970 focus primarily on the control of emissions and ambient concentrations of six pollutants: sulfur oxides, suspended particulates, carbon monoxide, nitrogen oxides, unburned hydrocarbons, and photochemical oxidants. The regulatory strategy embodied in the amendments has two components. First, the administrator of EPA is directed to establish primary and secondary ambient air quality standards which are to apply to the nation as a whole. The primary standards establish maximum allowable concentrations of the pollutants in the atmosphere so as "to protect the public health . . . allowing an adequate margin of safety. . . ." The more stringent secondary air quality standards have the objective of protecting ". . . the public welfare from any known or anticipated adverse effects. . . ." Under these amendments, states are also permitted to establish air quality standards that are more strict than the national primary and secondary standards.

The second element of the strategy calls for states to establish implementation plans (SIPs) which, when carried out, would assure that emissions within each state would be reduced sufficiently to attain at least the national primary air quality standards by 1975. Each state's implementation plan has to be submitted to the administrator of EPA for approval.[2] EPA can also grant extensions of the deadline for achieving national primary standards for up to two years.

Although other approaches are possible within the framework of the law, all of the states chose to follow a regulatory-enforcement strategy in the implementation plans they have submitted to EPA. States identified major individual emitters and categories of sources of those pollutants contributing to the violation of national air quality standards. The states also estimated the reductions in emissions necessary to achieve the standards. Emissions reductions were then embodied in permits issued to indi-

---

[1] For an informative discussion of the evolution of air and water pollution control laws, a more complete description of the present laws, and a discussion of the political factors helping to shape pollution control policy, see J. Clarence Davies III and Barbara S. Davies, *The Politics of Pollution* (2nd ed., New York, Pegasus, 1975).

[2] As of early 1976, EPA had granted complete approval to only twenty-three of the fifty-five implementation plans submitted by states and other jurisdictions. See U.S. Environmental Protection Agency, *Progress in the Prevention and Control of Air Pollution in 1975,* Annual Report of the Administrator (July 1976).

vidual emitters. These permits require emitters to reduce emissions to specified levels by some deadline. In some instances, the permits also establish schedules for achieving certain interim steps toward final compliance, for example, submission of emissions control plans, start of construction for control equipment, and the like.

The implementation plans also contain provisions for monitoring ambient air quality and emissions from individual sources, initiating enforcement actions where necessary, and imposing sanctions on emitters who fail to comply with the terms of their permits.

In addition to permitting states to set clean air targets that are more strict than the national primary and secondary standards, the law also permits differences both among states and within a state in the clean-up requirements or emissions standards imposed on *existing* individual sources. However, the law requires uniform national emissions standards to be imposed on all *new* sources of air pollutants. These new-source performance standards, as they are called, are to be based on technological and cost factors. Specifically, the law calls for "the degree of emission limitation achievable through the application of the best system of emission reduction which (taking into account the cost of achieving such reduction) the administrator determines has been adequately demonstrated."

The law does not limit regulatory action to the six pollutants mentioned above. The administrator is permitted to identify additional pollutants which have adverse effects on the public health or welfare and, after following certain procedures, to establish national primary and secondary ambient air quality standards for them. It would then become the responsibility of states to revise their implementation plans so as to achieve sufficient control of these new pollutants to meet the standards.

Finally, the administrator of EPA is authorized to identify "hazardous air pollutants" which "may cause, or contribute to, an increase in mortality or an increase in serious irreversible, or incapacitating reversible illness." For any pollutants so identified, the administrator of EPA is required to establish uniform national emissions standards so as to protect public health (including a margin of safety). So far the administrator has designated asbestos, beryllium, mercury, and vinyl chloride as hazardous pollutants and established national emissions standards for them.[3]

The Federal Water Pollution Control Amendments of 1972 represent a radical departure from past air and water pollution policy. Before 1972

---

[3] See chapter 4.

the federal law governing water pollution was similar in approach to the provisions of the 1970 Clean Air Amendments governing stationary source air pollution. The major difference between the Water Pollution Control Act of 1965 and the Clean Air Amendments of 1970 was the relative roles of the federal government and the states. There were two main activities for the states under the 1965 law—standard-setting and enforcement. Each state was required to draw up minimum water quality standards for all bodies of water within its borders. These standards could, however, vary for different bodies of water. Although the law was not specific on this point, the standard-setting requirement gave states the opportunity to weigh the benefits and costs of attaining different water quality levels. The 1965 act also laid the primary responsibility for enforcement of the standards on the individual states. After setting water quality standards, states were to determine the maximum discharges of various pollutants consistent with meeting these standards. The total allowable discharges would then be divided among the major sources of discharges on some basis. Dischargers would receive permits specifying the quantity of wastes they could legally discharge. Detecting violations of the permits, taking offending dischargers to court, and imposing fines where necessary were also the responsibilities of the states.

The 1972 Water Pollution Amendments represented a major departure from this approach in three main respects: goals, methods, and federal responsibility. First, the act established as a national goal the elimination of *all* discharge of pollutants into navigable waters by 1985. However, none of the major implementation provisions of the act is designed specifically to achieve this goal. The operational goal of the act is expressed as follows, "that wherever attainable, an interim goal of water quality which provides for the protection and propagation of fish, shellfish, and wildlife and provides for recreation in and on the water be achieved by July 1, 1983."

Second, the means for achieving this "fishable-swimmable waters" goal is a system of *technology-based* effluent standards to be established by the administrator of EPA. By basing effluent limits on technological factors rather than water quality objectives, the 1972 amendments do away with the need for regulators to estimate assimilative capacity of water bodies and the relationship between discharges and water quality. The amendments call for the application of the same standards to all dischargers within classes and categories of industries rather than a plant-by-plant determination of acceptable discharges based on water quality considerations.[4]

According to the 1972 Water Pollution Amendments, the technology-based standards are to be achieved in two stages. By 1977, industrial dischargers were to be meeting effluent limitations based upon the best practicable control technology currently available (BPT). However, in determining what is practicable, EPA must consider "the total cost of application of technology in relation to the effluent reduction benefits to be achieved." Effluent limitations for publicly owned treatment works call for "secondary treatment" by 1977. By 1983, effluent limitations for industrial dischargers are to be based upon the "best available technology economically achievable" (BAT), while publicly owned treatment works must meet effluent limitations based upon the "best practicable waste treatment technology." However these 1983 deadlines have been changed in several important respects by new amendments enacted at the end of 1977. These changes will be discussed in a later section of this chapter. In addition to the BPT and BAT requirements for existing sources, the 1972 amendments also call for EPA to establish effluent standards for new sources. New source performance standards are to be based on the "best available demonstrated control technology."

The third major departure from past policy is that, at least initially, the major responsibility for issuing permits to dischargers lies with EPA. All dischargers must hold permits and comply with their terms. EPA issues the permits, the terms of which are determined by the BPT and BAT effluent standards. The law calls for EPA to turn over the responsibility for issuing permits to individual states when these states meet certain standards. As of 1977, twenty-eight of fifty-four states and territories had satisfied these requirements and taken over the permit-issuing responsibility.

While making major changes in the objectives and approach to enforcement, the 1972 Water Pollution Amendments also continue and strengthen a complementary element of the federal policy toward water pollution control, namely, subsidies to cities and towns for treating municipal wastes. Since 1956 the federal government has sought to encourage the construction of public facilities for municipal waste treatment. This

---

[4] There is one exception to this statement. The 1972 Federal Water Pollution Control Amendments also call for even more stringent effluent limitations in those cases where the technology-based effluent standards are inadequate to achieve already established water quality standards.

encouragement has taken the form of grants from the federal government
to subsidize a portion of the construction costs for waste treatment plants.
By 1965, federal grants could cover up to 55 percent of the cost of plant
construction. The 1972 amendments raised the federal share to 75 percent
and substantially increased the amounts authorized to be spent. The
authorizations for the fiscal years 1973 through 1975 were $5 billion, $6
billion, and $7 billion, respectively. More recently a total of $24.5 billion
has been authorized for the five years ending in 1982. This contrasts with
a level of spending of about $1 billion per year before the passage of 1972
amendments.

Ends and Means: Some General Issues

What kinds of pollution control policies are best? The answer clearly depends on what we wish to accomplish through them. Our objectives must
be stated before the means of achieving them can be identified and evaluated. A clear statement of objectives provides the yardstick by which the
performance of policy instruments can be measured.

Objectives

The question of objectives emerges in two forms in the current debate on
pollution control policy. The first and more obvious is the question of how
far we should go in reducing pollution. Are the pollution control goals
embodied in present policy too strict? Or are they too lenient? The second
form concerns the way in which objectives are stated in the law. In the
present air and water pollution control laws, the statements of objectives
are sometimes ambiguous, and they reveal congressional ambivalence
toward the framing of objectives in economic terms. For example, the objective "to protect the public welfare" is ambiguous because welfare is not
defined. Also the congressional statements of objectives reflect ambivalence concerning the extent to which the costs of controlling pollution
should be taken into account in implementing the pollution control policies. Is the objective to control pollution regardless of cost? Or is it to
achieve some balance between benefits and costs? Ambiguity and ambivalence in congressional statements of policy objectives place a substantial
burden on the administrator of EPA as he carries out his legal responsibilities. If objectives have not been clearly stated by Congress, the political
conflict over objectives continues during the process of policy implemen-

tation by EPA. And this continuing political conflict can impede the effective implementation of pollution control policies.

[There are two points which should be kept in mind about the selection of objectives. The first is that the choice of objectives is ultimately a political one. In the absence of a universally accepted rule for determining what ought to be done, the reconciliation of different views must be accomplished through a political process. The second point is that what ought to be done is constrained by what can be done. This is the economic aspect of the problem. Economic considerations can be subordinated to other objectives through conscious political choice; but they cannot be ignored.

Pollution control is costly. Devoting more of society's scarce resources of labor, capital, administrative and technical skills, and the like, to pollution control necessarily means that less is available to do other things also valued by society—either collectively or as individuals. Because pollution control is costly, it is in society's interest to be "economical" in its selection of pollution control objectives.

There are two senses in which this is true. First, whatever pollution control objectives are chosen, the means of achieving them should be chosen so as to minimize the cost. Using more resources than are absolutely necessary to achieve pollution control objectives is wasteful. Yet as we will show, current air and water pollution control policies are wasteful in several respects. Second, society should be economical about its choices of environmental objectives. If society is to make the most of its endowment of scarce resources, it should compare what it receives from devoting resources to pollution control with what it gives up by taking resources from other uses. It should undertake pollution control activities only if the results are worth more in some sense than the gains we forgo by diverting resources from other uses. This is the universal core of truth in the benefit–cost approach to pollution control policy.

Although in this context, benefit–cost analysis is simply common sense, the term is ordinarily used to describe a more narrowly defined technical, economic calculus which attempts to reduce all benefits and costs to a common monetary measure, that is, dollars. If all benefits and costs could be measured in dollars, benefit–cost analysis might be an appropriate basis for making policy decisions. But, benefit–cost analysis as a decision rule breaks down when there is no agreed-upon rule for converting into monetary terms noncommensurable effects such as aesthetic improvements or savings of human life, or when lack of data or inadequate empirical techniques prevent the empirical estimation of benefits or costs.

In these cases policy decisions must be made through some kind of political process. But even then economic reality cannot be avoided. Political
choices have economic implications.

Consider the following example. Assume that the present level of pollution in an urban area is 10 "units" and that this concentration causes excess mortality of 50 deaths per year.

Concentra- tion of pollutant ("units")	Excess mortality (deaths)	Cost of control	Incremental cost of control	Incremental cost per death avoided
10	50	0	—	—
7	25	$10 million	$10 million	$400,000
3	10	$40 million	$30 million	$2 million
0	0	$100 million	$60 million	$6 million

If pollution is reduced to 7, at a cost of $10 million, excess mortality
would be reduced by 25 deaths per year. The cost per death avoided can
be computed from the second and third columns in the table. For example,
in moving from a pollution level of 7 to 3, an additional 15 deaths are
avoided, at an extra cost of $30 million—or $2 million per death avoided.

What level of pollution control should be chosen? One way to answer
the question is to say that it depends upon the monetary values assigned to
the lives saved. If the value per life saved is $2 million, the appropriate
policy is to reduce pollution to 3 units. Reductions beyond that level cost
more ($6 million per additional life) than the value of lives saved. One
might be repelled by the thought of basing policies on monetary calculations concerning human life. But it is important to recognize that one cannot avoid the monetary implications of policy choices about the saving of
life. These choices can be hidden, but they are inescapable. For example,
suppose a political decision were made to reduce pollution to 3 units. Em-
bedded in such a decision is the implication that the value of life is at least
$2 million but less than $6 million. Even if society decided to reduce pollution to zero, there is still the question of what other things, including other
means of saving lives, could have been bought with the extra $60 million.

To summarize, in pollution control policy as elsewhere, the relationship
between benefits and costs is an important aspect of policy choice. It is not
possible to avoid tradeoffs between economic costs and various noncommensurable forms of beneficial effects. The tradeoffs can be implicit and
hidden, or they can be made explicit and debated openly. We believe that
policy could be improved if Congress were to recognize this economic
reality. Congress should be more explicit and consistent about whether

costs should be taken into account in environmental decision making. Moreover, Congress should provide more guidance as to how costs should be weighed against beneficial effects in establishing pollution control objectives. There are two ways in which this would result in better policy. First, it would reduce much of the ambiguity and ambivalence in the present law and make possible a more coherent set of choices. Second, as we will show in later sections of this chapter, there are several cases where present policy calls for incurring massive and certain costs in order to achieve small and uncertain benefits. These cases represent a substantial misallocation of resources. Society's welfare could be improved if these resources were shifted to other, more productive uses.

We are not advocating that Congress require calculations of benefits and costs in dollars. Such calculations are often too difficult to make because of poor data, problems of attaching values to noncommensurables, and other reasons. But crude estimates and even qualitative and descriptive statements of expected beneficial and negative effects of a policy could be helpful to decision makers concerned with making the best use of society's scarce resources.

Instruments

Once pollution control objectives have been established, Congress must devise means to induce polluters to take the actions necessary to achieve the objectives. The policy instruments chosen by Congress help to define a range of options for dischargers and a structure of incentives, rewards, and perhaps penalties associated with these options. How well a policy instrument will work depends on the interaction of these options and incentives and how polluters respond to them.

There are two broad classes of policy instruments that can be used to attain pollution control objectives. One is based on regulations and the threat of penalties or sanctions for noncompliance. The other, often referred to as the effluent charge strategy, works by altering the set of prices faced by firms, thereby exerting its pressure more directly through the profit motive.[5]

[5] Allen V. Kneese and Charles L. Schultze are perhaps the best-known advocates of greater reliance on charges and other economic incentives. See their *Pollution, Prices, and Public Policy* (Washington, D.C., Brookings Institution, 1975); see also Frederick R. Anderson and coauthors, *Environmental Improvement Through Economic Incentives* (Baltimore, Md., Johns Hopkins University Press for Resources for the Future, 1977). But for a more critical perspective, see Susan Rose-Ackerman, "Effluent Charges: A Critique," *Canadian Journal of Economics* vol. 6 (1973) pp. 512–528; and her "Market Models for Pollution Control: Their Strengths and Weaknesses," *Public Policy* vol. 25, no. 3 (1977) pp. 383–406.

In the regulation-enforcement approach, the pollution control authorities must carry out four steps:

1. determine those rules and regulations governing the behavior of each discharger (installation of certain types of pollution control equipment, limitation of sulfur content in fuel, or maximum allowable discharges of certain substances) that are necessary to achieve the given pollution control objectives
2. establish a set of penalties or sanctions to be imposed for noncompliance with the regulations and requirements
3. monitor the actions of dischargers so that instances of noncompliance can be detected or establish a system of self-reporting with spot checks and audits
4. seek the aid of the courts in imposing penalties.

In deciding how to respond to a system of regulations and enforcement, dischargers must compare the costs of various degrees of compliance with the likely costs of noncompliance. The former may be substantial; but the latter are likely to be uncertain and problematical. Instances of noncompliance might not be detected by the pollution control authorities. Minor violations, even if detected, might be ignored by the pollution control authority if it is devoting its limited enforcement budget to more serious violations. The pollution control authority might seek actions short of major fines or injunctions. Finally, the court, after hearing the discharger's side of the story, might be more lenient than the pollution control authority would wish.

In order to utilize economic incentives like effluent or emission charges, the pollution control authority must do three things:

1. determine a set of charges or prices per unit of discharge of each polluting substance that is predicted to induce the necessary abatement actions on the part of dischargers[6]
2. monitor the discharges, or establish a system of self-reporting with spot checks and audits
3. collect a sum equal to the charge per unit of pollutant times the amount of the pollutant discharged during each reporting period.[7]

[6] It is likely that charges will have to be differentiated by substance as well as by location of the discharger. The degree of differentiation and what factors must be taken into account depend upon the nature of the pollution control objectives, among other things.

[7] Also, some decision must be made about the use of the charge revenues. This is likely to be of considerable political importance.

The major problem with the charge approach is determining the level of the charge. This problem has both analytical and political aspects. The information and analytical techniques required depend on the objective the charge is meant to serve. For example, if the charge is being used to attain ambient air quality standards, information regarding costs of control, atmospheric dispersion models, and data on existing air quality are all needed in order to compute the appropriate charge structure. Hypothetical charge structures have been computed in several case studies for both air pollution and water pollution.[8] But to date, none of these charge structures has been validated by experience in the United States. The political aspect concerns who is to set the charge. If it is to be set administratively, appropriate procedures must be followed during which affected parties would have the opportunity to challenge assumptions and data, and the like. Alternatively, if the charge is set legislatively, a tremendous burden for technical analysis is imposed on the legislature and its staff.

The charge strategy has long been attractive to economists because: (a) it provides a certain and graduated incentive to firms by making pollution itself a cost of production; (b) where several sources are discharging into the same medium, they will be induced to minimize the total cost of achieving any given reduction in pollution;[9] and (c) it provides an incentive for innovation and technical change in pollution control.

This last point deserves more emphasis. The present state of technology helps to determine the costs of meeting pollution control objectives and, in some cases, defines the objectives themselves. Innovation which lowers the cost of achieving given pollution control targets is obviously desirable. Despite the importance of technology, there are several ways in which present policies inhibit technological innovation, and even the adoption of existing advanced technologies.

Economic reasoning suggests that technological innovations and adaptations will be responsive to economic incentives. Other things being equal,

[8] See, for example, Edwin L. Johnson, "A Study in the Economics of Water Quality Management," *Water Resources Research* vol. 3, no. 2 (1967) pp. 291–305; Henry W. Herzog, Jr., "Economic Efficiency and Equity in Water Quality Control: Effluent Taxes and Information Requirements," *Journal of Environmental Economics and Management* vol. 2, no. 3 (1976) pp. 170–184; and Scott E. Atkinson and Donald H. Lewis, "Determination and Implementation of Optimal Air Quality Standards," *Journal of Environmental Economics and Management* vol. 3, no. 4 (1976) pp. 363–380.

[9] This is because each discharger will control discharges up to the point where its marginal or incremental cost of control is equated with the given charge. If all dischargers face the same charge, they will have equated the marginal cost of pollution control across dischargers. This is the condition for cost minimization in pollution control. There is no reallocation of the responsibilities for reducing discharges which will achieve the same total reduction at lower total cost.

more resources will be devoted to discovering ways to economize on costly and scarce inputs than on abundant and cheap inputs. This is because the potential payoff—that is, the cost savings resulting from successful innovative discoveries—is higher in the former case. Also, firms are likely to devote resources to research on new technology only if they can capture the benefits of innovation in the form of lower costs, expanded markets for new products, and higher profits. There are several respects in which present pollution control policies either fail to provide positive incentives for innovation or, even worse, penalize innovation. Several of these are discussed below and in chapter 3. In each case it seems likely that some form of charge or fee could improve the incentives to innovation.

We have outlined two very different approaches to pollution control, one based on economic incentives and the other on regulation. There are many variations and hybrid strategies which combine some of the characteristics of both approaches. For example, the pollution control authority could issue a limited number of pollution permits or "tickets" and auction them off to the highest bidders. Dischargers could also buy and sell permits among themselves. This system of marketable discharge permits could result in an allocation of pollution rights which would meet the ambient environmental quality target while minimizing the total costs of pollution control.[10] Of course, the authority would still face the problems of monitoring dischargers and imposing sanctions on those who violated the terms of their permits.

Another alternative would be to impose a graduated charge or "noncompliance fee" only on discharges above the amount permitted each discharger. This scheme would not have the automatic cost-minimizing properties of a pure effluent charge, but it could be administratively simpler to impose and could provide a more certain and graduated incentive for compliance than would the inflexible system of court-imposed penalties. Such policy instruments would also differ with respect to the incentives they would provide for innovation in pollution control technology.

Regulations and the Delegation of Authority

With one exception (the congressional specification of the auto emissions standards), the pollution control laws have followed the pattern of much

---

[10] When dischargers are located at different points in space, the permit system must be modified to take location into account. See Thomas H. Tietenberg, "The Design of Property Rights for Air Pollution Control," *Public Policy* vol. 22 (Summer 1974) pp. 275–292.

of the recent federal regulatory legislation. Typically, Congress has established the criteria and objectives for regulatory action while delegating the authority to set regulations and make specific decisions to an administrative agency. For example, it is the administrator of EPA who has the authority to set ambient air quality standards. It is his judgment that settles the question of what is necessary to "protect the public health." Similarly, the administrator has the authority to determine what substances are considered to be hazardous and to establish effluent limitations for individual dischargers subject only to some broadly defined test of technological practicability or availability. It is understandable that Congress would not wish to immerse itself in the technical details of pollution control technology for specific industries. But the complexity of the questions to be decided and the consequent efforts to delegate responsibility for detailed decision making to the executive branch raise two kinds of problems for the implementation of pollution control policy.

The first problem stems from the Constitutional principle of the separation of powers. Governmental actions that regulate and modify the rights and responsibilities of individuals gain their legitimacy principally from the sanction of the legislative body. Under the separation of powers principle it is the Congress which passes the laws that regulate individual rights and responsibilities, while the executive branch merely executes and enforces the laws. But as the role of government has expanded into areas such as environmental protection, and as the problems under consideration become more complex, it has become increasingly difficult to strike the appropriate balance between specific statements of legislative intent and the flexibility to deal with a wide variety of individual cases under rapidly changing circumstances. Congress must tread a fine line between excessive specificity and excessive flexibility. The former can prevent the government from responding adequately to changing circumstances and special cases, while the latter can lead to Constitutional challenges on the basis of excessive delegation of legislative power. As a consequence almost every action Congress takes concerning environmental policy raises questions about its intent. This is especially true if Congress is ambiguous in its statement of objectives. These questions can only be resolved by clarifying legislation or, more frequently, by judicial interpretation. In either case, the result is to delay the effective implementation of the law until questions of congressional intent have been settled. For example, although the 1972 Water Pollution Amendments called for industrial dischargers to be *meeting* BPT effluent limitations by July 1977, it was not until February 1977 that the U.S. Supreme Court settled the first major challenge to EPA's authority to establish uniform effluent limitations for broad categories of industrial dischargers.

The second problem raised by delegation of authority is how to protect individuals and corporations from essentially arbitrary exercises of bureaucratic or administrative power. Traditionally individuals have been protected by the opportunity to seek judicial review of actions affecting their own rights. More recently the Administrative Procedures Act has, among other things, given individuals more access to administrative decision making so that they can seek to protect their rights in advance of administrative decisions. But these administrative and judicial safeguards have serious implications for the implementation of environmental policies. There are literally thousands of decisions to be made affecting individuals' rights. If each individual is to be granted access to the decision-making process and the right to judicial appeal, implementation may be slowed and valuable administrative and bureaucratic resources shifted away from implementation and into the procedural and judicial mechanisms. For example, the National Commission on Water Quality noted that there were over 250 court cases challenging various provisions of the effluent guidelines established by EPA under the 1970 Water Pollution Amendments.

We cannot offer any simple solution to the problems raised by congressional delegation of authority. The issues are legally and politically complex. However, we believe that these issues are important for the evaluation of policy alternatives because different types of policies may place quite different burdens of decision making and discretion on both the legislative and the executive branches.

Stationary Source Air Pollution

With 247 air quality regions and six pollutants for which air quality standards have been set, it is difficult to summarize the present status of air pollution control efforts. There are some data on trends of total emissions and air quality readings (both national averages and for individual air quality regions) which give some indication of the overall effectiveness of air pollution policy.[11] However, these data must be interpreted with care since

[11] These data are presented and discussed in more detail in EPA, *Progress in the Prevention and Control;* Council on Environmental Quality, *Environmental Quality—1976* (Washington, D.C., 1976); and U.S. Environmental Protection Agency, *National Air Quality and Emission Trends Reports, 1975,* Publication No. EPA-450/1-76-002 (November 1976).

TABLE 2-1   Summary of National Emission Estimates, 1970–1975

(million tons)

Year	Particulates	SO$_x$	NO$_x$
1970	26.8	34.2	22.7
1971	24.9	32.3	23.4
1972	23.4	36.7	24.6
1973	21.9	35.6	25.7
1974	20.3	34.1	25.0
1975	18.0	32.9	24.2

Source: U.S. Environmental Protection Agency, National Air Quality and Emissions Trends Reports, 1975, Publication No. EPA 450/1-76-002 (November 1976) p. 47.

emissions are affected by factors other than pollution control policy—for example, the level of economic activity, and the availability and prices of different types of fuels. Air quality also depends on meteorological conditions, and these can vary substantially from year to year. There are also data on the extent of compliance with national air quality standards. Although these data give a direct indication of progress toward achieving pollution control objectives, they do not reveal the reasons for any failures to meet policy targets.

Table 2-1 summarizes data on total national emissions of particulates, sulfur oxides, and nitrogen oxides.[12] Emissions of particulates decreased continuously from 1970 through 1975. Both sulfur oxides and nitrogen oxides show mixed patterns with some periods of increasing emissions during the six-year period. Figure 2-1 shows the trends in total emissions and the contributions of major categories. The major source of sulfur oxides is fuel combustion for space heating and electrical power generation. The increase in emissions from this category in 1972 was due to changes in the prices and availabilities of low-sulfur versus high-sulfur fuels. Emissions from both stationary and mobile sources of nitrogen oxides increased slightly until 1973. Although emissions standards for new cars were first applied in 1973, the major source of the decrease in emissions since then has been stationary source fuel combustion.

The downward trends in emissions are also reflected in ambient air quality measures. The composite annual average for total suspended particulates has declined from 80 micrograms per cubic meter (μg/m^3) to 62 μg/m^3 over the period 1970–75. The latter figure is below the national primary standard of 75 μg/m^3. Most of the improvement in the composite

---

[12] Since the automobile is the major source of carbon monoxide, unburned hydrocarbons, and photochemical oxidants, discussion of trends in emissions and air quality for these pollutants will be deferred to chapter 3.

FIGURE 2-1   Calculated Total Emissions of Three Pollutants by Source Category, 1970 through 1975

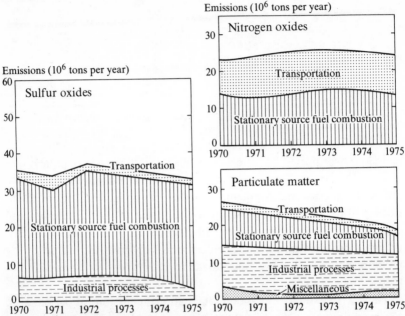

Source: U.S. Environmental Protection Agency, *National Air Quality and Emissions Trends Reports, 1975,* Publication No. EPA-450/1-76-002 (November 1976) p. 54.

average is attributable to lower readings at monitoring sites which were initially recording the worst air quality. However almost 25 percent of these sites still record annual average particulate levels above the national primary standard.

The downward trend in particulate levels is also reflected in a measure of the degree of exposure of the population to polluted air. Table 2-2 shows that the percentage of the national population living in areas where the national primary standard for particulates is violated has decreased substantially over the past six years.

Composite annual average readings for sulfur dioxide decreased by about a third over the period 1970–1975. The 1975 composite annual average was only about a third of the national primary standard for sulfur dioxide. But most of this improvement occurred in the first two years of the period. The composite average has been relatively stable since 1973. These averages conceal a good deal of variation in the experiences of cities

TABLE 2-2   Trend in National Population Exposure to Particulate
Matter Levels Above the Health-Related Standard

Year	Percentage of population
1970	45
1971	43
1972	37
1973	32
1974	30
1975	28

Source: U.S. Environmental Protection Agency, *Trends in the Quality of the Nation's Air* (Washington, D.C., 1977) p. 5.

and urban areas versus rural areas. Figure 2-2 shows trends in the annual averages for five major cities that illustrate the intercity variation.

A comparison of the trends in nationwide sulfur emissions and composite average air quality—which is heavily weighted toward urban areas—suggests the possibility that sulfur dioxide pollution in nonurban areas is not improving and might be getting worse. Emissions have been substantially reduced in urban areas; but there are many major sources in nonurban areas where air quality monitoring networks and data on trends are not nearly so extensive. The data on sulfate particulate concentrations in both urban and rural areas tend to support this explanation. The sulfate particulate problem will be discussed in the next section.

Finally, concerning the attainment of air quality standards, EPA estimates that over half of the air quality control regions in the nation will fail to achieve the national primary standard for total suspended particulates. In about half of these cases, the major cause of failure is windblown dust from agriculture, construction sites, unpaved roads, and the like, rather than industrial point sources. Thirty-five air quality control regions will fail to attain the national primary standard for sulfur dioxide, given existing trends in air quality.

There are two reasons why an air quality control region might not be in compliance with one or more of the national primary standards. The first is that individual sources might not be in compliance with the terms of their permits and emission limitations as specified by state implementation plans. (The noncompliance problem will be discussed in a later section.) The other reason is that the state implementation plan itself may be inadequate. For example, because of inaccuracies in air quality modeling,

*FIGURE 2-2   Composite Average Sulfur Dioxide Trends for Selected
Metropolitan Areas*

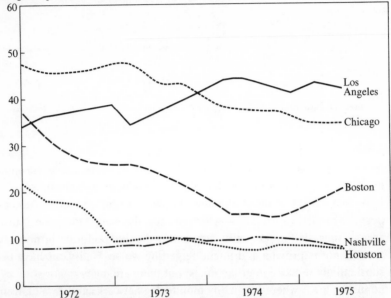

Concentration
(micrograms per cubic meter)

Source: U.S. Environmental Protection Agency, *National Air Quality and Emissions Trends Reports,
1975,* Publication No. EPA 450/1-76-002 (November 1976) p. 34.

the implementation plan and permits might have been based on an underestimate of the reductions in emissions necessary to achieve the standards.
Also, the state pollution control authority might have used an incomplete
inventory of emissions sources. EPA estimates that there are more than
200,000 minor sources of emissions (those discharging less than 100 tons
per year), many of which have not been brought under the effective control of the state implementation plan and permit system. Where the implementation plans are found to be inadequate to achieve primary air quality
standards, plans will have to be revised, new and more stringent permits
issued, and new compliance schedules negotiated with sources.

Air Quality Standards

Currently air pollution control strategies have as their target the attainment of national primary and secondary ambient air quality standards
established by EPA. These standards help to determine the costs associated with pollution control policies as well as the beneficial effects which

are anticipated. Thus, any assessment of present air pollution control policies should begin with a consideration of the empirical basis and the assumptions underlying these standards.

If full and accurate information on the monetary values of benefits and costs of alternative levels of air quality were available, the administrator of EPA could employ an explicitly economic approach to standard-setting by comparing the *additional* benefits associated with each small reduction in pollution levels with the *additional* costs of achieving them. If the additional benefits were greater than the additional costs, stricter standards would be justified. Since both benefits and costs can vary across regions (because of differences in population levels, composition of industry, and atmospheric conditions), it is possible—even likely—that this economic approach would lead to different air quality standards for different regions.

In the absence of data on the monetary value of benefits, it may still be possible to base decisions on standards on an examination of the tradeoffs between known costs of controlling pollution and some quantitative description of beneficial effects—estimates of reduced mortality, for example. What is required is that the costs of meeting alternative standards be estimated, and that the relationship between air quality on the one hand and mortality, morbidity, materials damages, and crop losses, on the other, be known. Then the administrator must make the value judgment as to where the balance is to be struck between costs and damages avoided.

In the case of air quality, Congress has rejected the economic tradeoff approach by specifying that primary air quality standards be set so as "to protect the public health," and secondary standards be set so as to protect against "*any* known or anticipated adverse effects" to public welfare. A basic assumption underlying this decision by Congress was that there were threshold levels of pollution below which there would be no observable or detectable adverse effects. The threshold concept can be illustrated by reference to a "dose-effect" or damage function. This is a function which relates some physical measure of damage or adverse effect to the level of air pollution which caused it. Figure 2-3 shows two hypothetical dose-effect functions. They relate mortality to pollution levels. Even with zero pollution there is some level of natural mortality. The dose-effect function labeled A shows that as pollution increases up to a point, there is no increase in mortality. Beyond this threshold point, further pollution increases mortality rates. The second curve labeled B shows no threshold. Mortality is an increasing function of pollution throughout its range.

The threshold concept was a source of controversy in 1970 when the Clean Air Amendments were passed. There was some support then for the

FIGURE 2-3   Threshold and No-Threshold Dose-Effect Functions

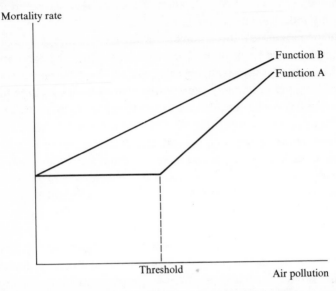

threshold concept coming from evidence regarding the acute health effects from short-term exposures to relatively high levels of air pollutants. But since 1970, a growing body of evidence has emerged which suggests that the threshold concept is invalid, especially with regard to the more subtle health effects associated with low-level exposures over long time periods. For example, the principal health effect of carbon monoxide is related to the impairment of oxygen transport in the blood. The degree of impairment and the resulting stress on the human body form a smooth continuum, ranging from zero impairment at zero levels of carbon monoxide to high impairment with high carbon monoxide levels. For normal, healthy individuals, low levels of impairment and stress may have no overt symptoms or lasting effects, but for the elderly and those with existing health problems—cardiac patients for example—even low levels of *additional* stress can have important consequences. The legislative history of the Clean Air Amendments makes it clear that Congress intended that air quality standards be set to provide protection even to particularly sensitive groups of individuals. Thus for the population as a whole, including sensitive groups, the concept of a threshold for carbon monoxide must be rejected.

Lave and Seskin's research on the relationship between mortality and sulfur compound and suspended particulate air pollution also casts considerable doubt on the threshold concept for these two classes of pollutants. They compared the mortality rates in various American cites with each city's air pollution, using multivariate regression analysis. They found a positive relationship between these two forms of air pollution and mortality. Specifically, they found that the no-threshold function (labeled B in figure 2-3) better fit the data than the relationship depicted by function A. They also found that the positive association between pollution and mortality persisted even in those cities that were meeting the national primary standards. In other words, they found significant health effects occurring at pollution levels *below the supposed threshold that was used to establish the national primary standards.*[13]

With respect to damages to plants and ecological systems, there is also some evidence of potentially serious adverse effects at levels of air pollution below national ambient air quality standards. For example, nitrogen fixation by alfalfa plants has been found to be reduced by as much as 40 percent at ozone concentrations below the national primary and secondary standards.[14]

If there are no thresholds for some pollutants with respect to certain types of health and ecological effects, what does this imply for air pollution control policy? First, it implies that at least some of the present national primary and secondary air quality standards are inconsistent with a literal interpretation of the law. Second, it implies that if the standards for these pollutants are to be revised to be made consistent with the law, they will have to be set at zero pollution. This is because the evidence suggests that for any positive level of pollution, the public health and welfare could be further improved by reducing pollution. Third, setting standards at zero pollution implies extremely high costs for controlling emissions to meet these standards. If standards were actually set at zero, the question of costs versus benefits would take on increasing importance. Congress will have to decide whether it is willing to impose these costs on the public, that is, whether the objective is "public health at any cost." If it is not, then the legal basis for setting air quality standards will have to be revised so as to permit some consideration of costs in the standard-setting process.

---

[13] Lester Lave and Eugene Seskin, *Air Pollution and Human Health* (Baltimore, Md., Johns Hopkins University Press for Resources for the Future, 1977) appendix B. Also, for a brief review of evidence relating to the questions of safety margin and threshold, see House of Representatives, Committee on Interstate and Foreign Commerce, *Report: Clean Air Act Amendments of 1976,* H. Rept. 94-1175, 93 Cong. 2 sess. (1976) 85–91.
[14] EPA, *Progress in the Prevention and Control of Air Pollution.*

There are two other respects in which the present air quality standards do not adequately reflect present knowledge about the effects of these pollutants. First, the standards do not explicitly take into account synergistic effects between two or more pollutants or interactions between pollutants and other environmental factors such as humidity and temperature. Synergistic effects occur when two pollutants in combination cause more harmful effects than would be expected by examining separately the effects of each. For example, moderate levels of sulfur dioxide alone have relatively minor health effects. But the presence of moderate levels of sulfur dioxide greatly enhances the damaging effects of suspended particulates. Similarly, sulfur dioxide and ozone have a strong synergistic relationship.[15] The air quality standards for these substances were based primarily on studies of the health effects of each taken separately. But sulfur dioxide typically occurs in combination with suspended particulates or ozone. Hence, existing standards are probably not adequate to protect against the synergistic effects of these combinations.

Second, air quality standards for suspended particulates are based on the total mass or weight of particles per cubic meter irrespective of particle size. A few large particles make a big contribution to the total mass of particulate matter in the atmosphere; but it is the smallest particles (3 microns and less) which pass most easily into the lungs and have the most damaging effects on human health. To compound the problem, existing techniques for controlling particulate emissions are most effective for the large particle sizes. They can achieve major reductions in the total mass of particulate emissions (for example more than 90 percent) without achieving effective control of the finest particles. Air quality standards should be revised to take into account the effect of particle size as a determinant of the health damages of suspended particulate air pollution.[16]

Noncriteria Pollutants

The administrator of EPA has authority to identify additional substances as pollutants and to establish national primary and secondary ambient air

[15] Bertram D. Dinman, "The SO_2 Ambient Air Quality Standard, with Special Reference to the 24-Hour Standard—An Inquiry into the Health Bases," in American Statistical Association, *Statistics and the Environment,* Proceedings of the Fourth Symposium (Washington, D.C., March 3–5, 1976) pp. 42–48; and H. Report 94-1175.

[16] The health effects of fine particles also depend upon the chemical composition of the particulate matter. Fine particulates may contain certain toxic trace metals and sulfates which have substantial health effects. Ideally, standards should reflect the chemical composition as well as the size of suspended particulate pollution. But present knowledge of these effects is probably inadequate to justify any specific standard.

quality standards for them. To date, no pollutant has been added to the original list of six.[17] One of the leading candidates for addition to the list is sulfate particulate matter.[18] Sulfur dioxide gas in the atmosphere is transformed over time into sulfuric acid and a variety of sulfate compounds. The nature and speed of these reactions depend upon atmospheric conditions such as temperature and humidity, as well as the availability of other substances with which the sulfur dioxide can react. These sulfate particles have a long residence time in the atmosphere and can be transported great distances from the original source of the sulfur emissions.

Present control strategies aimed at reducing sulfur dioxide emissions will not necessarily be effective in bringing sulfate particle pollution within safe levels. While sulfur dioxide levels have been reduced in most urban areas, sulfate particle readings in these areas have stayed relatively constant over the past several years; and there are also many instances of high levels of sulfate particles occurring in nonurban areas. Many of these areas have persistent readings of sulfate particles at levels at which significant health effects are thought to occur. Sulfate particles are also apparently a major contributor to the increasingly acidic rainfall being recorded over much of northeastern United States. The long-term consequences of acid rain for agricultural and forest productivity and ecological balance cannot be predicted at present. Nevertheless, they are potentially quite serious.

The sulfate particle problem is especially important since a major source of sulfur compound emissions is fuel combustion for electrical energy generation. Even if new generating stations using Western coal are designed to meet ambient air quality standards for sulfur dioxide in the vicinity of the plant, they may make substantial contributions to sulfate particle levels in more distant regions. Sulfate particulates should be taken into account explicitly in designing control strategies for new and existing fossil fuel generating stations. Unfortunately there is no legal basis for doing so until or unless national ambient air quality standards are established for sulfate particles.[19]

[17] These so-called "criteria pollutants" are carbon monoxide, nitrogen dioxide, hydrocarbons, photochemical oxidants, sulfur dioxide, and suspended particulates.
[18] Another is airborne lead. As a result of a suit brought by the Natural Resources Defense Council, EPA has begun the standard-setting process for lead.
[19] Establishing ambient air quality standards for sulfate particles will not be simple, since as noted above, the health effects depend importantly on particle size as well as composition. In fact one researcher has stated, "the simple fact is that the response to sulfate compounds differs so widely that the term 'particulate sulfate' is toxicologically meaningless." See Mary O. Amdur, "Toxicological Guidelines for Research of Sulfur Oxides and Particulates," in American Statistical Association, *Statistics and the Environment* Proceedings of the Fourth Symposium (Washington, D.C., March 3–5, 1976).

In conclusion, national air quality standards are based on an invalid premise, namely, the threshold effect. Standards do not reflect the more recent evidence on the subtle, long-term health effects of air pollutants. Nor do existing standards reflect the complexity of the physical, chemical, and biological phenomena involved. Finally, the standard-setting mechanism has not been utilized so as to add substances such as sulfate particles to the list of regulated pollutants as new evidence becomes available.

We believe that it is time for a thorough review of the scientific and legal basis for setting air quality standards. Such a review should focus on three questions. First, is Congress willing to accept the cost implications of absolute protection in the absence of threshold effects? If not, then the administrator must be given authority to weigh beneficial effects against the costs of attaining them. Second, what are the beneficial effects and the costs of reducing pollution levels below the present national standards for the six criteria pollutants? Consideration of this question could lead to a relaxation of standards for some pollutants, and a tightening for others. Third, what are the beneficial effects and the costs of reducing concentrations of noncriteria pollutants below present levels?[20]

Noncompliance Charges

Suppose an industrial source is found to have emissions in excess of the terms of its permit or is behind in meeting the deadlines in its compliance schedule. Under present law, both the state in which the source is located and EPA have enforcement authority. Although the procedures vary among states and between the state and federal levels, enforcement generally involves the use of administrative and judicial procedures (1) to determine that a violation exists, (2) to issue a compliance order (which is a redundancy), and (3) to impose sanctions if necessary. These procedures are time consuming. Moreover, the delays involved often work to the economic advantage of the emitter while the violation continues. In addition, these procedures strain the legal resources of the pollution control authority. It can only pursue vigorously a limited number of enforcement actions at any one time. Some violators may go unattended; for others, the backlog of cases can lead to further advantageous delay.

[20] The 1977 amendments require the administrator to review and revise if appropriate all existing ambient air quality standards by the end of 1980 and at least every five years thereafter. They also specify that a number of other substances, including sulfates, radioactive pollutants, polycyclic organics, cadmium, and arsenic, be considered for inclusion under the various regulatory provisions of the act. The amendments do not change the statutory basis for establishing ambient air quality standards.

Finally, the enforcement procedures may give the pollution control authority relatively little flexibility in dealing with specific cases. The authority may be faced with a limited range of options—imposing stiff fines, shutting down the offending operation, or accepting continued operation and further delays in compliance, for example.

A pure emission charge system would be advantageous in these cases. Charges would be imposed and collected administratively and on a regular basis rather than through the courts. These charges would reduce the incentives and rewards for delaying compliance. In addition, the charge system would eliminate the need for making all-or-nothing choices such as that between accepting pollution or shutting a plant down. Emission charges would have the further desirable property of giving emitters more flexibility in their choice of techniques for controlling emissions and the extent to which individual emitters cut back on emissions. The total costs of achieving any given reduction in emissions would be minimized. And finally, if the charge is set at the appropriate level, total emissions can be reduced sufficiently to meet ambient air quality targets.

As we argued above, however, scrapping the present regulatory-enforcement approach and substituting a pure emission charge would be a major and difficult change in pollution control policy. However, it would be possible to obtain a number of the advantages of an emission charge system with a relatively minor modification of the existing regulatory-enforcement approach. The modification would be to add one more enforcement option to the regulatory authority's arsenal, namely, an administratively levied noncompliance charge.[21] A noncompliance charge would be levied automatically on any emitter who is not in compliance with the terms of its emission permit and would be based on the amortized capital costs and operating and maintenance costs of whatever control equipment is necessary to meet the emission limitations. For emitters who are in partial compliance, the noncompliance charge would be reduced on a pro rata basis. If the charges are properly calculated, they eliminate the economic incentive for emitters to delay compliance. If the noncompliance charges are levied administratively, they reduce the burden on the enforcement staff of the pollution control agency. Although there may be some difficulty in estimating the costs of compliance in advance in order to set the

[21] The State of Connecticut has a system of charges or penalties which can be levied administratively at the discretion of the head of its environmental agency. In many respects these penalties are like the charges discussed here. But the selective and discretionary nature of their application makes them markedly different from a true economic incentive system.

noncompliance charge, estimates can be checked against actual costs later. Some versions of the noncompliance charge provide for retroactive adjustment of the schedule of charges on the basis of actual compliance costs. However, identifying compliance costs even after the fact may be difficult if compliance were achieved through process changes rather than add-on control equipment.

While the noncompliance charge has much to offer within the context of an ongoing regulatory-enforcement strategy, it is not a perfect substitute for a full-fledged system of emission charges. Since the charge is based only on the speed with which the source achieves compliance, it does not have the cost-minimizing properties of a regular emission charge. Since the charge drops to zero when compliance is achieved, it does not provide an incentive for innovation and technological change in pollution control or for continued effective operation of the new equipment.

The 1977 Clean Air Amendments call for the administrator or the states to levy noncompliance penalties on sources not in compliance by July 1, 1979. These penalties are similar to those described earlier, except that the administrator is required to hold formal hearings for each source before levying any penalty.

Nonattainment Areas

State implementation plans issued in conformance with the 1970 Clean Air Amendments must provide for preconstruction review and disapproval of new or modified air pollution sources that would "interfere with" the attainment of national ambient air quality standards. In air quality regions which are not presently in compliance with national air quality standards, this would seem to preclude new sources of emissions, even though the sources might have been designed to achieve the relatively stricter new source performance standards. The effect of this provision of the law is to prevent major plant expansions or the entry of new industries into regions which are presently not in compliance.[22]

In response to political concerns with what was perceived as a "lid" on regional development, EPA has issued a set of rules which would make it possible for new sources to be constructed in nonattainment areas without

---

[22] The same argument would apply to the regions which were just barely in compliance with national standards. The EPA policy described below applies only to nonattainment areas. However, the marketable permit system described below could be used to assure the maintenance of existing air quality as well. The argument also applies to rivers where currently mandated effluent reductions are not adequate to achieve ambient water quality standards—the so-called water-quality-limited waters.

slowing down progress toward achievement of the national air quality standards. These rules were given congressional sanction in the 1977 amendments. The rules require that any new source in a nonattainment area:

1. control emissions to the lowest achievable emission rate for that type of source, without regard to economic feasibility (these emission limitations are more strict than the new-source performance standards)

2. show that its new emissions are more than offset by new emission reductions from existing facilities in the region beyond those required by existing permits and compliance plans.

In other words the new source must show that its increment to the total amount of emissions in the region will be more than offset by extra reductions elsewhere in the region.

The offset or tradeoff policy gives firms desiring to expand or enter a region an incentive to find additional ways to reduce emissions from existing sources in the region. The responsibility for finding offsetting emission reductions lies with the firm proposing the new source. The offsets need not be limited to reductions at other sources owned by that firm. The firm is free to seek offsets from other existing sources as well. This is what gives the offset policy a special interest to economists. It appears to set the stage for a system of marketable discharge permits.

The new policy creates an opportunity for existing sources to "sell" emissions reductions to new sources. One firm would be willing to enter into a contract with another to reduce its emissions provided that its costs of emission reduction were less than the payments it would receive from a new firm. New sources would be willing to buy offsetting reductions provided that the price were less than the anticipated advantage from locating in that region. Such a system would induce those sources with the lowest control costs, that is, those most able to control pollution, to undertake the largest emission reductions. But these firms would not be penalized for their extra pollution control efforts since they would be compensated through the sale of their offsets to new sources.

If emission offsets can be bought and sold, there seems to be no barrier to extending the role of the market to all air quality regions whether in compliance or not. A regional discharge permit market would operate in the following manner. The pollution control authority would calculate total emissions that are allowable consistent with attaining air quality standards. Permits for this total of emissions would be auctioned to the highest bidders. Firms' willingness to pay for permits would depend upon their emissions control costs. Those with the highest control costs would be willing to pay the most for permits. Those with the lowest control costs would buy the fewest permits and would undertake the most emission reduction. In this way, the total cost of achieving the emission reduction in the region would be minimized.[23]

The Nondegradation Policy

The main thrust of the 1970 Clean Air Amendments is to reduce emissions in dirty air areas so as to bring air quality at least up to the level of the national primary standards. There are many parts of the country where air quality was and still is better than even the national secondary air quality standards. None of the regulatory provisions of the 1970 amendments applies to these clean areas. But the statement of purpose of the act includes the following phrase: "to *protect* and enhance the quality of the nation's air resources. . .".[24] As a consequence of a suit brought by the Sierra Club, EPA has been directed by the courts to develop regulations to assure the protection of existing air quality in clean air areas, that is, to develop and implement a policy of nondegradation of air quality.

If the terms "protection" and "nondegradation" are given a literal interpretation, they seem to require that EPA bar all potential major sources of air pollution from locating in any areas presently cleaner than the national secondary standards. This would seem effectively to prevent economic development based on heavy industry in presently underdeveloped regions. More significantly, it would pose a major barrier to the development and exploitation of Western coal resources, either by generating power locally or through coal conversion.

From an economic perspective, a literal interpretation of the Clean Air Amendments would rule out the weighing of the benefits and costs of permitting new sources in presently clean areas. If we assume that the facility will be built and that the choice is whether to locate it in a clean or dirty region, the economic criterion can be stated in the following manner. Calculate the benefits of locating in the clean area, that is, whatever advantages in productivity are associated with locating the facility in the clean

---

[23] An alternative would be to distribute permits to all sources on some basis, and to encourage the development of an aftermarket among firms. In fact this version of the scheme is closer in spirit to the EPA emission offset policy. For further discussion of the marketable permit approach, see Thomas H. Tietenberg, "The Design of Property Rights," pp. 275–292.

[24] Actually this phrase first appeared in the Clean Air Act of 1967.

rather than dirty area.[25] Then adjust this figure for the difference in environmental damages between the two regions due to pollution from the facility. If environmental damages would be greater in the dirty area—for example, because of its larger population at risk—the difference in damages would be an additional benefit due to locating in the clean area.

Because of political concerns about preventing regional development and impeding the development of Western energy resources, and to allow some consideration of benefits and costs, EPA sought to develop a policy which would regulate the introduction of new sources of sulfur oxides and particulates into clean air regions rather than prevent it. EPA issued regulations which defined three classes of clean air regions:

Class I.   where practically any air quality deterioration would be considered significant, and therefore not allowed

Class II.   where the deterioration in air quality that would normally accompany moderate growth (for example, one coal-burning power station) would not be considered significant, that is, would be permitted.

Class III. where air quality would be permitted to deteriorate to the national secondary standards, thus allowing more intensive, concentrated industrial development.

New sources of emissions locating in Class II and Class III were required to meet emission standards that were stricter than the new source performance standards. They were required to utilize the best available control technology without regard to cost. EPA initially designated all areas of the country as Class II. States were allowed to reclassify areas as Class I, or Class III if they found that the social and economic benefits of development warranted the latter classification.

The EPA regulations were challenged in court. Because of the uncertainties involving the outcome of the court challenges, and because the

---

[25] For example, if the proposed development is an electric generating station located near a coal mine, the benefit would be the cost saving for this location compared with shipping the coal to another location for use there. Additional population, employment, and income in the region should not be counted as benefits because they would exist somewhere else even in the absence of the project. The project simply relocates people and jobs from one place to another. If there are unemployed factors in the region which then become employed, or if labor can be employed more productively with this project than would be the case elsewhere in the absence of the project, the extra productivity and the added jobs do constitute real economic benefits. These would normally be a small part of the total economic consequences of the project.

EPA regulations involved substantial elements of policy making, Congress moved to establish its own nondegradation policy through the 1977 amendments. These amendments retain the three classes of the EPA regulations but are more specific as to allowable increments to pollution levels. They also mandate Class I status for the larger national park and wilderness areas, initially place all other areas in Class II, and allow states to alter some of the classifications. Finally the amendments provide for the extension of the nondegradation requirements to the other criteria pollutants within two years.

In order to assess the specific provisions of the congressionally sanctioned nondegradation policy, one must consider the objectives they are meant to serve. Once the objectives have been identified, it then becomes possible to consider whether the operational requirements of the amendments are the best means to attain those objectives. One possible objective is the protection of national parks and other unusual national lands.[26] Some national lands could be considered to be so unusual, ecologically fragile, or valuable in their present use that any air quality deterioration would result in costs outweighing any potential benefits. The 1977 amendments recognize a national interest in such lands and call for mandatory designations of certain national parks, wilderness areas, and other lands as Class I.

Another possible objective, one playing a prominent role in the House committee report, is to prevent damages to public health and to agricultural crops and forests that are thought to occur from exposure to pollutants below the levels of the national secondary air quality standards and from exposure to noncriteria pollutants such as sulfate particles. In this respect the 1977 amendments represent an improvement over the EPA regulations. EPA allowed Class III air quality to deteriorate up to the level of the national secondary standards. The amendments do not define new ambient air quality standards but rather establish maximum decrements to existing air quality. In many instances, the allowable decrements would still leave air quality better than national secondary standards.

From a broader perspective, if the argument about the inadequacy of the secondary standards is correct, the congressional approach to the problem is contradictory. If Congress believes that protection of health and prevention of agricultural and forest damages is a primary national objective of pollution control policy, and if Congress believes that present pri-

[26] The four objectives identified here are distilled from H. Report 94-1175.

mary and secondary air quality standards do not achieve those objectives, the logical course of action is to direct that those standards be modified for all areas of the country, not just the present clean air regions. In fact, given those findings, a higher priority should be given to reducing pollution in the present nonattainment areas. This is because most of the nonattainment areas are urbanized, with large populations exposed to high pollution levels. The large number of people exposed implies a substantial benefit from reducing pollution in these areas first.[27] The congressional approach to nondegradation might be justified on the grounds that the benefits of obtaining stricter air quality standards outweigh the costs in the present clean air areas, but are less than the costs of further improvements in air quality in those parts of the country not covered by nondegradation policy. But no evidence has been offered to support that contention, nor was that line of reasoning made explicit in the congressional debate.

A third possible objective of a nondegradation policy is to prevent states from competing for new industry by offering more relaxed environmental standards and to protect states from environmental "blackmail" by industrial sources threatening to relocate facilities in states with more lenient standards. This, of course, has been one of the objectives behind federal intervention in air and water pollution policy from the very beginning. However, the existing requirements for new-source performance standards would meet this objective.

A fourth possible objective is to permit states to maintain some parts of their territory at higher air quality levels than the national standards. But this option is already present in the 1970 Clean Air Amendments. States may set ambient air quality standards equal to or stricter than the national air quality standards. The objectives of flexibility and local option are already served by existing provisions of the 1970 Clean Air Amendments.

In summary, the EPA nondegradation provisions were developed in response to a court order to implement a vague and general statement of congressional intent. The EPA effort suffered from the absence of any more specific statements of the objectives to be served by a nondegradation policy. In developing its own version of a nondegradation policy, Congress sought to make more explicit statements of objectives. The objective of protecting certain valuable national lands is well served by certain provisions of the 1977 amendments. But other stated objectives are either already adequately served by existing provisions of the law, or, as

[27] On the other hand, the costs of reducing pollution are also likely to be higher.

in the case of additional protection of human health, poorly served by the 1977 amendments.

Sulfur and the Scrubber Controversy

The controversy over the economic feasibility of flue-gas-desulfurization (removing sulfur oxides from exhaust gas streams by scrubbing) is probably the clearest example of problems caused by inappropriate incentives for technological innovation. The earliest efforts to control sulfur emissions from combustion processes relied primarily on fuel switching, that is, switching to low-sulfur-content coal, or oil, or natural gas. The increased demand for these fuels soon caused low-sulfur coal and oil to carry a premium on the market.[28] The rising relative price of low-sulfur oil and complications resulting from the Arab oil embargo of 1973–74 caused many utilities to seek variances to permit them to burn high-sulfur-content fuels.

Of course, the burning of naturally occurring, low-sulfur fuels is not the only way to limit sulfur emissions. It is technically possible to pre-treat oil and coal to remove naturally occurring sulfur. Moreover, stack gas scrubbers can be used to remove sulfur combustion products from exhaust gas streams. EPA has been a major source of financial support for research and development on flue-gas-desulfurization processes. For several years, EPA has argued that the processes are technically and economically feasible and reliable in commercial operations. But for the most part, the utility industry has resisted the adoption of this technology. This can best be explained by the absence of positive incentives to industry to seek out the best technologies for controlling emissions. As long as high-sulfur fuel variances and delays in compliance schedules can be obtained, they represent the cheapest option facing dischargers. EPA has very limited authority to force the adoption of the scrubber technology on unwilling utilities; and utilities have the incentive to claim that the EPA-developed technology is inadequate, untested, unreliable, and too costly.

The issue of the technological feasibility of sulfur controls is becoming increasingly important as we learn more about the adverse health effects of sulfur oxides and their atmospheric by-products. In addition, present energy policies are placing greater emphasis on the development of our coal resources; but much of the accessible coal reserves contain substantial quantities of sulfur. Given these problems, an emissions charge on sulfur

---

[28] Interstate natural gas prices are regulated by the Federal Power Commission.

has very attractive properties. First, as we pointed out above, a charge provides incentives for more rapid compliance with existing permits and pollution control requirements. Second, at least for combustion sources of sulfur, monitoring the emissions is quite straightforward. Sulfur input can be measured by examining the sulfur content of fuel and measuring total fuel use. Emissions must be equal to sulfur input less any sulfur products recovered by flue-gas-desulfurization.

Third, and perhaps most important, an emission charge would create the appropriate incentives for technological development in the area of sulfur control. If EPA is correct about the economic and technological feasibility of flue-gas-desulfurization, utilities would adopt the process voluntarily in order to reduce their sulfur charge payments. If EPA is wrong about flue-gas-desulfurization, utilities and others would have the appropriate economic incentives to modify the technology to make it work, or to seek other technologies for controlling sulfur emissions.

Implementation of the sulfur charge at the federal level would require amendments to the 1970 and 1977 clean air legislation since EPA does not presently have authority to impose one. President Richard Nixon proposed such a charge to Congress in 1973 but the proposal languished because of lack of congressional and administration support. Other sulfur charge proposals have also been introduced at various times, without notable success. There is nothing in the Clean Air Act that would prevent a state from using a sulfur charge as part of its state implementation plan. It is to be hoped that some state will seize the opportunity for such an innovative approach to pollution control policy.

Water Pollution

Although the present federal policy was established by Congress in 1972, substantial federal efforts at regulating industrial water pollution and stimulating construction of municipal treatment plants date back to 1956. These earlier efforts were apparently at least somewhat successful. The results of EPA's first National Water Quality Inventory conducted in 1973 indicate that there have been significant improvements in most major waterways over the preceding decade, at least in terms of the organic wastes and bacteria that were the primary targets of the earlier efforts at pollution control.[29]

[29] For further discussion of available data on water quality and trends, see CEQ, *Environmental Quality*.

It is too early to assess the impact of the 1972 amendments on trends on water quality. Industrial dischargers were not required to meet the first stage, BPT effluent limitations until mid-1977. Because of the time lags in data compilation and publication, the latest water quality data available are for 1975. Hence our primary assessment of the 1972 Federal Water Pollution Control Amendments must be in terms of how well the administrative machinery is functioning in meeting the requirements of the act.

With respect to its first major deadline, it appears that the law has not been a success. The law requires that all industrial dischargers be in compliance with effluent limitations based upon the best practicable control technology currently available (BPT) by July 1, 1977. Publicly owned treatment works were to be in compliance with effluent limitations based on secondary treatment by the same date. The National Commission on Water Quality (NCWQ) expected that about 20 percent of the industrial dischargers would be unable to meet the 1977 deadline.[30] The report of the commission staff suggested that industrial compliance with BPT limitations is not likely to be achieved until 1980.[31] Only about half of publicly owned treatment works are expected to be in compliance with secondary treatment by the 1977 deadline. Under present arrangements, the date on which municipalities will be in full compliance depends primarily on the level of funding from the municipal treatment grants program. The problems faced by municipalities in achieving compliance, and the consequences of the municipal grant program will be discussed in a separate section of this chapter.

There are several reasons why full industrial compliance with the deadline has not been achieved. First, effluent limitations on each source are to be based upon "effluent limitation guidelines" for each category of source. The guidelines were to have been prepared by EPA within one year after the enactment of the law. Because of the complexities of the task, no effluent limitation guidelines were published before the deadline.[32] Even at this writing, guidelines for some categories of sources are still being prepared, and others already issued, are being revised.

A second factor has been the numerous legal challenges to both the guidelines and the limitations actually imposed on individual sources. The National Commission on Water Quality reported that there are currently

[30] National Commission on Water Quality, *Report to the Congress* (Washington, D.C., NCWQ, March 1976) p. 16.
[31] National Commission on Water Quality, *Staff Report* (Washington, D.C., NCWQ, March 1976).
[32] Some of these complexities will be discussed in the next section.

about 250 court cases pending that challenge the effluent limitations already promulgated. In some cases, the courts have remanded effluent limitations to EPA for revision. And in any case, implementation of the limitations will be delayed as long as court suits are still pending.

Another factor in the delay has been the sheer enormity of the task of issuing permits to more than 60,000 industrial and municipal sources. EPA has reported that as of March 31, 1976, it had issued permits to only 67 percent of all industrial dischargers. The percentage was higher for major industrial sources—over 90 percent.[33] But many of these permits were written before the applicable effluent limitation guidelines were promulgated. In some of these cases permits were issued which are inconsistent with the effluent limitation guidelines eventually adopted. Permits are subject to periodical review and revision. But in the meantime, some dischargers may be in nominal compliance with the terms of their permits, but not in compliance with the applicable BPT effluent guidelines.

The 1972 Water Pollution Amendments also establish additional goals and requirements for 1983. The law states the following goal, ". . . that wherever attainable, an interim goal of water quality which provides for the protection and propagation of fish, shellfish, and wildlife and provides for recreation in and on the water be achieved by July 1, 1983." This has been nicknamed the "fishable-swimmable" goal. In furtherance of that goal, industrial dischargers are to comply with effluent limitations based upon the best available technology economically achievable (BAT) by 1983; municipalities are to comply with best practicable treatment by the same date.[34]

The fact that the 1977 BPT requirements have been so difficult to achieve raises some questions about the 1983 requirements. In fact, questions can be raised about both the objectives (fishable-swimmable) and the means (BAT effluent limitations). The National Commission on Water Quality has recommended what it called "mid-course corrections" in the form of more flexibility both for deadlines and for effluent limitations for individual dischargers. In the ensuing three sections, we give a more detailed analysis of existing policy and possible alternatives. The next section deals with the objectives of water pollution control policy. The section following that deals with means of achieving control of industrial

[33] CEQ, *Environmental Quality,* p. 15.
[34] Amendments to the 1972 Federal Water Pollution Control Act were enacted in December 1977. These amendments included some changes in the details and timing of the BAT requirements. The following discussion is still generally applicable. Specific aspects of these changes will be noted as appropriate below.

sources—technology-based effluent limitations and alternatives. The final section on water pollution deals with means to achieve control of municipal sources, especially the federal municipal treatment grant program.

Goals of Water Pollution Policy

The first sentence of the amendments states that the goal is "to restore and maintain the chemical, physical, and biological integrity of the Nation's waters." This is followed by two more specific statements of operational objectives. The first is to achieve the elimination of all discharge of pollutants into navigable waters by 1985. The second is related to the desired uses of the nation's water bodies and helps to define the nature of the benefits sought from controlling pollution. It calls for "fishable and swimmable" waters by 1983. These objectives are to be attained by imposing and enforcing effluent standards on all dischargers—the BPT standards by 1977 and the BAT standards for 1983.

Actually the distinction between goals or ends (fishable-swimmable, and the like) and means (BPT and BAT) is blurred in the 1972 amendments. For example, the objective of elimination of all discharges (EOD) is not directly related to the benefits of improving water quality and perhaps more logically should be considered a means of achieving the objective of "restoring and maintaining the . . . integrity" of our waters. More important, although the BPT and BAT effluent standards seem logically to be a means of achieving "fishable-swimmable" water or some other water quality objectives, some statements by supporters of the effluent limitation approach seem to raise the standards to the status of objectives—that is, something to be achieved irrespective of their effect on water quality. Technology-based effluent limitations replaced an earlier strategy in which effluent reductions were calculated so as to achieve ambient water quality standards. The congressional debate makes it clear that supporters of the 1972 amendments saw them as an explicit rejection of ambient water quality standards, either as a feasible basis for determining effluent reductions or as a basis for enforcement. Rather, if technology allows an effluent limitation to be achieved, it should be done.

It is this disagreement concerning the appropriate objectives of water pollution policy that is the basis of Senator Edmund Muskie's strong dissent from the recommendations of the majority of the National Commission on Water Quality.[35] The majority recommended, in essence, a more

---

[35] National Commission on Water Quality, *Report to the Congress.*

flexible approach to the application of technology-based standards as a means for achieving water quality objectives, while Senator Muskie defended them as objectives *per se*. Rational debate on the means of achieving policy objectives is difficult in the absence of agreement on the nature of the objectives to be achieved.

A more sensible approach would be to make the prevention of adverse effects of water pollution the primary objective of water pollution policy, with the proviso that the nature and magnitude of these adverse effects be compared with the costs of their prevention. That is, benefits and costs would be balanced at the margin. Adverse effects depend on the nature and concentrations of polluting substances in the water. Hence this objective can be stated in terms of ambient water quality standards. We turn now to a discussion of the EOD and fishable-swimmable objectives of the 1972 amendments in terms of the statement of overall objectives.

The EOD objective is really a form of effluent standard, one set at zero. As such, it should be assessed in terms of its contribution to the achievement of water quality objectives. From this perspective, the validity of EOD as a proximate goal depends on specific circumstances. There are some substances such as DDT or polychlorinated biphenyls (PCBs) which are highly toxic, persistent in the environment, and which accumulate in food chains. For such substances, zero discharge is probably justified in terms of the nature and magnitude of the potentially adverse environmental effects.[36] For other substances EOD is relatively simple to achieve; in fact, it has been incorporated into the BPT or BAT requirements for some categories of sources.[37]

In general, however, the costs of additional treatment or removal of waste products from any given effluent stream rise rapidly as 100 percent removal is approached (see figure 2-4). Removal of waste products from a water stream leaves residuals to be disposed of in some other manner. The possible adverse effects of incineration or land disposal of these residuals must be weighed against the benefits of improved water quality. For those substances for which waters have some assimilative capacity, the adverse effects of low levels of discharge may be small, perhaps even negligible. In such cases, the costs of achieving EOD probably substantially outweigh any benefits.

Finally, EOD is at the outer limits of, or beyond, the technological capabilities of industry in many cases. If it is to be pursued as a goal in its own

[36] See also chapter 4.
[37] See National Commission on Water Quality, *Staff Report* p. II-138.

FIGURE 2-4   *Example of Marginal Costs of Pollution Control*

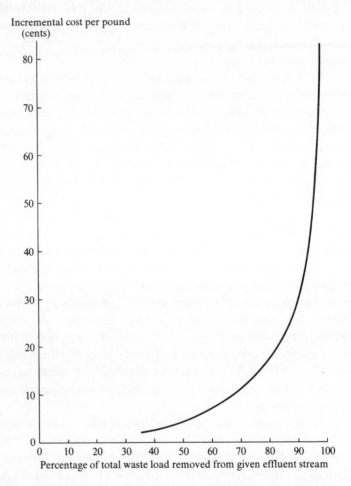

Source: Adapted from Steve H. Hanke and Ivars Gutmanis, "Estimates of Industrial Waterborne Residuals Control Costs," in Henry Peskin and Eugene Seskin, eds., *Cost Benefit Analysis and Water Pollution Policy* (Washington, D.C., Urban Institute, 1975) p. 241.

right, incentives must be provided for the technological developments which would make it possible. Effluent charges are ideally suited for providing this kind of long-term, continuing incentive for innovation in waste control technology.

The benefit–cost approach can also inform us as to the desirability of achieving fishable-swimmable waters by 1983 and the advisability of achieving the BAT effluent limitations by that date. The answers to these questions must be found by examining costs and benefits on a case-by-case basis. The benefit–cost ratios are likely to vary both across water bodies for a given type of source, and across different categories of sources. For example, for some categories of sources, the major difference between BAT and BPT lies in the level of control of biochemical oxygen demand (BOD) and total suspended solids. Water bodies have some degree of natural assimilative capacity for these pollutants. There are other cases where BAT involves imposing controls on additional substances not controlled under BPT—for example, sulfides, fluorides, nitrates, and manganese from the iron and steel industry. It may be desirable to bring these additional substances under control without necessarily increasing the limitation on BOD and total suspended solids.

There are three possible reasons why moving to BAT might not be desirable from a benefit–cost perspective. First, there are a number of water bodies for which it appears that achieving BPT effluent limitations will be sufficient to achieve fishable-swimmable waters. In these cases there may be no point in going beyond BPT, at least in controlling BOD and total suspended solids. Even in these cases, however, it may be desirable to invoke those portions of BAT requirements which involve the control of additional substances.

Second, there are likely to be bodies of water for which BAT will not be sufficient to achieve fishable-swimmable waters. This would mean that the costs of BAT would be incurred without realizing the corresponding benefits. This could be for one of two reasons. First, it could be that, even with BAT, the total volume of industrial and municipal discharges may still be too high to permit the attainment of the fishable-swimmable standard. The 1972 Water Pollution Amendments actually anticipate this possibility by requiring even stricter effluent limitations for these cases. However, the administrator is required to examine the relationship between costs and benefits and may choose not to require the additional effluent limitations.

The second possible reason for not attaining fishable-swimmable water with BAT could be pollutants from *nonpoint sources,* since these are not covered by the technology-based effluent limitations. Nonpoint sources are those which are diffuse, unlike specific industrial locations. These include runoff from cultivated agricultural land, from silvicultural activities, and urban storm runoff. Of course, the larger the nonpoint sources of pollution relative to point sources in any water body, the less impact control of point sources will have on ambient water quality. The National Commission on Water Quality *Staff Report* includes estimates of total waste loads for the nation as a whole after achieving BPT for several forms of waste. The relative importance of nonpoint sources can be seen by looking at nonpoint sources as a percentage of total discharges. The percentages for several pollutants are as follows:[38]

Pollutant	Nonpoint sources as percentage of total discharges
Suspended solids	92
Fecal coliforms	98
Total nitrates	79
Total phosphates	53
BOD	37

Since these are nationwide averages, the relative importance of nonpoint sources of substances such as BOD may be substantially higher in certain water bodies. In such cases, it is unlikely that additional control of point sources will have a significant effect on water quality.[39]

The third possible reason for recommending against BAT is that fishable-swimmable waters may be technically attainable with the application of BAT, yet not desirable. This could be either because the benefits of achieving fishable-swimmable waters are low or the costs of BAT are high, or both.

The major questions considered by the National Commission on Water Quality concerned the economic, social, and environmental effects of achieving BAT and fishable-swimmable waters by 1983. The commission chose to recommend that the fishable-swimmable goal be retained but that the deadline for achieving BAT be postponed by five to ten years. The commission also recommended that during the time allowed by the postponement, efforts should be made to improve the control of toxic substances, that BPT requirements be reviewed and upgraded to reflect technological innovations, and that more stringent effluent limitations be applied selectively where they can be shown to have a significant beneficial effect in achieving water quality standards. The commission also called for a further study of the results actually achieved by the eventual attainment of the 1977 requirements and to consider whether uniform application of BAT or other more stringent effluent limitations is justified and desirable.

[38] National Commission on Water Quality, *Staff Report,* II-138.
[39] The question of means of control of nonpoint sources will be taken up in the next section.

In the discussion supporting these recommendations, the commission stated:

> The Commission believes existing uncertainty over estimated social and economic effects, adverse and beneficial, can best be resolved by allowing adequate time for collection and analysis of data to determine changes resulting from substantial achievement of the 1977 requirements. . . . Any adverse water quality impact in delaying the 1983 requirements will likely be minimal. . . . Considerable evidence . . . suggests that meeting the 1977 requirements may, in many cases, produce the desired water quality. . . . Wise use of total national resources would support the imposition of only those levels of control or treatment that actually produce the intended result. Additional investment with marginal identifiable benefits or improvements could operate to the detriment of competing demands of other worthwhile national programs, such as energy conservation and air pollution control.[40]

The 1977 Water Pollution Amendments are at least partly responsive to these recommendations. They permit EPA to relax the secondary treatment requirement for municipalities which discharge into deep marine waters if they can show that "fishable-swimmable-drinkable" water quality standards can still be attained. They provide for various extensions of the 1983 deadline for BAT for industry—in some cases to as late as 1987. Finally, they permit the modification of effluent limitations for conventional pollutants (BOD, suspended solids, bacteria, and pH) after consideration of such factors as "the reasonableness of the relationship between the costs . . . and the benefits derived. . . ."

Means

The principal means for attaining water quality objectives in the Federal Water Pollution Control Amendments of 1972 are the establishment and enforcement of technology-based effluent standards. These standards are quantitative limits imposed on all dischargers where the quantities are determined by reference to present technology. To put it simply, standards are set on the basis of what can be done with available technology, rather than what *should* be done to achieve ambient environmental quality standards, to balance benefits and costs, or to satisfy any other criteria.

Technology-based standards in general must spell out the degree of technological sophistication to be embodied in the standard. The standard could be based on present normal practice, best current practice, best

---

[40] National Commission on Water Quality, *Report to the Congress* p. 21.

available or demonstrated technology, and so forth. If the legislation governing the standards called only for technological considerations, it would be a *purely* technology-based system. But often, as in the case of the 1972 amendments, technological requirements are tempered by economic considerations and qualifications. These two aspects, the technological and economic, illustrate a major difficulty in the technological approach to defining effluent and emission standards. Although technology-based effluent standards may appear to be determinate and objective, in practice both the definition of the technology to be employed and the economic qualifications that are usually attached are imprecise and ambiguous. "Best practical" and "best available" or "reasonable costs" are not objective, scientific terms. Such language grants a tremendous amount of discretion to the officials charged with the implementation of technology-based standards. In addition, the wording places a very large responsibility on those officials to interpret a bewildering assortment of engineering, scientific, and economic information.

Industrial and environmental representatives have raised many questions as EPA has moved toward the promulgation of specific effluent limitations. Four major questions have emerged as being of general and perhaps overriding concern. This discussion of these questions is intended only to illustrate some of the problems and complexities that are involved in translating legislation into action.

The first question concerns the EPA's use of "exemplary plants" as the basis for standard-setting. Industry groups have argued that the "starting point" for determining what is practicable in an industrial category should be "a survey of at least a representative sample, if not all, of existing performance. . . . except where present practices throughout the industry are inadequate."[41] The issue is whether "practicable" is to be defined in terms of common practice or in terms of best observed practice.

The second set of questions concerns whether Congress intended that BPT guidelines provide specific numerical values to be applied uniformly across broad industrial categories or that they provide ranges of possible performance within which specific limits would be set on a case-by-case basis. The latter could take into account the particular conditions of industrial subcategories and individual plants. EPA has chosen the uniform approach. One legal challenge which has reached the Supreme Court has been decided in favor of EPA.

[41] National Commission on Water Quality, *Staff Report* p. V-124.

The third major controversy concerns the extent to which EPA should consider in-plant modifications and process changes in drawing up effluent limitation guidelines for BPT. Industrial groups and congressional critics have argued that EPA exceeded its statutory authority when it considered in-plant modifications, process changes such as recycling and alternative uses of water, and materials recovery from wastewater streams as elements of practicable technology.

Finally, industry has raised numerous legal challenges to effluent guidelines based on the claim that EPA failed to consider adequately the costs and benefits associated with proposed BPT regulations. The language of the amendments requires only that costs, benefits, environmental impacts, and energy requirements be considered. It does not say what weight they are to be given. There are many controversial judgments and decisions that must be made in deciding questions of technology. The problem of judgment is compounded when technology is to be weighed against economic factors such as costs and benefits. Congress has said that this must be done; but it has not given guidance as to how the value judgments are to be made, that is, what relative weights are to be given to costs, benefits, and so forth. Lacking adequate congressional guidance, it is inevitable that the role of costs and benefits has become a major source of controversy in the implementation of supposedly technology-based effluent limitations.

This discussion of the controversial issues surrounding the BPT and BAT standards is intended to demonstrate an important point. Whenever legislation provides general guidance that must be translated into specific terms at the discretion of a bureaucracy, there will be many opportunities for legal challenges to bureaucratic decisions in which it can be argued that the bureaucracy misinterpreted the legislative intent, failed to give adequate weight to particular evidence, exceeded its authority, failed to utilize its authority, and so forth. These legal challenges serve to slow down the process of implementation. This is in part because the bureaucrats, hoping to forestall excessive litigation, will attempt formally or informally to negotiate agreements with affected parties. Also, litigation itself is time consuming. The result is that implementation of the law may be held up until the key issues are resolved by the courts, often only after lengthy review and appeal.

The major criticism of technology-based standards from an economic standpoint is that they are virtually certain to result in higher than necessary total costs for any particular level of water quality. There is nothing in the logic or the procedures for setting technology-based limits to assure that the conditions for cost minimization will be satisfied. One set of studies prepared for the National Commission on Water Quality shows a substantial potential for cost savings (30 to 35 percent for the nation as a whole) by the selection of a cost-minimizing pattern of effluent reductions to achieve the same pattern of water quality improvement.[42]

A major question concerning technology-based effluent standards is their effect on innovation and technological change in pollution control. On the positive side, it could be argued that by requiring dischargers to control their discharges to levels that engineers say can be achieved, a technology-based policy forces the adoption of the best available technology. The statement is true but misses the point. The statement refers to the static process of adoption of existing technology. Technological change is a dynamic process which involves the search for and discovery of new and innovative ways of doing things.

During a congressional hearing, John Quarles, then deputy administrator of EPA, was asked about the incentives for innovation. He responded ". . . we do not mandate the type of technology required to achieve compliance with our standards. We base our standards on available technologies; but if someone chooses to use a different technology, then we allow him to do so, so long as he meets the standards."[43] It is true that firms are free to use alternative technologies to meet the established effluent limitations. However, the National Commission on Water Quality found that "in many cases, the abatement [technology] which is *actually* being installed is equivalent to the suggested *technologies,* rather than being designed to meet the *limitations* per se."[44] This is so even though there is evidence that some of the technologies suggested by EPA may not be adequate to meet the legal effluent limitations. Thus, firms may be responding in a perverse way to the technology-based limits. The firms may reason that if they do not meet the effluent limitations, they will be safe from EPA prosecution so long as they have demonstrated a good faith effort to achieve the standards by adopting the technology used by EPA

[42] See Ralph A. Luken, Daniel J. Basta, and Edward H. Pechan, *The National Residuals Discharge Inventory,* (Washington, D.C., National Research Council, 1976) chapter 9. Earlier studies comparing the costs of uniform treatment policies with cost-minimizing alternatives found the former to be sometimes two to three times larger than the latter. See Allen V. Kneese and Blair T. Bower, *Managing Water Quality: Economics, Technology, Institutions* (Baltimore, Md., Johns Hopkins Universtiy Press for Resources for the Future, 1968) pp. 158–164, 224–235.

[43] *Implementation of the Federal Water Pollution Control Act,* Hearings before the Subcommittee on Investigations and Review of the House Committee on Public Works, 93 Cong. 2 sess. (1974) pp. 486–487.

[44] National Commission on Water Quality, *Staff Report* p. II-68.

in establishing the standards. Thus, rather than encouraging innovation or the development of alternative technologies to meet effluent limitations, the existing policy may encourage a risk-averting strategy of adopting the sanctioned technologies even when these technologies may not be expected to meet the standard.

None of this discussion speaks to the problem of positive incentives for innovation and technological change in pollution control. Once technology-based limits are established by EPA, there is no incentive for the private sector to develop new technologies which make possible even more stringent control of effluents. In fact, if anything, there is a negative incentive because once the technologies become known, EPA is required to upgrade the technology-based standards, thus imposing new costs on all dischargers.

All of this is in contrast to the structure of incentives created by a comprehensive system of effluent charges. If charges are levied on all discharges, even those consistent with the attainment of water quality objectives, dischargers have a continuing incentive to reduce this element of their costs. It would not be in dischargers' interests to choose the EPA-suggested control techniques if they had reason to believe that the techniques would not be successful in meeting effluent limits.[45] In the longer run, firms would have continuing incentives to seek out and adopt new technology as long as the extra cost of the new technology is less than the reduction in effluent charge payments it makes possible.

Once effluent limitations have been promulgated for individual dischargers, EPA faces the task of enforcing the terms of the permits. Since permits are often accompanied by agreed-upon schedules for compliance, monitoring progress toward compliance is relatively easy. EPA inspectors must simply observe whether deadlines for such things as starting construction or completing installation have been met. If compliance deadlines are not met, EPA must either ignore the violation or seek sanctions through the judicial system. A system of noncompliance charges like that described above could help to reduce the burden on the enforcement staff of EPA and the states while providing dischargers with positive incentives to achieve compliance, perhaps even before the stated deadlines.

Another enforcement problem is how to ensure that the treatment equipment is operated in a satisfactory manner. Monitoring performance

---

[45] However, firms would choose such techniques if they minimized the total costs of pollution control to the firm—including the costs of the charge. But in these circumstances, this is a desirable outcome.

is possible, and necessary. But if periods of poor operation and noncompliance with the effluent limitations are detected, the agency must seek to exercise its enforcement powers in the courts. This is a time-consuming process with an uncertain outcome. Often enforcement officials will negotiate consent orders, new compliance schedules, and so forth, rather than attempt to push the judicial enforcement process through to its logical conclusion, the imposition of civil or criminal penalties.

In making day-to-day decisions about levels of operation for treatment systems, firms must weigh the extra costs of effective operation against the probability that violations of standards will be detected and enforcement actions undertaken. They must also consider the length of procedural delays, and the likely penalties, if any. Any step that raises the expected costs to firms of failing to meet effluent standards is likely to bring about more effective continuing operation of treatment systems. Higher penalties and more streamlined enforcement procedures are one set of options. Yet there are limits to the extent to which the judicial system can or should be altered in this way. For example, judges may be reluctant to impose stiff fines which are out of proportion to the perceived seriousness of the offense.

Administratively levied effluent charges would be an attractive alternative. Such charges could be levied on all discharges—so as to include an incentive for innovation—or only on discharges above the effluent limitation. In the latter case they would still provide a continuous incentive to operate treatment systems effectively. These charges would be very much like the noncompliance fees described above; but they would apply to the operation of treatment systems as well as their installation.

As noted above, water quality improvements in some river basins can only be obtained through control of nonpoint source pollutants. For some types of nonpoint source pollution, the technological aspects of control are relatively straightforward. Control might require changes in agricultural practice to control farm runoff or better harvesting procedures to reduce soil erosion from forest areas. For other nonpoint sources, urban runoff, for example, control technologies are known but are extremely costly.

The main barrier to controlling nonpoint sources is not technological. It is the absence of an effective institutional and regulatory framework. The principal tool for dealing with nonpoint sources in the 1972 Water Pollution Amendments is Section 208 which calls for the "development and implementation of area-wide waste treatment management plans."

Section 208 makes explicit reference to nonpoint sources. The requirement for comprehensive planning and the assignment to Section 208 planning agencies of responsibility for issuing permits and for other aspects of the implementation of waste management plans create at least the opportunity for a coordinated attack on nonpoint as well as point sources.

To date there has been little progress in implementing Section 208. One factor has been EPA's preoccupation with establishing effluent limitations and standards and with issuing discharge permits to meet the deadlines established in the 1972 amendments. Now that these initial tasks are complete or at least under control, EPA has indicated that it is giving the highest priority to implementation of Section 208 planning and management. A second factor in the slow progress has been that many states had to create new regional agencies which lacked institutional and political support. A third difficulty is that although federal funds are available to support planning activities, the states must finance the implementation phase. Financial considerations may limit the range of implementation activities undertaken by Section 208 agencies.

It is too early to tell whether these difficulties can be overcome. But as an institutional innovation, the agencies deserve support, not only because of their capacity for developing more coordinated and cost-effective approaches for achieving water quality objectives, but also because of their potential as a vehicle for integrated environmental and resource management.

The Municipal Grant Program

The problem of pollution from municipal wastes has been treated differently from industrial pollution in one important respect. As an incentive to achieve compliance and to ease the financial burden on local government, the federal government will pay up to 75 percent of the design and construction costs for municipal treatment plants. The ability of municipalities to achieve secondary treatment is tied, therefore, to the level of funding for the municipal grant program. If grant funds are not available, lack of funds becomes a justification for the failure to construct the necessary treatment facilities. Apparently only about 50 percent of the municipalities in the country have met the 1977 deadline for secondary treatment. The primary reasons are the shortage of grant funds and delays in obligating and spending the available funds.

The 1972 Water Pollution Amendments authorized the expenditure of $18 billion over the three-year period 1973–1975. In combination with

TABLE 2-3   *Construction Grant Program: Authorizations, Allotments, Obligations, and Outlays*

(billion dollars)

Fiscal year	Authorization	Allotments[a]	Obligations	Outlays
1973	5.0	2.0	1.6	0.0
1974	6.0	3.0	1.4	0.1
1975	7.0	4.0	3.6	0.9
1976	0.0	9.0	6.4[b]	1.5
1977	0.0	0.0	5.0[c]	n.a.
Total	18	18	18	2.5

Note: n.a. = not available.

Source: National Commission on Water Quality, *Staff Report* p. V-34.

a The president's impoundment and the later Supreme Court ruling explain the delayed pattern of allotments.

b EPA estimates.

c No estimates available. Figure represents total available to be obligated.

matching funds from state and local governments, this would have been sufficient to fund the construction of $24 billion worth of treatment facilities. Actually, through fiscal year 1976 less than 15 percent of the authorized funds had actually been spent. The authorizations, allotments, obligations, and actual outlays are in Table 2-3.

Although the authorizations seem large relative to actual expenditures, they are small relative to estimated needs. The National Commission on Water Quality estimates that constructing the facilities needed to meet the secondary treatment requirement by 1985 (and to provide for more stringent treatment where necessary) will cost $39.2 billion in 1976 dollars. (EPA's estimate for the same category is $34.2 billion.)[46] The commission estimates that an additional $47.7 billion will be needed for correction of infiltration problems in sewers, sewer rehabilitation, and new collector and interceptor sewers. (The comparable EPA estimate is $43.4 billion.) By far the largest category of estimated capital requirements is that for the separation of combined sanitary waste and storm sewers and for the control of storm waters. The National Commission on Water Quality estimates that $262.0 billion will be required for this task. (The comparable EPA estimate is $72.4 billion.)

The disparity between estimated needs and available authorizations would suggest that a substantial increase in authorized grants is in order.

---

[46] These data are from the U.S. Environmental Protection Agency, *Cost Estimates for Construction of Publicly-Owned Wastewater Treatment Facilities—1976 Needs Survey* (1977).

The commission recommended that Congress authorize additional grants of at least $5 billion per year and perhaps as much as $10 billion per year for at least five more years. The 1977 amendments authorize a total of $24.5 billion in grants spread approximately evenly over the five years ending in 1982. While this extension of the grant program is desirable on balance, the present form of the grant program has resulted in several problems. It would be desirable to examine these problems and to consider some possible improvements in the form of the program and the way it is administered.

The first problem is that the grant program distorts the incentives faced by municipalities and may bias their choice of treatment technologies. Federal grants subsidize the capital cost but not the cost of operating and maintaining treatment plants for municipal wastes. As a result cities have an incentive to choose treatment technologies which have high capital costs relative to operating and maintenance costs even though their total costs might be substantially higher than other alternatives. This is because the federal government shares in a greater percentage of the total costs when capital costs are high.[47]

Is there some way to modify the grant program so as to reduce or eliminate this capital bias? There are two approaches. The first is to lower the grant rate, say from 75 percent to 50 percent. While this reduces the bias, it also reduces the overall flow of aid to cities. The alternative is to extend the subsidy to cover operating and maintenance costs as well. A 75-percent subsidy of operating and maintenance costs would greatly expand the flow of aid to municipalities, since operating and maintenance costs could be as much as 75 percent of the total lifetime system cost. The budgetary implications of an operating and maintenance subsidy of that magnitude are staggering.

A combination of a reduction in the overall subsidy rate with an extension of the subsidy to cover operating and maintenance costs could be worked out in such a manner that total aid to municipalities is the same as that provided by the present grant program. The time pattern of aid would be different, involving a lower level of "front end" expenditure by the federal government and more borrowing by municipalities to cover a larger share of capital costs. Because interest on municipal bonds is exempt from federal taxation, this form of implicit federal subsidy would be increased.

[47] For an example, see Richard Raymond, "The Impact of Federal Financing Provisions in the Federal Water Pollution Control Act Amendments of 1972," *Public Policy* (Winter 1974) pp. 109–119.

The distribution of aid among municipalities would also be somewhat different since towns whose circumstances dictated a more capital-intensive technology would receive relatively less aid than under the present program. However, the total costs of meeting secondary treatment standards across the country would be lower.

There is a danger in subsidizing operating and maintenance costs, though. If actual expenditures each year become the basis for subsidy, municipalities will have a reduced incentive to avoid waste and to operate their plants efficiently. In this respect a subsidy of actual operating expenses may not be cost effective. Alternatively, at the time of construction, an *expected* rate of operating and maintenance expenditures could be calculated as the basis for the subsidy. With the amount of the subsidy fixed, municipalities would have incentives to minimize their operating and maintenance costs.[48] However, maintaining the incentive for minimizing operating and maintenance costs is not an unmixed blessing.

The effectiveness of waste treatment (that is, the percentage of waste actually removed from the effluent stream) depends in part on the level of operation and maintenance expenditures. If municipalities are too frugal in their operating and maintenance expenditures, the result may be a failure to achieve effluent limitations and water quality targets. This is simply one aspect of a more general problem. There is now an accumulation of evidence that many municipal waste treatment plants are operated at levels of effectiveness well below their designed standard. For example, the Council on Environmental Quality reports, "GAO [U.S. Government Accounting Office] conducted a detailed study of five plants and found that none met design performance standards 'because of poor operation and maintenance, plant overloading, or possible faulty design'."[49] EPA has also reported that, of the operating plants inspected as part of the routine construction grant follow-up, 30 percent of those plants with sufficient data for analysis were not achieving designed effluent quality.[50] Incentives for proper performance are weak, especially in comparison with the incentives for keeping operating and maintenance expenditures "in line."

The question of the effectiveness of municipal plant operation is just one aspect of the overall problem of incentives to achieve targeted effluent

[48] Provisions would have to be made for indexing operating and maintenance costs to take account of general price inflation over the life of the project.

[49] CEQ, *Environmental Quality* p. 18.

[50] Quoted in EPA, *Economic Report—Alternative Methods of Financing Wastewater Treatment* (1975) p. IV-37. The reported source is EPA's *Review of the Municipal Wastewater Treatment Works Program* (November 1974) p. 16.

limitations. Since effluent limitations from municipal plants are written into the permits they must hold, one approach to achieving compliance is monitoring and enforcement. We have already discussed some of the limitations of the enforcement approach. We have also commented on the incentives for better performance provided by a system of effluent charges. Effluent charges could be imposed either by the federal government, or by the states as part of their programs for implementing the national permit system. A federal charge system would require the enactment of new legislation by Congress. There is nothing in the 1972 amendments to prevent a state from enacting an effluent charge system that would include coverage of municipalities. One advantage of the state system would be the ability of the state to control the use or redistribution of the effluent charge revenues. Revenues could be used to fund state pollution control programs, or they could be returned to municipalities, for example, on the basis of population. As long as funds are not returned on a dollar-for-dollar basis, there would be no net financial drain on municipalities. Considered in aggregate, there might be some redistribution effects; but the incentive for effective operation would be maintained.

The grant program as it has been administered contains incentives to build plants with excess capacity. It makes sense to build plants with a capacity to handle the waste from a population larger than the present one so as to accommodate expected economic and population growth in the service area. The question is: what planning horizon is most appropriate for use in deciding on plant capacity? In the past the tendency was to use a twenty-year design for treatment plants and a fifty-year period for interceptor lines as rules of thumb. If plants are designed with the capacity to handle the expected growth in population over twenty years, and the projections of growth are accurate, the plant will have excess capacity for nineteen years.[51] The economic question is: what is the optimum degree of excess capacity? On the one hand, expanding an existing plant to increase its capacity is likely to mean high incremental costs. On the other hand, building in excess capacity ties up resources which are unused, and in a sense, wasted until demand grows to the capacity level. With the federal subsidy of capital (capacity) costs, state and local governments together only bear 25 percent of the cost of excess capacity.

[51] This statement and the example that follows are both based on the assumption that population growth is not affected by the development of treatment capacity. But the existence of excess capacity can be an attraction to real estate development, particularly when it takes the form of sewer connectors and trunk lines installed to serve future expected populations.

The interest rate or cost of capital is a crucial variable in choosing the optimum degree of excess capacity. Consider a very simple example. Suppose the interest rate at which municipalities can borrow is 6 percent. Suppose that the cost of increasing the capacity of a plant that is about to be built so that it can handle the increment to population expected in the period between fifteen and twenty years from now is $100. Suppose further that the cost of expanding the existing plant fifteen years from now to handle that increment would be $200. Should the larger plant be built now? Or should the municipality wait to expand the plant when the need actually arises? Despite the doubling of the incremental costs, the municipality should wait. If it were to take the extra $100 now, and lend it at an interest rate of 6 percent, in fifteen years the amount would have grown to $240 with interest. This would more than pay for the expansion of capacity at that date. Somewhat more complicated calculations based on this line of reasoning have shown that optimal design periods could be as short as five years and rarely as long as twenty years, depending upon cost conditions and the interest rate. EPA has now begun to require each municipality seeking grant funds to perform these kinds of calculations to determine the optimal design.

The final problem associated with the municipal grant program is the lack of effective planning and coordination in the allocation of grant funds. There has not yet been developed an effective mechanism for allocating grant funds where they are most needed to improve ambient water quality. Because of the time lags involved in preparing projects and grant applications, and the slow rate of obligation of grant monies, there is a tendency for grants to be made on a first-come, first-served basis, with little regard to environmental needs or cost effectiveness.

This is unfortunate because Congress anticipated the need for planning in carrying out such an ambitious strategy as that embodied in the 1972 Water Pollution Amendments. In fact, planning is essential for coordinating the permit system, construction grants, control of nonpoint sources, and so forth. Requirements for planning occur in several places in the 1972 amendments, including Section 208. However the National Commission on Water Quality found, "that planning has not functioned [in the manner anticipated] so far can be attributed to two factors: (1) the diffuse and uncoordinated planning requirements of the Act and (2) the delay, by EPA, in implementing Section 208, the areawide planning provision."[52]

---

[52] National Commission on Water Quality, *Staff Report* p. I-64.

Effective planning requires resources and time to bear fruit. The Section 208 planning process was not given high priority by EPA in the early stages of implementing the 1972 law. It was predictable that the Section 208 area-wide planning apparatus would not be developed and in place in time to have much impact on the allocation of the $18 billion in municipal grants, given the timing of the authorizations. This is perhaps another demonstration of the adage, "haste makes waste."

The 1972 amendments included two provisions regarding the financing of municipal treatment plants that are decided improvements over previous practice. First, where industrial sources make use of municipal treatment plants which were built under the treatment grant program, municipalities are required to recover the federal share of capital costs allocated to treating the industrial wastes through user charges based on quantities of waste treated. The effect of a user charge is to provide the industrial discharger with a financial incentive to reduce the volume of wastewater flows and their pollutant content. This is desirable. However the provision applies only to the federal share of capital costs, and it applies only to the allocated construction costs, not the interest cost on capital.

The second provision requires that municipalities operating federally funded plants must establish a system of user charges to recover the operating and maintenance costs from all users, domestic, commercial, and industrial. Again, the user charge provides a beneficial incentive to reduce waste flows. Many municipalities have had difficulty in implementing a system of user charges because of the lack of a capability for metering discharges. The typical solution for residential users is to base the user charge on metered water consumption. This may be unfair to many lawn waterers; but separate metering for residential sewers is probably not justifiable on cost grounds. The 1977 amendments permit municipalities to recover residential users' shares of operating and maintenance costs through ad valorem taxation of real property. But Congress wisely declined to extend this exception to major industrial and commercial users.

Conclusions

In this chapter we have discussed a number of specific issues and made recommendations for several kinds of changes in present policy. Here we attempt to summarize and synthesize these recommendations in terms of the establishment of pollution control objectives and the selection of means for achieving them.

The justification for governmental intervention to control pollution is that the beneficial effects (broadly defined) to society as a whole from such action outweigh the costs. The issue is whether this justification should be accepted as a presumption for any and all proposed environmental targets (swimmable-fishable waters, elimination of discharges, prevention of all adverse health effects) or whether this should be considered an open question for which evidence should be gathered and judgments rendered on a case-by-case basis. We believe society should recognize that not all interventions in behalf of environmental protection are desirable per se. Some may cost more than they are worth—not only in terms of the private calculus of market values but also in terms of individual and social welfare. Examination of costs and beneficial effects should become an integral part of the process of establishing pollution control objectives.

If this position were accepted, we could then turn to a consideration of the objectives established under the 1970 Clean Air Amendments and the 1972 Federal Water Pollution Control Amendments. In the case of the latter, this would mean both an end to our commitment to uniform effluent standards as well as a case-by-case review of the decision to move to BAT. This review would consider the pollutants to be controlled, the costs of control, and the impact on water quality in each river basin. We hazard the guess that, at least for some river basins, this would result in less emphasis on additional control of degradable organic materials and suspended solids and relatively more attention to toxic substances, heavy metals, and other exotic pollutants. In the case of air pollutants, consideration of new evidence on long-term health effects and ecological damages might lead to the control of new substances and the establishment of stricter standards for some of the existing criteria pollutants. A reevaluation of environmental policy would also lead to an abandonment of the flawed threshold assumption, and a reconsideration of the criteria for establishing air quality standards.

We have seen that in both air and water pollution control, progress toward attaining objectives has been slow. Timetables have not been kept, and deadlines have been reached and passed without full compliance with the legislated objectives. These shortfalls in implementation are due in substantial part to the complexities of the task. But a major share of the responsibility for the slow pace of progress must be assigned to the inappropriate incentive structures created by the regulatory approach to pollution control. In both air and water pollution control there are opportunities for restructuring incentives through the imposition of various types of charges for pollution. We have suggested:

—noncompliance charges for dischargers not meeting existing deadlines for cleanup

—marketable discharge permits or quotas to facilitate regional development and industrial expansion in regions where present ambient air or water quality standards are being violated or just barely met

—charges on all pollution discharges to strengthen the incentives for proper operation of treatment systems and for innovation and technological change in methods of reducing pollution.

Finally, we have seen that the emphasis on equal treatment of dischargers or uniformity of cleanup requirements has meant that the costs of reaching existing environmental quality objectives will be substantially higher than necessary. This means fewer of society's resources are available for other valuable uses. More emphasis should be given to the development of cost-effective means of achieving targets. We have discussed the potential role of charges in moving toward a more cost-effective pollution control policy. Yet even if charge strategies are not adopted, substantial savings can be realized through more selective rather than uniform application of discharge standards such as BAT.

CHAPTER 3

Automobile
Air Pollution Policy

EUGENE P. SESKIN

In July 1977, Washington and Detroit were again face-to-face over the issue of emissions controls on automobiles. The automakers were not prepared to meet the tighter statutory emissions standards for 1978 models that were to go into effect. At the same time, few believed that either Congress or the administration would shut down the nation's largest industry. At 2:20 A.M. on August 3, 1977, House and Senate conferees decided to give the automobile industry two more years to clean up emissions from its cars. The questions that immediately come to mind are: how did we get ourselves in this standoff position, why did Congress once again move back the deadline, and where can we go from here?

This chapter will address these questions. In the next section we will examine the history of mobile-source air pollution.[1] Then, a discussion of the benefits and costs of automobile emissions controls is followed by a section concentrating on the question of technology forcing. After discussing implementation and enforcement aspects of mobile-source control policy, we investigate alternative regulatory policies to control automobile exhausts. We then examine the application of economic incentives to mobile-source pollution control. In the final section we summarize our findings and draw some conclusions.

Depending on which air pollutant is under consideration, the transpor-

[1] The chapter focuses primarily on automobile emissions controls since they (rather than those on trucks, motorcycles, trains, or airplanes) represent the dominant mobile-source air pollution problem and have been the focal point of clean air legislation.

tation sector, in general, and light-duty, gasoline-powered vehicles, in particular, contribute a varying portion of total emissions into the atmosphere. Table 3-1 shows estimates of these relative contributions to total emissions by specific air pollutant during 1973. As the table shows, the automobile is a major contributor to total emissions of certain air pollutants, such as carbon monoxide, while for others, such as sulfur oxides, it contributes little.

Table 3-2 presents a breakdown of the relative importance of mobile and stationary sources of air pollution in large urban areas during the late 1960s. It can be seen that the highest proportions of mobile-source emissions are generally found in the South and West; whereas the contributions of stationary sources are highest in the East and Midwest.

The focus of mobile-source air pollution policy is the control of three air pollutants: hydrocarbons (HC), carbon monoxide (CO), and nitrogen oxides (NO_x), and we are concerned about each because of their ultimate effects on public health. Carbon monoxide is of interest in and of itself. Its inhalation increases the level of carboxyhemoglobin (COHb) in the blood, thus reducing the amount of free hemoglobin available for carrying oxygen to the body tissues for normal activity. The saturation of the blood with COHb is known to put a strain on the heart and to affect performance on standardized tests (for example, it impairs coordination, reduces one's ability to judge time, slows down reaction time, and affects mental abilities). However, these effects have been demonstrated only for relatively high concentrations of carbon monoxide (or COHb in the blood). Much less is known about the health effects of carbon monoxide levels typically experienced in urban atmospheres.[2]

Hydrocarbons and nitrogen oxides are primarily of interest because they are precursors to the formation of photochemical oxidants.[3] The health effects of oxidants are hypothesized to be similar to those of carbon monoxide, although the detailed physiological mechanism through which oxidants operate is not fully understood. Relatively little work has been done on the health effects of hydrocarbons and nitrogen oxides themselves.

[2] Lester B. Lave and Eugene P. Seskin, *Air Pollution and Human Health* (Baltimore, Md., Johns Hopkins University Press for Resources for the Future, 1977) appendix A.

[3] The prevailing view seems to be that HC is the more important of the two. See F. P. Grad, A. J. Rosenthal, L. R. Rockett, J. A. Fay, J. Heywood, J. F. Kain, G. K. Ingram, D. Harrison, Jr., and T. Tietenberg, *The Automobile and the Regulation of Its Impact on the Environment* (Norman, Okla., University of Oklahoma Press, 1975) p. 36.

TABLE 3-1 *National Emissions by Air Pollutant, 1973*
(absolute figures in tons)

Source	Air pollutant				
	Particulates	Sulfur oxides	Nitrogen oxides	Hydrocarbons	Carbon monoxide
Mobile sources	1,156,240	646,539	9,649,050	14,209,967	75,987,164
Percentage of total emissions	7.3	2.0	44.4	59.8	78.3
Gasoline-powered, light-duty vehicles	687,560	172,415	5,844,508	9,117,521	54,507,863
Percentage of total emissions	4.3	0.5	26.9	38.3	56.2
Point sources	12,395,280	29,603,741	10,208,208	6,340,806	15,242,825
Percentage of total emissions	77.9	90.5	46.9	26.7	15.7
Total[a]	15,922,841	32,696,630	21,746,991	23,778,764	97,020,190

Source: U.S. Environmental Protection Agency, *1973 National Emissions Report*, publication no. EPA-450/2-76-007 (1976).
[a] Also includes other relatively minor area and point-source emitters.

TABLE 3-2   Relative Importance of Mobile and Stationary Sources in Large Urban Areas

(all figures except totals in percentage)

Region	Study year	CO Mobile	CO Sta-tionary	HC Mobile	HC Sta-tionary	NO$_x$ Mobile	NO$_x$ Sta-tionary
Chicago	1967	94	6	81	19	35	65
Denver	1967	93	7	78	22	48	52
Los Angeles	1966	95	5	72	28	73	27
New York	1965	96	4	84	16	38	62
Philadelphia	1967	70	30	47	53	27	73
Washington, D.C.	1966	96	4	86	14	44	56
Dallas	1967	97	3	93	7	80	20
Phoenix-Tucson	1967	94	6	87	13	71	29
Portland, Oregon	1968	72	28	64	36	79	21
Cincinnati	1967	85	15	83	17	34	66
Louisville	1967	75	25	83	17	35	65
Miami	1968	90	10	7	93	60	40
Atlanta	1968	89	11	86	14	71	29
Houston	1967	75	25	58	42	43	57
New Orleans	1968	47	53	49	51	56	44
Oklahoma City	1968	98	2	49	51	69	31
Pittsburgh	1967	80	20	70	30	29	71
St. Louis	1967	77	23	80	20	48	52
Charlotte	1968	92	8	86	14	28	72
Hartford	1967	95	5	82	18	52	48
Indianapolis	1967	85	15	86	14	52	48
Providence	1967	95	5	88	12	56	44
National level		65	35	46	54	38	62
National totals (millions of tons)		98	53	17	20	9	15

Source: F. P. Grad and coauthors, *The Automobile and the Regulation of Its Impact on the Environment* (Norman, Okla., University of Oklahoma Press, 1975) p. 154.

Over the past several years, ambient concentrations of carbon monoxide and photochemical oxidants have declined.[4] At the same time, emissions of HC, CO, and NO$_x$ in the transportation sector have also exhibited a modest downward trend (see figure 3-1). The question that naturally arises is whether current automobile emissions control policy has played a significant role in this trend. There is limited evidence suggesting that it has. This is largely based on the fact that between 1970 and 1973, NO$_x$ emissions significantly increased during roughly the same time period that emissions control devices were put on 1968–72 model-year cars to reduce

[4] Council on Environmental Quality, *Environmental Quality—1976: The Seventh Annual Report of the Council on Environmental Quality* (Washington, D.C., 1976).

FIGURE 3-1   Calculated Total Emissions of Nitrogen Oxides, Hydro-carbons, and Carbon Monoxide by Source Category, 1970 Through 1975

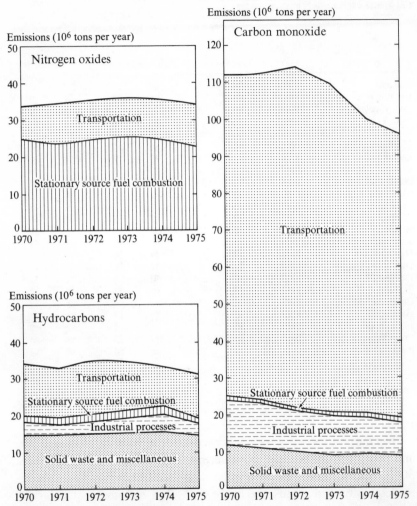

Source: U.S. Environmental Protection Agency, *National Air Quality and Emission Trends Report, 1975*, Publication No. EPA-450/1-76-002 (November 1976).

HC and CO emissions. Since these devices also had the effect of *increasing* NO_x emissions, this pattern would be expected if the control devices significantly affected emissions trends.

There are three basic ways in which emissions from mobile sources can be controlled: (1) modify the internal combustion engine and exhaust system; (2) adopt a "radically" different engine system; or (3) regulate the amount of driving, especially in seriously polluted areas. Current policy has focused primarily on the first approach—modification of the internal combustion engine.

A major difficulty in controlling emissions from internal combustion engines are the inherent tradeoffs involved. For example, high engine temperatures discourage HC and CO emissions but encourage NO_x emissions, and vice versa. In addition, there are other important tradeoffs between emissions controls and such features as (1) fuel economy, (2) engine performance (for example, acceleration and top speed), (3) vehicle drivability (including the propensity to hesitate, stall, or surge, and the relative ease of starting the engine), and (4) cost of manufacturing.

As we would expect, the various technical tradeoffs in control technologies strongly affect the particular emissions control packages selected by manufacturers. For example, one of the most important considerations in selecting an emissions control system concerns the ultimate effect on fuel economy. To illustrate, one study reports the following losses in fuel economy due to emissions controls: for smaller vehicles (less than 3,450 lbs.), there has been no significant trend over the period 1967–74; for intermediate and standard size cars (greater than 3,450 lbs.), there has been about a 14 percent loss in fuel economy over this period for urban driving.[5] Unfortunately, these estimates are extremely crude. Fuel economy varies considerably from vehicle to vehicle because of weight, type of transmission, driving habits, length of trip, cold or warm engine start, and other conditions. Consequently, precise values are subject to considerable debate. Nevertheless, it is probably safe to say that there is convincing evidence that the application of emissions controls to the automobile has resulted in significant reductions in fuel economy. As a consequence, national fuel consumption has been affected, although the magnitude of this effect is difficult to estimate.

History

The first legislation dealing with the control of mobile-source emissions was passed by the California state legislature in 1961.[6] The law required a

---

[5] Grad and coauthors, *The Automobile*, pp. 133–135.

[6] This discussion is based in large part on material found in: E. S. Mills and L. J. White, "Government Policies Toward Automotive Emissions Control," (paper prepared for the Workshop on Air Pollution and Administrative Control) Massachusetts Institute of Technology, Cambridge, Mass., December 1976; H. D. Jacoby, J. D. Steinbruner, and others, *Clearing the Air: Federal Policy on Automotive Emissions Control* (Cambridge, Mass., Ballinger, 1973); and Grad and coauthors, *The Automobile*, chapter 8.

simple crankcase device on vehicles marketed in California. In 1963 a law was passed in California requiring that exhaust emissions control systems be installed on all new cars sold in California one year after the state had certified that at least two such devices were practical and available at reasonable cost. In March 1964, the automobile companies told the state that the 1967 model year was the earliest that they would be able to install such devices. However, in June 1964, the state certified four exhaust control devices developed by independent parts manufacturers, which, according to the 1963 legislation, made such devices mandatory on the 1966 models. Then in August 1964, the automobile companies announced that they would be able to provide their own exhaust control devices for the 1966 model year.

However, national interest in automobile emissions control lagged behind California's concern. The only reference to such controls in the Clean Air Act of 1963 involved the appointment of a liaison committee by the secretary of the Department of Health, Education and Welfare (DHEW) to work with industry representatives on this issue. Consequently, as it became apparent that the industry would meet requirements in California, pressures grew for a national policy. Finally, the 1965 Amendments to the Clean Air Act directed the secretary of DHEW to set emissions standards for automobiles. Subsequently, the secretary set standards for hydrocarbons and carbon monoxide, effective January 1, 1968 (see table 3-3).

By 1970, the environmental movement was in full swing. The climate was one in which public officials found it politically expedient to express dissatisfaction with the lack of progress in controlling automobile emissions.[7] In February of 1970, the Nixon administration proposed regulations for 1975 cars, extending controls to NO_x emissions and tightening existing standards for HC and CO emissions. Moreover, emissions goals for 1980 were published, and the administration proposed federal funding to develop a new "clean-engine" technology by 1975.

In August of 1970, the Muskie subcommittee produced a bill that essentially moved the Nixon goals for 1980 ahead to 1975. The final result was Title II of the 1970 Amendments to the Clean Air Act. This legislation, officially labeled the National Emissions Standards Act, was enacted in 1970. In the act, Congress detailed a timetable for automobile *exhaust*

---

[7] For an interesting political perspective on the automobile emissions history, see H. Margolis, "The Politics of Auto Emissions," *The Public Interest* (Fall 1977) p. 3.

emissions standards.[8] Specifically, it mandated 90 percent reductions in both HC and CO emissions (from 1970 levels) by 1975 and a 90 percent reduction in NO_x emissions (from 1971 levels) by 1976. These emissions reductions were based in large part on a report by D. S. Barth and co-authors.[9] The appendix to this chapter discusses the analysis behind their findings. It was widely recognized that these 90 percent reductions were beyond the technical capabilities of the automobile industry at that time.

Nevertheless, the Environmental Protection Agency (EPA) began to administer the requirements of the act. In 1972, the automobile companies requested that the effective dates of the standards be delayed one year, which they were entitled to do under the provisions of the act. Their request was denied by the EPA administrator. However, the automobile companies appealed and a circuit court remanded the case to the EPA. Finally, in April 1973, the EPA administrator granted a one-year delay in the 1975 deadline for the HC and CO standards, and in July 1973, the administrator granted a one-year delay in the 1976 deadline for the NO_x standard. While granting this delay, the administrator also set the 1975 interim standards (1975-I in table 3-3).

It should be noted that the only grounds permitted in the legislation for delaying the enforcement of the emissions standards were technological infeasibility. Yet, the EPA administrator granted these delays shortly after certifying that the Japanese-made Honda CVCC engine met the original 1975 standards. We can only speculate as to what might have happened

[8] We have stressed "exhaust" because there are two other significant types of hydrocarbon emissions—crankcase and evaporative. Crankcase or "blowby" emissions are discussed later in this chapter. The two sources of evaporative emissions are related to temperature changes of the fuel tank and carburetor system. Evaporative emissions standards were introduced in 1971. In August 1976, the EPA issued new standards for hydrocarbon evaporation from cars and light trucks that required further reduction by approximately 70 percent below current levels, beginning in 1978. The EPA stated that some current models could meet the standards, while others would require only minor adjustments such as tighter sealing gasoline tank caps and improved canisters to collect vapors. It estimated that they would increase sticker prices for new cars and light trucks by $7.30 and cost the industry $2.2 million over a five-year period for test equipment. Fuel economy would not be affected. A more stringent standard imposing a 90 percent reduction that was originally to take effect in 1979 was postponed due to technical infeasibility, cost, and lead time. (See "EPA Issues Auto Evaporative Emission Limits, Sets Air Standards for Supersonic Planes," *Air/Water Pollution Report,* August 23, 1976, p. 334.)

[9] D. S. Barth, J. C. Romanovsky, E. A. Schuck, and N. P. Cernansky, "Federal Motor Vehicle Emission Goals for CO, HC, and NO_x Based on Desired Air Quality Levels," *Air Pollution-1970,* Part 5, U.S. Senate, Committee on Public Works, Subcommittee on Air and Water Pollution, 91 Cong., 2 sess. (Washington, D.C., GPO) p. 1639.

TABLE 3-3   Automobile Emissions Control Standards

	Exhaust[a]					
	HC		CO		NO$_x$	
Model year applicable	Grams/ mile	Percentage reduction[b]	Grams/ mile	Percentage reduction	Grams/ mile	Percentage reduction
Pre-1968[c]	8.7	—	87	—	4.4	—
1968	6.2	29	51	41	NR[d]	—
1970	4.1	53	34	61	NR	—
1972	3.0	66	28	68	NR	—
1973	3.0	66	28	68	3.1	30
1975-I[e]	1.5	83	15	83	3.1	30
1975-C[f]	0.9	90	9	90	2.0	55
1976	1.5	83	15	83	3.1	30
1977	1.5	83	15	83	2.0	55
1978[g]	1.5	83	15	83	2.0	55
1979	1.5	83	15	83	2.0	55
1980	0.41	95	7	92	2.0	55
1981 and beyond	0.41	95	3.4	96	1.0[h]	77

Note: (−) = not applicable.

a As measured by the federal constant volume sampling, cold- and hot-start test procedure.

b Percentage reduction from average precontrolled vehicle emissions.

c Emissions from vehicle population per vehicle mile in year before standards were introduced. Evaluated in July 1967 for HC and CO, and July 1972 for NO$_x$.

d No requirement.

e Interim standards set by EPA April 1973.

f California standards.

g Had Congress not acted to amend the law in August 1977, the requirements for the 1978 model year (and beyond) would have been: 0.41 grams per mile (gpm) HC, 3.4 gpm CO, and 0.4 gpm NO$_x$.

h Research objective of 0.4 gpm NO$_x$ retained.

had an American manufacturer developed an engine that met the original standards.

In 1973 the Organization of Petroleum Exporting Countries (OPEC) instituted the oil embargo, which resulted in the "energy crisis" of 1973–1974. In June of 1974, Congress, aware of the tradeoff between emissions controls and fuel efficiency, granted an additional year's delay in the enforcement of all emissions standards.[10] Meanwhile, to meet the stricter California standards the automobile industry installed catalytic converters on 1975 model-year cars sold in California. In April of 1975, the EPA administrator granted another year's delay in enforcement of the HC and CO standards because it was feared that catalytic converters might generate serious sulfur oxide emissions.[11] Thus the original 1975 HC, CO, and NO$_x$

[10] This was done as part of a new law, the Energy Supply and Coordination Act of 1974.

[11] Specifically, in an EPA report, "Estimated Changes in Human Exposure to Suspended Sulfate Attributable to Equipping Light Duty Motor Vehicles with Oxi-

emissions standards—three times postponed—were now scheduled for 1978.

When the administrator granted the 1975 delay, he urged Congress to enact a graduated schedule of emissions standards to culminate in the ultimate compliance with the 1970 goals by 1982 models. He also suggested that the 1982 NO_x standard be left to the discretion of the EPA administrator and promised to impose a standard for limiting sulfate emissions from catalytic-equipped cars.[12]

As part of the legislative hearings on new amendments to the Clean Air Act, an air pollution bill giving the automobile industry more time to meet the strict emissions standards originally set forth in the 1970 amendments was passed by both houses of Congress and signed by President Carter on August 8, 1977.[13] The new timetable for emissions standards calls for still another extension of the current 1977 standards for two more years, followed by stricter HC and CO standards in 1980, and further tightening of the CO and NO_x standards in 1981 and beyond (see table 3-3). The original NO_x emissions goal of 0.4 grams per mile (gpm) was retained as a research objective. Furthermore, the Environmental Protection Agency was empowered to waive the stricter CO standard for 1981 on a model-line basis if it finds that this would not endanger public health and that it would be in the national interest. The recent amendments also gave financially troubled American Motors Corporation two additional years to meet the NO_x standard, and at the same time contained a waiver that could give diesel and other "innovative technology" cars a four-year delay to meet the 1.0 gpm NO_x standard, as long as emissions do not exceed 1.5 gpm.

Benefits and Costs

As pointed out in chapter 2, reducing mobile-source emissions, like most government policies, confers benefits and imposes costs. Accordingly, we

---

dation Catalysts" (mimeo., n.d.), there were indications that automotive catalytic control systems designed to reduce hydrocarbons and carbon monoxide emissions converted sulfur dioxide to sulfur trioxide and that direct emissions of sulfur trioxide would result in increased local concentrations of sulfuric acid and sulfate salts in the vicinity of roadways. EPA has since concluded that the contribution to sulfate levels in urban areas by catalytic-equipped automobiles is negligible.

[12] However, EPA has not proposed a sulfate emissions standard because it believes too many uncertainties remain (especially with regard to health effects) and because most evidence verifies that the original problem was overstated.

[13] See "Air Conferees Adopt Senate Auto Standards, Limit Scope and Effect of 'Breaux' Plan," *Air/Water Pollution Report,* August 8, 1977, p. 312.

are led to ask two important and related questions: (1) what are the "best" levels of emissions controls? and (2) what are the best strategies for achieving them?

The benefits associated with control of mobile-source emissions include improvements in human health, reduced damage to plants and animals, longer lives for various materials and structures, and perhaps reduced cleaning costs.[14] In addition, there are other, less easily valued benefits— improved visibility, more frequent clear skies and sunny days, and possible reductions of noxious odors[15]—being the most prominent examples.

The costs associated with the control of mobile-source emissions include the costs of required hardware (for example, catalytic converters), those necessitated by the modification of existing equipment (engines, for example), special fuels and fuel penalties, extra maintenance (including the owner's time), consumer dissatisfaction if controls affect performance or other important automobile characteristics, and finally, the costs associated with administering the program.[16]

Benefits

Several steps are required in the difficult process of quantifying the benefits discussed above. First, reduced emissions must be translated into impacts on ambient air pollution concentrations.[17] Second, the physical effects of these reduced concentrations must be determined. For example, crops susceptible to air pollution damage must be identified. Third, these physical impacts must be quantified meaningfully (the percentage of crops lost to air pollution might be established for a particular region, with allocation of the losses by specific air pollutants, for instance). Fourth, these quantitative effects must be translated into a useful measure of benefits. This final step usually involves the assignment of dollar values to the losses,

---

[14] Mobile-source emissions do not generate significant particulate emissions; hence, the effects on cleaning costs are not likely to be large.

[15] Sulfur oxides are usually associated with noxious odors; and again, mobile sources are not important emitters of these compounds.

[16] If control programs cause plant shutdowns, or net unemployment, additional costs may be imposed on employees as well as regions whose economic base is affected.

[17] There is a host of difficulties in estimating the resulting effects on ambient air quality. Current models of diffusion and atmospheric chemistry are not sufficient to give confident estimates of the change in air quality caused by a change in air pollutant emissions. Furthermore, natural sources also produce air pollution and it is difficult to isolate their contribution.

which, as pointed out in chapter 2, should accurately reflect individuals' willingness to pay in order to avoid them.

The literature on the health effects of mobile-source air pollutants is much less extensive than that on the health effects of such stationary source air pollutants as sulfur oxides and suspended particulates.[18] It is important to note that although investigators may one day discover strong associations between serious health effects and automobile emissions (as represented by ambient levels of carbon monoxide, nitrogen oxides, hydrocarbons, and photochemical oxidants), no strong associations have as yet been demonstrated. However, current evidence *does* suggest that air pollution attributed to mobile sources exhibits associations with short-term health effects such as headache, cough, and eye and chest discomfort.[19] With regard to effects such as eye irritation, it should be noted that even in the presence of a strong association between the levels of mobile-source emissions and health effects in certain areas of the country, this does not necessarily imply that such health effects are significant in all parts of the country.

Although there is evidence that mobile-source air pollution damages both plants and animals, it is again difficult to estimate the extent of the damage. Similarly, it is difficult to quantify and value the damage to materials and structures from mobile-source emissions.[20]

In spite of the difficulties, there have been attempts to quantify the potential benefits associated with control of such emissions. One of the first of these was a study entitled, *Cumulative Regulatory Effects on the Cost of Automotive Transportation* (RECAT). Piecing together information from several earlier studies, the RECAT report presented estimates of total benefits for the decade 1976–85 that ranged between $18.3 and

[18] See Lave and Seskin, *Air Pollution,* especially chapter 10 and appendix A.

[19] See, for example D. I. Hammer, V. Hasselblad, B. Portnoy, and P. F. Wehrle, "Los Angeles Student Nurse Study," *Archives of Environmental Health* vol. 28 (1974) p. 255; and D. I. Hammer, B. Portnoy, F. M. Massey, W. S. Wayne, T. Oelsner, and P. F. Wehrle. "Los Angeles Air Pollution and Respiratory Symptoms," *Archives of Environmental Health* vol. 10 (1965) p. 475. Evidence of chronic effects from mobile-source-related air pollution is practically nonexistent.

[20] For a more detailed discussion of mobile-source air pollution damage to plants and animals as well as to materials and the general value of property, see Lave and Seskin, *Air Pollution,* chapter 10; and National Academy of Sciences, *Air Quality and Automobile Emission Control,* vol. 4, *The Costs and Benefits of Automobile Emission Control,* Report by the Coordinating Committee on Air Quality Studies, National Academy of Sciences, National Academy of Engineering, serial no. 93-25 (Washington, GPO, 1974) chapter 5, hereafter referred to as the 1974 NAS study.

$46.3 billion.[21] For the first year after this "conversion decade" the esti-
mated annual benefits ranged between $3.5 and $9.1 billion (page xxi of
the RECAT report). It should be noted that the RECAT figures were
computed under the assumption that the emissions-controlled 1976 vehicles would be essentially "zero-polluting" (p. 28 of the RECAT report).
As a result, it was recognized that the benefits were exaggerated somewhat.

To date, the most comprehensive benefit–cost analysis of mobile-source
emissions control was the one undertaken by the National Academy of
Sciences in 1974.[22] Benefit estimates in the NAS study were based on two
different valuation techniques. The first involved a direct assessment of
the economic damages to health, vegetation, and materials from mobile-
source air pollution. The second technique attempted to measure benefits
by observing differences in property values and wage rates across areas,
under the assumption that these differences would reflect the benefits of
improved living and working conditions associated with enhanced air
quality.

The NAS study presented an estimated range for the direct damages to
human health from mobile-source air pollution that was between $360
million and $3 billion annually.[23] Taking the midpoint of this rather wide
range, one obtains a value of $1,680 million. At the same time, the "best"
estimate of the annual vegetation losses due to mobile-source air pollutants was $200 million.[24] Finally, the "ballpark" estimate of the annual

[21] *Cumulative Regulatory Effects on the Cost of Automotive Transportation*
(RECAT), final report of the Ad Hoc Committee, prepared for the Office of
Science and Technology (Washington, D.C., GPO, 1972) hereafter referred to
as the RECAT report. The two most notable earlier studies were: L. A. Caretto,
and R. F. Sawyer, "The Assignment of Responsibility for Air Pollution," paper
presented at the Annual Meeting of the Society of Automotive Engineers, Detroit,
Mich., 1972; and L. R. Babcock, Jr., "A Combined Pollution Index for Measurement of Total Air Pollution," *Journal of the Air Pollution Control Association*
vol. 20 (1970) p. 653.

[22] A benefit–cost study that looks at benefits only in terms of reductions in the
concentrations of HC, CO, and NO_x is D. Harrison, Jr., *Who Pays for Clean Air?*
(Cambridge, Mass., Ballinger, 1975). In K. A. Small, "Estimating the Air Pollution Costs of Transport Models," *Journal of Transport Economics and Policy* (May
1977) p. 109, a methodology similar to that of the RECAT study was employed.
The Small paper also used updated pollutant severity factors estimated by L. R.
Babcock, Jr., and N. L. Nagda in two studies they published: (1) "Response:
Rating of Pollutants by Effect," *Journal of the Air Pollution Control Association*
vol. 22 (1972) p. 727; and (2) "Cost Effectiveness of Emission Control," *Journal
of the Air Pollution Control Association* vol. 23 (1973) p. 173. Both the Harrison
and the Small analyses rely on cost data from the 1974 NAS study.

[23] This estimate included morbidity effects such as headache, cough, eye and
chest discomfort, as well as mortality effects. With regard to the valuation of the
latter effects, the estimate embodied a value of human life equal to $200,000.

[24] 1974 NAS study, p. 378.

losses to materials was approximately $1 billion.[25] Combining these three estimates produces an admittedly rough estimate of $2,880 million per year for the damages associated with this type of air pollution.[26]

In addition to these estimates of direct damages, the NAS report presented estimates based on the second valuation technique. Using models of the process by which wage rates and property values are determined, the NAS report concluded that the benefits of emissions control expressed through wages and property values ranged between $1.5 and $5 billion per year.[27] Furthermore, under the questionable assumption that health, vegetation, and materials effects were not fully embodied in the "market valuation" estimates, this range of benefits was combined rather than contrasted with the damage estimates discussed above. The final estimate of the total benefits from reducing mobile-source emissions was calculated to be $5 billion per year.[28]

As suggested above, this figure probably represents an overestimate of the actual benefits that would be realized from control of mobile-source emissions. In part, this is due to the method that was used to estimate the benefits (see footnote 26, below). However, even more critical is the assumption that "in-use cars" would actually meet the emissions standards as they were instituted, thereby reducing ambient levels of mobile-source air pollutants. Unfortunately, there is considerable evidence that the average emissions from controlled cars already on the road exceed even the relatively less strict standards applicable to them.

Costs

The costs of mobile-source emissions control are somewhat easier to quantify than the benefits discussed above. The early RECAT study presented a cost estimate of automotive emissions control over the 1976–85 decade totaling $95.1 billion for meeting the original standards legislated in the 1970 amendments. The annual costs after this period were estimated to be $10.1 billion.[29]

[25] 1974 NAS study, p. 397.
[26] The health "damages" were not based on total abatement, but rather on various scenarios (see the 1974 NAS study, pp. 356–360). The estimates for vegetation and materials losses represent total damages and are therefore overestimates of the value of the incremental benefits associated with abatement of air pollution associated with mobile sources.
[27] 1974 NAS study, p. 412.
[28] This value incorporates a slight downward adjustment because it was recognized that some double-counting was probably involved.
[29] RECAT report, p. xxi.

The 1974 NAS study also developed cost estimates (including equipment, fuel, and maintenance costs) based on the best available data at that time. In some cases, estimates were based on technology that is not now in major production; however, the NAS felt that although specific numbers might change, the general conclusions were likely to remain unaltered.[30]

Keeping these caveats in mind, some of the major findings of the NAS study were:

1. If the law ultimately requires 0.4 gpm of NO_x (see table 3-3), vehicles meeting that standard may cost $850 more over their lifetimes than vehicles meeting the 1970 standard. Total national expenditures for automobile emissions control would be approximately $8 billion per year by 1985 if no catalyst replacements are required, and as much as $11 billion annually if all vehicles must change catalysts at 50,000 miles.[31]

2. If the most stringent standard requires only 2.0 gpm NO_x (the current 1977 standard), total national expenditures for automobile emissions controls would be approximately $4.7 billion per year by 1985 without catalyst replacements and as much as $7 billion per year with catalyst replacements.

3. If the most stringent standard requires only 3.1 gpm NO_x (the 1975 interim standard), total national expenditures would peak in the 1970s, and by 1985, would amount to $3 billion per year without catalyst replacement, and $4.5 billion per year with catalyst replacement.

Thus, cleaning up mobile-source emissions is a costly undertaking. The annual cost of meeting the strictest standards of the Clean Air Act Amendments (including a 0.4 gpm NO_x standard) could be as high as $11 billion per year. Furthermore, these estimates are likely to understate the "true" cost of the program since they ignore consumer dissatisfaction with inferior performance characteristics as well as costs associated with the owners' time and inconvenience because of additional maintenance requirements.[32]

[30] 1974 NAS study, p. 115.

[31] Current technology suggests that some type of catalytic converter will continue to be relied on to meet the stricter emissions controls.

[32] There is also evidence that the cost estimates in the 1974 NAS study are too low because fuel penalties were based on a comparison of controlled cars with relatively uncontrolled 1970 vehicles, rather than with uncontrolled automobiles that would now be in existence whether or not emissions controls were mandated. See Mills and White, "Government Policies," pp. 17–18.

Comparing the Benefits and Costs

In 1972 the RECAT Committee's benefit–cost analysis raised significant questions concerning the mobile-source emissions control program. It concluded that the United States was "embarked on an air pollution-control program of enormous scope, complexity, and cost with little measure of the relative harmfulness to health of the several pollutants being considered."[33]

According to the 1974 NAS study two years later, the benefits of reduced mobile-source emissions were determined to be in the neighborhood of $5 billion. At the same time, the NAS findings indicated that the annualized costs required to meet the strictest standards specified in the 1970 Amendments to the Clean Air Act were approximately $8 billion by 1985 if no catalyst change is required and $11 billion if such a change is required at 50,000 miles.

Today, little evidence has been developed that would alter the basic conclusions of these studies. Under the present law, the probable benefits of mobile-source emissions control may be considerably lower than the projected costs. This does *not* mean that no abatement of automobile emissions is worthwhile. What seems more likely is that the current strategy may be too strict when considered as a whole and that a slight relaxation of the emissions standards or some alternative policy may be called for. This would be the case, for example, if certain standards could be relaxed with little or no reduction in benefits while at the same time achieving important cost savings. We will consider such a possibility later in this chapter.

The Question of Technology Forcing

It is evident that the 1970 Amendments to the Clean Air Act precipitated the discovery of new technologies for the control of automobile emissions. In view of such positive effects, some analysts conclude that it is prudent to maintain full legislative pressure. It is clear that the 1970 amendments "got tough" with the automobile manufacturers through stringent standards, tight deadlines, provisions requiring them to supply data, and language requiring the automakers to show a good faith effort to comply with standards regardless of technical difficulties.

Because the success of current automotive emissions control programs is closely linked to technology, it is important to ask what the history of

[33] RECAT report, p. xx.

technical developments in this area really tells us.[34] Concern with mobile-source emissions as a significant contributor to air pollution began in the 1950s.[35] Initially, the automobile manufacturers denied that automobiles were an important factor in the creation of smog. Nevertheless, in 1953 they formed a joint committee to study the problem. Then, in 1955, they signed a cross-licensing agreement ensuring that all manufacturers would have access to new developments on a royalty-free basis.

From the point of view of maximizing profits, the industry's actions were quite rational. Emissions control devices would only serve to increase costs, while doing little to make cars more attractive to buyers.[36] On the contrary, often the control devices had undesirable side effects such as fuel penalties. Thus, the industry as a whole sought to make emissions controls look unnecessary, impractical, and costly. Yet, at the same time, there was some incentive—in the form of public relations, profits on patents, and fleet sales to the public sector—for individual manufacturers to be the first to develop new control systems if they were eventually required.

In 1959, blowby was "discovered" as a significant source of hydrocarbon emissions. Blowby refers to the collection of unburned and partially burned hydrocarbons in the crankcase. If they are allowed to remain there, they contaminate and thin the crankcase oil; hence, manufacturers vent these hydrocarbons to the atmosphere via a blowby port. In fact, blowby accounts for between 20 and 25 percent of hydrocarbon emissions from an uncontrolled car. What is interesting to note is that although the technology to control these emissions had been known since the 1930s, and although devices had actually been installed on commercial and industrial vehicles to prevent these emissions, it took until the 1960s for such controls to be installed on automobiles. Specifically, in 1961 positive crankcase ventilation (PCV) devices were installed on all new cars sold in California, and in 1963 these devices were installed on all new cars in the nation.

The industry's joint committee combined with its cross-licensing agreement were largely successful in delaying progress in emissions control.

[34] The reader is referred to Mills and White, "Government Policies," section II for a more detailed discussion of the history of automotive emissions control efforts.

[35] The process that generated photochemical smog in Southern California was identified by Dr. A. J. Haagen-Smit in 1951.

[36] One could argue that some benefits would accrue to the industry or an individual manufacturer in terms of good public relations for demonstrating concern about air pollution.

This problem was addressed in a 1969 antitrust suit filed by the Department of Justice. The suit was later settled by a consent decree, without admission of guilt by the manufacturers. However, the major impetus to the control of automobile emissions was to be provided by the passage of the 1970 Amendments to the Clean Air Act.

Congress' response to the slow pace at which achievements in mobile-source emissions control were being made was to pass a law that essentially told the automobile manufacturers that they had better reduce emissions by specific amounts by specific dates, or "else." The question we wish to consider here is whether this strategy has provided the proper incentives to realize the ultimate goal of cleaner cars and, presumably, cleaner air.

Unfortunately, the legislation passed by Congress has probably impeded progress in mobile-source emissions control. This is the case because the imposition of a $10,000 fine for each automobile not meeting emissions standards is simply not a realistic sanction to use against automobile makers. If such fines were levied, the result would be a complete shutdown of the manufacturer in question. Given the importance of automobile manufacturing to the total U.S. economy (approximately 10 percent of GNP), neither EPA nor the Congress would find it politically feasible to take such extreme measures. This conclusion is certainly borne out by history.

For example, in 1973, EPA granted a one-year delay for meeting the original HC and CO standards of the act, largely because Chrysler was unable to meet them. At the same time, it was generally apparent that General Motors could have met the standards. Quite simply, EPA was not prepared to shut down the Chrysler Corporation. Furthermore, there have been cases in which foreign manufacturers have demonstrated the ability to meet emissions standards, while domestic manufacturers were unable to provide adequately controlled vehicles.[37] In such cases, delays have actually had the effect of serving to protect U.S. automobile manufacturers.

A recent NAS report concluded that the delays that have been granted thus far have undoubtedly led to a slackening in the automobile manufacturers' efforts to develop the technology necessary to meet the strict NO_x standard of 0.4 gpm mandated in the 1970 amendments.[38]

---

[37] The introduction of the Honda CVCC is a case in point, and there is now an example involving the Swedish car, Volvo.

[38] National Academy of Sciences, "Report of the Conference on Air Quality and Automobile Emissions to the Committee on Environmental Decision Making," mimeo. (Washington, D.C., NAS, May 5, 1975).

TABLE 3-4   Summary of Typical Emissions Modifications

Model year added	Modification
1963	"Open" crankcase ventilation system
1968	a Leaner mixture carburetor calibration b Intake air preheat to constant temperature c Intake manifold preheat d Retarded idle timing e "Closed" positive crankcase ventilation (PVC) system
1970	a Decreased compression ratio b Air injection (on some models) c Modified spark advance control
1971	Fuel evaporative control system
1972	a Antidieseling solenoid b Fast acting choke c Air injection
1973	a Exhaust gas recirculation (EGR) b Hardened valve seats c Spark advance control
1974	a Precision cams, bores, pistons b Improved EGR systems

Source: F. P. Grad and coauthors, *The Automobile and the Regulation of Its Impact on the Environment* (Norman, Okla., University of Oklahoma Press, 1975) p. 124.

Thus, the current policy has actually created perverse incentives for the manufacturers.[39] Given that they are unlikely to be shut down, their interests are best served by presenting a public image of putting forth a "good faith effort" in developing emissions controls while privately dragging their feet. The stringent deadlines forced manufacturers to respond with short-term, high-cost solutions rather than longer term, less costly technologies. Specifically, congressional pressures resulted in a sequence of modifications and additions to the conventional, carbureted, spark-ignition engine (see, for example, table 3-4) which consisted of relatively minor changes in engine design with more substantial changes in engine operating conditions. Furthermore, there is increasing evidence that the catalytic-converter technology chosen by U.S. companies to meet the current emissions requirements is relatively costly compared to such alternatives as stratified-charge engines. Nevertheless, it was rational for manufacturers to choose the former, since the latter were considered to be much

[39] We shall discuss later in the chapter how other control policies such as economic incentives can induce more efficient innovation in terms of total resource usage and allocation patterns.

riskier technologies.[40] In addition, the other options would no doubt have required considerable redesign, retooling, and other set-up costs.[41]

Implementation and Enforcement

Successful regulation of mobile-source emissions to improve ambient air quality will depend on four basic factors: the ability of the automobile industry to meet new standards; the durability of the control systems that are adopted; the rate at which older cars are phased out; and the way in which state and local governments deal with the problem of older cars or cars with deteriorated control systems.[42]

The 1970 Amendments to the Clean Air Act allude to three components of the implementation and enforcement of mobile-source emissions control: (1) prototype testing, (2) assembly line testing, and (3) on-the-road testing.

Under current procedures, manufacturers deliver prototype vehicles to EPA for certification, and these vehicles must meet the emissions standards applicable to their model year before any cars can be marketed. Any cars sold that have failed to meet the standards would be subject to a $10,000 fine per vehicle.[43]

Once the prototype vehicles are certified, there are no further testing requirements under the law. However, the EPA administrator has a number of other discretionary powers. For example, EPA began assembly line audits during the 1977 model year.[44] The administrator can recall any model vehicle of which a substantial number are found to be in violation of the relevant emissions standards.[45] Along these lines, EPA has now pro-

---

[40] In a 1977 article, Margolis also argues that such rationality explains the automakers' behavior throughout the time the 1970 legislation was pending, since it was in their interests to be faced with an impossible timetable rather than with a commitment to replace the internal combustion engine. See Margolis, "Politics of Auto Emissions."

[41] Moreover, some of the transition costs of emissions controls were probably shifted to the oil companies since the catalyst technology required more expensive lead-free gasoline.

[42] See Grad and coauthors, *The Automobile*, p. 338.

[43] No such fines have ever been levied.

[44] Prior to the assembly line audits, there was some incentive for manufacturers to send "cream puffs" to EPA for certification.

[45] In June 1977, as part of its assembly line audit program, the EPA ordered the Ford Motor Company to recall 21,000 1977 models to repair the ignition spark timing which was causing the cars to exceed the NO_x standards. See "Ford Ordered to Recall 21,000 New Cars to Correct NO_x Emission-Related Defect," *Air/Water Pollution Report*, June 13, 1977, p. 235. In July 1977, Ford was ordered to recall

mulgated new regulations requiring automobile manufacturers to notify the agency of virtually all emissions-related defects.[46] Taken together, these measures not only motivate manufacturers to produce new vehicles that conform to standards, but they also protect car owners from purchasing automobiles that will fail inspection tests.

It is still too early to tell how successful the recall and notification procedures will be. Nevertheless, EPA has other regulatory powers that can be effective in the control of mobile-source emissions. These include: requiring manufacturers to share technology through mandatory licensing; requiring the federal government to purchase "clean" cars;[47] and regulating fuels and fuel additives to conform with the needs of pollution control systems. To our knowledge, only the last of these powers has been exercised. This occurred when EPA instituted regulations governing the distribution of lead-free fuel to ensure its availability for catalyst-equipped automobiles.

There is considerable evidence that emissions control devices deteriorate substantially during the life of the automobile. Figure 3-2 illustrates this phenomenon by presenting a typical pattern of emissions control deterioration in the case of CO. This pattern of deterioration implies two things for enforcement. First, manufacturers must produce cars that with proper maintenance will *on average* have emissions below the standards, and second, owners must have incentives to perform the necessary maintenance.

Recognizing the deterioration problem, Congress specified in the 1970 amendments that emissions standards must be met for the "useful life of the car," which was translated to mean five years or 50,000 miles whichever came first (allowing for routine operation and maintenance).[48] By in-

---

220,000 1975 models that were in violation of NO_x emissions standards. See "EPA Orders Recall of 220,000 Fords to Correct NO_x Control System," *Air/Water Pollution Report,* July 18, 1977, p. 286.

[46] The regulations went into effect July 5, 1977 and require manufacturers to file an Emission Defect Information Report within fifteen days of learning that such a defect has affected at least twenty-five vehicles. If a manufacturer *voluntarily* begins to recall defective cars, a Voluntary Emissions Recall Report must be filed describing the defects as well as necessary repairs, and a copy must be sent to vehicle owners. See "Ford Ordered to Recall 21,000 New Cars to Correct NO_x Emission-Related Defect," *Air/Water Pollution Report,* June 13, 1977, p. 235.

[47] Once certain vehicles are certified as "low-emitters," the federal government must purchase them if the costs are no greater than 150 percent of the retail value of the least expensive alternative.

[48] The actual life of an automobile is about 100,000 miles or ten years. (See Grad and coauthors, *The Automobile,* p. 369.)

FIGURE 3-2   *Typical Pattern of CO Emissions Control Deterioration*

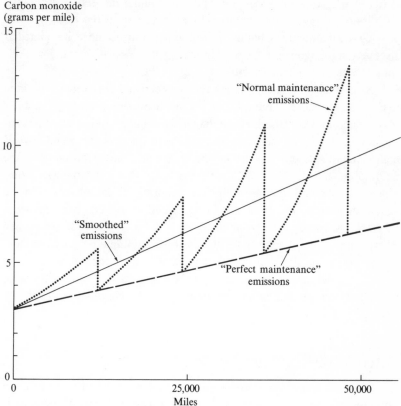

Source: H. D. Jacoby, J. D. Steinbruner, and others, *Clearing the Air: Federal Policy on Automotive Emissions Control* (Cambridge, Mass., Ballinger, 1973) p. 91.

cluding emissions control equipment in the warranty provision, Congress was placing the primary responsibility on the manufacturer for repair and upkeep of the emissions control systems.[49]

At the same time, EPA was also given the power to require states to perform in-use inspections of emissions control systems.[50] To encourage this

[49] A possible problem introduced by this provision could lead to distortions in the automobile service industry, if manufacturers required all repairs to be performed by dealers because emissions control systems are part of the overall engine system. While this has not been evaluated, the Clean Air Amendments of 1977 narrow the components of the system covered by the warranty and specify that other parts of the system are the responsibility of the owner and can be serviced at any facility of the owner's choosing.

[50] Despite this, only a handful of states currently have emissions inspection programs. Results of a pilot study in New Jersey indicated that 45 percent of the

activity, the administrator can make grants to state agencies covering two-thirds of the costs of developing and maintaining inspection programs. Such in-use testing is designed to reduce average emissions of cars by improving the maintenance habits of the public.[51] Furthermore, it is aimed at discouraging car owners from deactivating those parts of the emissions control system that are accessible.[52]

It is clear that in-use emissions have exceeded and are likely to continue to exceed the federal standards. On the one hand, enforcement of mobile-source emissions controls is easier than many other pollution situations because the number of automakers is few and because the technology is highly standardized. On the other hand, the size and importance of the automobile industry make hollow the threats to shut it down for noncompliance. In the end, the most effective incentive for compliance with the standards may be the good will to be earned by the company that first meets the standards in an economical way.

With regard to incentives for the car-owning public, effective mobile-source control policy will probably require state or local inspections to ensure that vehicles continue to meet the standards for which they were built. This will be true unless emissions control technology is drastically altered.

Alternative Regulatory Policies

As discussed earlier, it appears that the current method of controlling automobile emissions is difficult to justify on benefit–cost grounds. It is hard to arrive at an annual benefit figure in excess of $5 billion, while, as outlined above, the current legislation entails annual costs that probably range from one and one-half to more than twice this amount.

Our reluctance to spend a dollar-and-a-half to two dollars in search of each dollar of benefits is understandable. In this section we discuss policies designed to reduce mobile-source emissions that differ from the approach embodied in the Clean Air Act and its amendments. Our hope is

---

vehicles inspected failed the state standards using a 35-second test. After a "tune-up" costing approximately $20, virtually all vehicles could pass the test. See Allen V. Kneese, and Charles L. Schultze, *Pollution, Prices, and Public Policy* (Washington, D.C., Brookings Institution, 1975) p. 102.

[51] The motoring public finds it more difficult to accept emissions inspections than it does safety inspections because emissions from automobiles are generally intangible.

[52] Mechanics are forbidden by law from disconnecting emissions control systems.

that one or more of these policies will prove to be more efficient than the current approach.

The Two-Car Strategy

The current legislation specifies a single standard that is to apply to all light-duty vehicles.[53] Under a frequently discussed alternative, all automobiles would have to meet one of two separate standards. The objective would be to induce the use of low-emissions vehicles in areas where automotive pollutants are of major importance to ambient air quality, while permitting the use of lower cost, higher emissions vehicles in areas where air quality would not be significantly degraded by such vehicles.

Specifically, the 1974 NAS study analyzed a scenario in which a 0.4 gpm NO_x standard is required for the 37 percent of vehicles in the most seriously polluted areas, while a less strict 3.1 gpm NO_x standard is required elsewhere. The study estimated that $23 billion would be saved (over a uniform 0.4 gpm NO_x standard) during the 1975–85 period, exclusive of any catalyst changes anywhere. About $40 billion would be saved over this period if catalyst changes could be omitted in the less polluted areas. Further, by 1985, the savings from this two-car strategy, as opposed to a uniform strategy, would run over $3 billion per year without credit for elimination of catalyst changes.[54]

Moreover, while such a two-car strategy would drastically reduce the initial costs of emissions control, there is little evidence that such a strategy would significantly reduce the benefits of mobile-source emissions control. Nevertheless, the costs of implementing and administering such a program could be considerable. For example, some means of regulating vehicle ownership would be needed to ensure that vehicles registered in polluted areas met the stricter standard. In addition, there would probably be some costs associated with the inconveniences of two-tiered markets for new cars, used cars, and fuels. Decisions involving the implementation of a two-car strategy should be based on technical and economic issues. However, in reality, political issues would probably play a major role.[55]

[53] We are neglecting the fact that the state of California has for some time required stricter emissions standards than the national standards.

[54] The study also examined the possibility of varying maintenance requirements across the country under a one-car strategy. If catalyst replacement was required for only 37 percent of all vehicles meeting a 0.4 gpm NO_x emissions standard, total costs during the 1975–85 period would be $15 billion less than with a uniform maintenance requirement.

[55] In this regard it should be noted that most analysts do not believe that there are significant constitutional or legal issues which preclude the implementation of a two-car strategy. See Grad and coauthors, *The Automobile*, pp. 380–381.

Relaxing the NO Standard

As discussed above, a second method for reducing the costs of emissions control involves relaxation of the NO_x standard. If the standard were reduced from 0.4 gpm (the research objective) to 2.0 gpm (the 1977 level), the associated costs would be reduced to an annual level of about $5 billion (without catalyst changes at 50,000 miles) or $6 to $7 billion (with catalyst changes). Further, the NAS study pointed out that at the 2.0 gpm NO_x standard, new engine technologies (for example, stratified charge or diesel engines) might make emissions control almost costless by the latter part of the century.[56]

What is even more important from a benefit–cost viewpoint is the NAS conclusion that, on the basis of available data, the cost savings gained from easing the NO_x emissions standard probably exceed the loss in benefits from higher concentrations of NO_x. In short, current evidence indicates that there would not be a significant increase in benefits associated with lowering the NO_x standard below 2.0 gpm. Only a few urban areas such as Chicago and Los Angeles now have NO_x levels above estimated thresholds at which health-related damages are observed (see chapter 2 for a discussion of threshold effects). In such areas, the option of controlling NO_x emissions from stationary sources might provide a more cost-effective control strategy.

Smaller Cars

With the unveiling of President Jimmy Carter's energy program, it is apparent that there will be a significant trend toward smaller cars over the next several years.[57] The question immediately arises as to how this trend will affect policies designed to control mobile-source emissions.

Compact cars, it has been found, require smaller emissions reductions to meet CO and NO_x standards than standard size cars,[58] although the differences with respect to HC emissions reductions are negligible. Nevertheless, the 1974 NAS study concluded that switching to smaller cars would

---

[56] 1974 NAS study, p. 17.

[57] The largest U.S. manufacturer of automobiles, General Motors, took an active lead in this regard by introducing smaller cars for the 1977 model year. This trend continued in 1978 model-year cars.

[58] For example, emissions data from 1963–67 precontrol vehicles indicated that CO and NO_x emissions for tested cars weighing less than 3,000 lb. inertia weight, were 25 percent lower than emissions from tested cars weighing more than 4,000 lb. inertia weight. (HC emissions for these two weight categories were not significantly different.) See Grad and coauthors, *The Automobile*, p. 134.

not significantly affect emissions control costs, although it would have substantial impact on total motoring costs. For example, reducing the average new-car size from intermediate to compact by 1985 was estimated to save only $0.56 billion in emissions control costs for 1985 in comparing a uniform 0.4 gpm NO_x standard with the interim 1975 standard (3.1 gpm NO_x). At the same time, the savings in total motoring costs over the 1970–85 period were estimated to be more than $70 billion.[59] Clearly, as the size of the automobile changes in response to higher gasoline prices,[60] careful attention will be needed to see if significant interdependencies exist with regard to emissions controls.

New Technologies

"No single alternative to the conventional gasoline engine with pollution controls appears to be significantly better in all respects for all standards."[61] So claimed the NAS in their 1974 study and there is reason to believe the statement is still applicable in 1978.

In most cars the conventional gasoline engine has met the 1977 standards through engine modification and the addition of an oxidizing catalyst. Stratified-charge engines—either dual-carbureted (such as that used in the Honda CVCC) or fuel-injected (under development)—may be eventually able to meet these standards without a catalyst at lower overall costs.[62] Diesel engines (such as that used in the Peugeot) and rotary engines (such as that used in the Mazda) can also meet these standards without catalysts, but both systems have other unfavorable characteristics. Diesels have noise and handling problems, while rotaries appear to suffer from worn seals and fuel economy problems.

Most engines still have problems in meeting a 0.4 gpm NO_x standard, although the California Air Resources Board reported in May 1976 that Volvo had developed a nearly pollution-free automobile. The Swedish car employs the new Lambda-sond system that uses an American-made, three-way catalyst to eliminate CO, HC, and NO_x emissions simultaneously. Test cars equipped with the system averaged 0.2 gpm HC, 2.8 gpm

[59] 1974 NAS study, pp. 109–110.
[60] The Energy Policy and Conservation Act of 1975 specifies a fuel economy standard for 1978 of 18 mpg. According to EPA certification tests, the 1977 models averaged 18.6 mpg—6 percent better than the 1976 models. See "1977 Cars Get Six Percent Better Fuel Economy than 1976 Models," *Air Conservation* no. 85 (September–October 1976).
[61] 1974 NAS study, p. 116.
[62] There are a small number of 1977 models that can meet the 1977 standards without a catalyst by means of precise control of the fuel mixture.

CO, and 0.17 gpm NO_x. In addition, the test cars got 10 percent *better* gas mileage than the current models. Nevertheless, Volvo has noted that there are a number of problems in applying the system to a broad range of engines; hence, the technology will not have immediate and widespread application.[63] Furthermore, despite its apparent comparative advantage, Volvo has recommended a moratorium on emissions standards at 0.9 gpm HC, 9.0 gpm CO, and 2.0 gpm NO_x, as a compromise between emissions reductions, fuel economy, costs, and technology.

Public Transportation or Transportation Controls

The 1970 Amendments to the Clean Air Act allude to other approaches that might be used in reducing mobile-source air pollution in urban areas.[64] One of these deals with increasing the use of public transportation by making private transportation more expensive. There is little argument that shifting commuters from automobiles to buses or other public transportation would alleviate some of the mobile-source air pollution problems in downtown areas. However, studies have found that commuters generally are unwilling to shift from automobiles to buses or rapid rail transit for all but exceedingly large increases in the price of automobile use.

A related strategy involves instituting traffic controls in downtown areas. For example, in certain sections of the central business district long-term parking might be prohibited. Alternatively, steep parking fees for downtown lots might be levied. Unfortunately, students of the subject have found that strategies such as these are also unsuccessful in luring large numbers of drivers out of their automobiles.[65] In addition, it is sometimes noted that even if such control programs were effective in reducing traffic and mobile-source air pollution in the central business district, administrative costs and the costs of increased travel time and inconvenience could

---

[63] Specifically, the system was applied to a four-cylinder, in-line engine and application to a V-type engine would be significantly more difficult. See "Volvo Says Its Emissions Control System Not Widely Applicable," *Air Conservation* no. 89 (March–April 1977).

[64] Many of the points here are found in Mills and White, "Government Policies."

[65] The following sources are unanimous in rejecting either public transportation or transportation controls as an effective means to control the mobile-source air pollution problem: D. N. Dewees, *Economics and Public Policy: The Automobile Pollution Case* (Cambridge, Mass., MIT Press, 1974) chapter 6; Jacoby and Steinbruner, *Clearing the Air*, chapter 3; Grad and coauthors, *The Automobile*, chapter 5; and the 1974 NAS study, chapter 3.

be substantial. What is more important, such strategies might shift the pollution problem to suburban areas.[66]

Economic Incentives

In theory the ultimate goal of a policy to control automobile emissions should be to produce a fleet of "optimally clean" cars. That is, we would like a mix of automobiles for which the marginal costs of further emissions controls would be balanced by the marginal benefits of the controls in place. Thus, one important characteristic of such a policy should be to reward producers and consumers of "clean" cars and penalize producers and consumers of "dirty" cars. We have already discussed some of the inefficiencies in the current control policy and have examined several alternative regulatory policies that could replace it. We now turn to the use of emissions charges, of the sort discussed in chapter 2, to deal with mobile-source emissions and their control.

Allen Kneese and Charles Schultze noted that fifteen years ago economists at the Rand Corporation proposed a smog tax.[67] One version of the tax was based on periodic testing of vehicles and the assignment of a smog rating on the basis of the results. At the time of gasoline purchases, drivers would pay a tax according to their smog rating. Consumers could potentially reduce their tax payments by four methods: (1) purchasing "cleaner" cars; (2) retrofitting cars with emissions control systems; (3) maintaining existing control systems; or (4) driving less.

More recently, Mills and White have proposed a detailed system of charges for mobile-source emissions control, the basic elements of which are as follows.[68]

1. Emissions charges would be levied on all new cars sold and would be based on average measured emissions for a sample of each vehicle type.[69]

[66] This result is seen in several of the simulations undertaken by Grad and coauthors, *The Automobile,* chapter 5.

[67] Kneese and Schultze, *Pollution.* The original paper is reprinted as D. M. Fort and coauthors, "Proposals for a Smog Tax," in *Tax Recommendations of the President,* Hearings before the House Committee on Ways and Means, 91 Cong. 2 sess. (Washington, D.C., GPO, 1970) pp. 369–379.

[68] Mills and White, "Government Policies."

[69] The testing would be similar to the current procedure. A small fleet would be tested for 50,000 miles, and a larger one for 4,000 miles. The latter would then be extrapolated to 50,000 miles.

2. Any type of car could be legally sold as long as the proper emissions fee were paid.

3. The fee structure would be of the following form:

$$F = (F_{HC} \times HC) + (F_{CO} \times CO) + (F_{NO_x} \times NO_x)$$

where F is the total fee and F_{HC}, F_{CO}, and F_{NO_x} are the individual fees for HC, CO, and NO_x, respectively.[70]

4. Two fee schedules would be used, one for low-pollution areas and one for high-pollution areas.[71]

5. An emissions charge would also be applied to cars currently in use on the basis of annual testing.[72]

6. The emissions fees would be announced five years in advance, except in extraordinary circumstances, in order to permit planning, engineering, and design.[73]

7. Comparable federal or state emissions fees, or both, would be applied to other pollution sources.[74]

The proponents of smog taxes or similar emissions charge schemes point to a number of advantages of such systems. For example, they suggest that the car-buying public would demand "cleaner" cars; hence, manufacturers would have an incentive to produce them. Furthermore, consumers would have a very real incentive to maintain clean cars since it would directly affect the fees they would pay. Depending on the magnitude of the emissions fees, it might even pay consumers to retrofit older cars with emissions control equipment, an incentive that at present is lacking because individuals do not perceive any tangible effects on air quality from putting controls on cars.[75]

[70] The HC emissions would include both evaporative and blowby emissions.

[71] Ideally one would want more variation in the fees to correspond with a complete range of pollution problems. Mills and White suggest that one way to achieve this is by having a single federal fee schedule with states or smaller geographical units adding supplemental fees.

[72] These charges would be based on the number of miles driven as well as the actual emissions. Mills and White recognize that this would require a "tamper-proof" odometer.

[73] Obviously during the initial phases of such a plan, the five-year advance warning would not be possible.

[74] Assuming that the average annual automobile mileage is 12,000 miles, a charge of $6.33 gpm HC is equivalent to $0.053 grams per year HC; this fee could be levied on stationary sources of HC.

[75] This is an excellent illustration of the traditional "free-rider" problem in dealing with public goods. The public good, in this case, is air quality.

With regard to manufacturers, announcement of fee schedules several years in advance would mean that once the policy was in operation, companies would not face all-or-nothing deadlines as under the current law. Manufacturers would have flexibility as to the timing of introducing new technologies, and they would be able to make optimal tradeoffs in the control of individual pollutants. In essence, they could choose least-cost strategies for emissions control within the technological constraints available to them.

As a policy alternative, emissions fees have several favorable attributes in addition to those discussed above. Emissions standards under the current legislation designate specific emissions levels for specific pollutants applicable to a particular model year. These often lead to the adoption of a specific control technology for that year (see table 3-4). Once in place, and assuming proper maintenance, such equipment is associated with certain pollution emissions per mile driven.

However, ambient pollution levels are directly related to the number of miles driven as well as the emissions per mile. Consequently, the imposition of standards has no built-in incentive to influence total driving. On the other hand, emissions fees usually are accompanied by provisions that link them directly to the number of miles driven. Thus, such proposals incorporate a characteristic that directly provides incentives for individuals to reduce the fees they pay; hence, they may also decrease their total driving.

Emissions fees can also be designed to incorporate more wide-ranging aspects of cost effectiveness in pollution control. For example, we discussed earlier how manufacturers would be induced to "optimally" control the mix of emissions levels for the various pollutants being controlled. This notion can be easily extended, in that emissions fees would tend to equate marginal abatement costs across manufacturers. Those manufacturers for which abatement was cheapest would choose control strategies that led to the greatest reduction in emissions, while those for which abatement was expensive would choose to produce "dirtier" cars. Furthermore, this concept not only applies to automobile manufacturers, but also to other sources of pollution.[76]

Once an emissions fee system is instituted, the apparatus can also be used to handle other unpleasantries associated with automobile usage. For instance, in areas where congestion presents a serious problem, a congestion tax could be added as a component of the total emissions fee. Sim-

---

[76] See item 7 of the Mills and White proposal above.

ilarly, another tax increment might be added to handle the problem of noise pollution.

Emissions fee systems are not without difficulties, however. First, the fees themselves must be set. Ideally, they should be just high enough that the benefits associated with raising them slightly (and presumably reducing emissions slightly) are less than the costs of doing so. However, because of the uncertainty surrounding the estimates of the benefits and costs of mobile-source pollution control,[77] and because of the uncertainty of the behavior that will result from the imposition of the fees, it is very difficult to specify the fees precisely. Nevertheless, it should be emphasized that this problem also arises with regard to setting standards. Furthermore, some would argue that fee schedules are more easily adjusted than systems based on standards.

There is also the problem of what to do with the collected revenues if a fee system is adopted. Mills and White argue that although the earmarking of effluent fee revenues for pollution control efforts is not generally a good practice, they doubt it would introduce significant inefficiencies if it were done. Two specific uses of earmarked funds they mention are waste treatment facilities and pollution control research.[78]

Mention should also be made of the administrative costs of emissions control programs. Mills and White address this aspect of the problem with respect to their proposed program.[79] They indicate that some of the administrative costs associated with their proposal would be similar to those for the current program since testing procedures would be similar. However, they note that administrative costs associated with control of in-use cars would be higher than under the current program, since state or local inspections that are now optional in some places would be a necessary component of their system. Nevertheless, as discussed earlier, for the current system to be truly effective, increased inspections of in-use cars are necessary because of the inherent deterioration in emissions control systems (especially when they are not properly maintained).

Finally, there is the issue of the political acceptability of an emissions fee program on the part of the various groups involved.[80] By their very nature, economic incentives represent a more indirect approach to pollution control than do regulations. As a consequence, a regulatory agency

---

[77] This is particularly true with regard to the benefit estimates.
[78] See Mills and White, "Government Policies," pp. 72–73.
[79] See Mills and White, "Government Policies," pp. 69–71.
[80] For a more extensive discussion of this issue, see Mills and White, "Government Policies," pp. 77–80.

may view the use of economic incentives as a threat to its own power and authority. At the same time, some legislators still see fee systems as a "license to pollute." They seem determined to mandate legislation that dictates both standards and deadlines. Paradoxically, automakers were perhaps more efficient in fighting specific standards and deadlines than they would have been in avoiding compliance with an emissions fee system. Some environmentalists also view effluent fees with suspicion rather than as an efficient means of balancing social benefits and costs. Finally, consumers may view a charge system as only increasing out-of-pocket costs since they will not only pay for control equipment but also may be responsible for the emissions fee itself. In the end, it is difficult to find any interested party that is motivated to wave the banner for economic incentives.

Implications and Conclusions

This chapter has been concerned with air pollution policy as it relates to mobile sources. In particular, the focus has been U.S. environmental policy regulating automobile emissions.

We introduced the subject by illustrating the recent confrontation between Detroit and Washington. We also presented evidence that mobile-source control policy thus far has probably had some effects on air quality in certain areas of the United States. Finally, we stressed the tradeoffs inherent in the technology used to control automobile emissions—tradeoffs that make the control of such pollution a complex issue for environmental policy.

This was followed by a brief history of mobile-source air pollution legislation. From the first acts passed by the California legislature in 1961, to the latest air pollution bill clearing both chambers of Congress in August 1977, we have seen how strict emissions standards have been legislated and how the deadlines for their implementation have been postponed.

In discussing the benefits and costs of mobile-source pollution control, we have seen that it is much easier to enumerate the categories of benefits and costs than to quantify them. By placing heavy reliance on secondary sources, however, we presented evidence suggesting that under the present law, the probable benefits of control fall short of the estimated costs. Thus, although we may wish to limit automobile emissions to some extent, there is a strong possibility that some alternative to our current approach should be given careful consideration.

Before turning to some of these alternative policies, we looked at the question of technology forcing. That is, we examined the industry's response to the setting of emissions standards to see what role the legislation had in motivating technological advances. We concluded that the history indicates that the legislation created perverse incentives for the automobile industry. The all-or-nothing deadlines resulted in short-term, high-cost control technologies, rather than longer term, less costly solutions to the control of mobile-source emissions.

Next, we dealt with implementation and enforcement. Because present emissions control systems exhibit significant deterioration once in use, it appears that proper maintenance is essential if public policy is to have an important impact on air quality. Unfortunately, the 1970 legislation did little to actively encourage such in-use maintenance. Instead, it placed primary responsibility on the manufacturers since control systems were to be guaranteed to meet emissions standards for five years or 50,000 miles, whichever came first. In 1977, President Carter signed a new bill that not only postpones stricter emissions standards for two years, but also narrows the manufacturers' warranty to two years, or 24,000 miles, for all components of the emissions control system other than those installed for the sole or primary purpose of reducing vehicle emissions (for example, catalytic converters). It is difficult to see any justification for this aspect of the legislation. Even if one has doubts about the merits of the strictest emissions standards, their implementation in the absence of adequate enforcement procedures cannot be sound public policy.

The succeeding section examined alternative regulatory approaches to the control of mobile-source pollution: specifically, the two-car strategy, relaxation of the NO_x standard, the implications of driving smaller cars, the feasibility of other available technologies, and public transportation and transportation controls. We saw that the costs of automobile emissions control could be significantly reduced by the implementation of a two-car strategy or through the relaxation of the NO_x standard. In addition, we reviewed evidence suggesting that, while a policy requiring a shift to smaller cars would greatly reduce motoring costs (primarily because of their fuel economy), it would not solve the emissions problem in a cost-effective manner. Furthermore, there was some indication that the three-year-old conclusion of the National Academy of Sciences—that no single alternative to the conventional gasoline engine was better in all respects for meeting emissions standards—still held. Even Volvo, which had developed the nearly "pollution-free" Lambda-sond system, advocated a moratorium on emissions standards at the 1975 California standard, partially because of the cost that further reductions would entail. Finally, we presented arguments that suggested transportation control strategies were unlikely to be effective means of solving the mobile-source pollution problem. On cost-effective grounds, we conclude that of the various alternative *regulatory* policies, the adoption of a two-car (or multiple-car) antipollution strategy merits perhaps the most serious consideration.[81] To this end, further research should be undertaken to consider more carefully the implementation of such a scheme, including: the levels of emissions to be allowed, the proportion of vehicles to be stringently controlled, and the adminstrative mechanisms necessary for enforcement.

We next turned to possible economic incentives for control of mobile-source emissions. Specifically, we reviewed a proposal by Mills and White that would levy charges on mobile-source emissions and considered some of the advantages and disadvantages of their program. Weighing the pros and cons, we believe there is significant merit in such a program and that, at a minimum, it should be implemented on an experimental basis in some area of the country. Their scheme would provide a continuing incentive for both manufacturers and motorists to reduce emissions and might even reduce total driving. Furthermore, their incentive scheme could provide a mechanism by which more cost-effective measures could be introduced into the total air pollution control program.

To paraphrase a recent editorial in *Science*, while it is important that Detroit produce low-emissions cars, that is only part of the problem. What also matters is the performance of automobiles once they are in use. At a minimum, this requires strong inspection programs in the urban areas having serious mobile-source-related air pollution problems. The editorial continues:

> During the next decade we will spend hundreds of billions of dollars on pollution abatement, but most of it will be wasted unless there is better scientific understanding of the problems, a better analysis of costs and benefits, and an enforcement system applicable to all polluters.[82]

---

[81] More than five years ago, the RECAT study urged that a two-car strategy be given serious attention. See RECAT report, pp. 33–34.

[82] "Control of Automobile Emissions," *Science* vol. 197 (August 5, 1977).

APPENDIX TO CHAPTER 3

Analysis Behind Current Emissions Standards[1]

The mobile-source emissions standards as legislated in the 1970 Amendments to the Clean Air Act are based in large part on work done in a study by Barth and his coauthors.[2] With the objective of finding out to what extent 1980 auto emissions would have to be controlled in order to reach a specified level of desired air quality in 1990, Barth and his coworkers chose a simple "rollback" model.[3]

To obtain the desired percentage reduction in auto emissions, the researchers first determined the highest ambient reading in any city during 1967 (1967 max) for each air pollutant under consideration. This reading was then multiplied by an "emissions growth factor" to project what the automobile emissions would be in 1990 with no emissions controls. The factor that was used was 2.18 and was equal to the expected growth in the automobile population.

With the goal to provide the maximum possible protection to human health, they then chose desired levels (DL) of ambient concentrations of the air pollutants below which no study had found any adverse health effects. These desired levels were then subtracted from the 1990 projected levels to obtain the percentage reductions required. (An adjustment was also made for background levels [BL] of the air pollutants in question.) Finally, assuming that the maximum ambient readings in each city were attributable completely to automobile emissions, the required emissions reduction was calculated and applied to the current 1967 emissions rate from the automobiles (1967 rate) to obtain the desired emissions rate (DER). In mathematical notation:

$$DER = \left[1.00 - \frac{(2.18 \times 1967\,\text{max}) - DL}{(2.18 \times 1967\,\text{max}) - BL} \right] \times 1967\,\text{rate}$$

The above methodology can best be followed by applying it to a specific pollutant.[4] For example, Barth and his coauthors selected the current primary standard for carbon monoxide (CO) as the desired level of

---

[1] Much of the material in this appendix is taken from chapter 7 of Jacoby and Steinbruner, *Clearing the Air*.

[2] Barth and coauthors, "Federal Vehicle Emissions."

[3] Implicit in their model was the assumption that the automobile has a ten-year turnover rate.

[4] While we have chosen to discuss CO, the analyses for HC and NO_x present similar assumptions and conclusions despite the fact that the situation is more complex since control of these air pollutants is designed primarily to control the formation of photochemical oxidants.

ambient air quality (9 parts per million [ppm] or 10 milligrams per cubic meter [mg/m³]), based on a maximum eight-hour average. The maximum 1967 reading for CO was in Chicago and was equal to 51 mg/m³. The background concentration was determined to be 1 mg/m³. And the 1967 emissions rate for CO was said to be 82.6 gpm. Substituting these values into the above equation one obtains:

$$DER = \left[1.00 - \frac{(2.18 \times 51) - 10}{(2.18 \times 51) - 1} \right] \times 82.6 \cong 6.16 \text{ gpm.}[5]$$

This meant that a $[(82.6 - 6.16)/82.6] \times 100 = 92.5$ percent reduction from 1967 emissions of CO would be needed in 1980 to ensure that the desired level of ambient CO would not be exceeded in any city in 1990.

There have been many criticisms of the approach followed by Barth and his colleagues. First, the model assumes that all ambient concentrations of CO are contributed by automobile emissions. As table 3-2 indicates, mobile sources (including trucks and buses) accounted for about 94 percent of CO emissions in Chicago by weight. This implies that automobiles probably contributed to less that 80 percent of the actual concentrations of CO in Chicago. In addition, since the maxium reading was used in the calculations, this further overstates the contribution. For example, the 1975 reduction in total CO emissions in Chicago necessary to meet the air quality standard was as high as 68 percent or as low as 26 percent, depending on whether the historic high eight-hour average concentration of 44 ppm or the 1970 maximum of 21 ppm was used.[6] What is even more disturbing is the fact that the percentage contribution of the automobile to total emissions of HC and NO_x is far less than the relative contribution of CO emissions to total emissions. (See tables 3-1 and 3-2.) Hence, the bias introduced by the assumption that the automobile is the only source of emissions is far greater for calculations involving these two air pollutants.

Another bias is introduced into the analysis by the emissions growth factor. The highest concentration of CO in Chicago was recorded in the downtown area. Since the traffic situation in that area is already quite dense, it is not realistic to assume that 2.18 times as many automobiles could inhabit the area. Therefore, the projected emissions levels are prob-

[5] The approximation sign signifies the fact that we were unable to duplicate the calculation precisely despite the fact that these numbers are identical to those in the original article by Barth and coauthors, "Federal Vehicle Emissions." The calculation by Barth and coauthors for HC and NO_x led to desired emissions rates of 0.14 and 0.40, respectively.

[6] W. A. Daniel, and Jan M. Heuss, "Ambient Air Quality and Automotive Emission Control," *Journal of the Air Pollution Control Association* vol. 24 (1974) p. 849.

ably substantially overstated. In short, the assumption of a linear relationship between automobile population and ambient levels of pollutants associated with automobile emissions is probably not a very good one.

In fairness, it should be pointed out that proponents of the analysis argue that since the ultimate goal of mobile-source emissions control is to protect the public health, such biases only serve to provide additional "margins of safety." However, as discussed in this chapter the resulting standards are extremely costly to meet.

CHAPTER 4

Toxic Substance Policy and the Protection of Human Health

PAUL R. PORTNEY

IN A RECENT BOOK, William McNeill suggests that the demise of empires and civilizations past may have been due more to infectious disease than political or economic factors.[1] Many of the diseases of which he writes no longer pose serious threats to the inhabitants of developed nations. For example, the spread of waterborne diseases like cholera and diphtheria has been arrested by filtration and treatment of drinking water sources. In a similar fashion typhus, pneumonia, influenza, and tuberculosis gradually have come under the control of modern medicine.

Nonetheless, we are slowly becoming aware of a new and extremely serious threat to human health arising from our exposure to certain highly toxic substances in the home, on the job, and at play. Although the effects of these exposures may never topple a modern civilization, they have the potential to cause great numbers of deaths and widespread, profound human suffering.

This chapter discusses U.S. policies designed to control toxic substances. In the first section, we call attention to the problems that toxic substances pose and to the characteristics of these problems that make them so difficult to manage. We consider next two extreme and idealized kinds of responses to toxic substance problems—one where the govern-

[1] William H. McNeill, *Plagues and Peoples* (New York, Anchor Press/Doubleday, 1976).

ment does nothing and another where the government tries to legislate such substances out of existence. There we also discuss actual federal toxic substance policy, which lies, as we might expect, between these two extremes. In the third section, we point out the shortcomings of current federal policy, some of which are easily correctable while others are less so. There we make specific suggestions for policy reform.

Introduction

Mankind's acute, or immediate, vulnerability to certain substances is a matter of historical record. We know, for example, that Socrates died of hemlock poisoning and that the Borgias routinely dispatched their enemies with lethal mixtures. Such acute effects arise from accidental exposures to less well-known "poisons," as well. For example, more than 4,000 citizens of London died from an extended period of severe air pollution there in 1952. Fortunately, our knowledge of these acute effects continues to grow. Recent studies have linked temporal variations in air pollution within a metropolitan area to acute ophthalmological and other health problems.[2]

However, our knowledge of the chronic, or long-term, adverse effects of exposures to toxic substances is much less well developed. This is not at all difficult to explain. Latency and uncertainty make chronic toxic substances difficult to recognize and control. By latency we mean the period between exposure to a toxic substance and the manifestation of its effect. By uncertainty we mean our imperfect knowledge of the identity of toxic substances and the way in which they eventually affect health. These problems are discussed at length later in the chapter.

A number of the toxic substances discussed in this chapter are transmitted through air or water. Several were mentioned in chapters 2 and 3. In fundamental ways they often differ from traditional air and water pollutants, and their effects are sufficiently severe to warrant additional discussion. A number of these substances do not imperil their victims through the air and water to which we are all exposed but rather through occupational or voluntary exposures. For this reason, too, the subject of chronically toxic substances merits separate attention.

Two factors account for the increased attention being given toxic substances by Congress and federal administrative agencies. The first is the sheer volume of publicity such substances now receive. The current con-

[2] See, for example, Eugene P. Seskin, "An Analysis of Some Acute Health Effects of Air Pollution in the Washington, D.C. Area," *Journal of Urban Economics,* in press.

troversy surrounding the Food and Drug Administration's (FDA's) proposed saccharin ban is an example. Similar publicity was accorded the discovery that the pesticide Kepone was highly toxic not only to employees of the plant where it was produced but also to nearby residents and those eating fish from the river into which Kepone was discharged along with other municipal wastes. Somewhat less recent were the revelations about the carcinogenic effects of vinyl chloride on industrial workers, as well as the mercury poisoning suffered by the residents of Minamata, the Japanese fishing village.

It is doubtful that toxic substances generally would receive such publicity were it not that many are linked to cancer, a disease that Americans not unreasonably have come to fear more than any other. As table 4-1 indicates, cancer has increased dramatically as a cause of death in the United States. Although it caused less than 4 percent of all deaths in 1900, it accounted for more than 17 percent in 1970, and is now second only to heart disease as a killer of Americans. While some of this increase can be attributed to the aging of the population (as table 4-1 indicates, infectious diseases now kill fewer victims in childhood), much of it cannot.

Moreover, this has occurred at a time when the average life expectancy of Americans surprisingly has leveled off. Between 1900 and 1950, average life expectancy for white females rose from less than 50 years to 72 years; that of white males rose from 47 to 67 years during the same period. Between 1950 and 1970, there has been very little change in the expected life span of white females (although that of non-white females has risen); and there has been even less increase in the expected life span of white males (with no change in that for non-white males).

This would be of no relevance to the subject of this chapter were it not for our growing recognition of the environmental causes of cancer. Although heredity and viruses are thought to be responsible for some cancers, between 60 and 90 percent of all cancers are now believed to be caused by environmental factors, broadly defined.[3] For example, recent studies have found the variation in cancer death rates correlated with pork and beef consumption, cigarette smoking, atmospheric concentrations of ammonium, beta and ultraviolet radiation, and other factors.[4] Cancer

---

[3] World Health Organization, *Prevention of Cancer,* Technical Report, Series 276 (Geneva, 1974); Samuel Epstein, "Environmental Determinants of Human Cancer," *Cancer Research* vol. 34 (1974) pp. 2425–2435.
[4] Allen V. Kneese and William Schulze, "Environment, Health, and Economics— The Case of Cancer," *American Economic Review* vol. 67 (February 1977) pp. 326–332.

TABLE 4-1   Leading Causes of Death, 1900, 1960, and 1970

Rank	Cause of death	Deaths per 100,000 population	Percentage of all deaths
	1900		
	All causes	1,719.0	100.0
1	Pneumonia and influenza	202.2	11.8
2	Tuberculosis (all forms)	194.4	11.3
3	Gastritis, etc.	142.7	8.3
4	Diseases of the heart	137.4	8.0
5	Vascular lesions affecting the central nervous system	106.9	6.2
6	Chronic nephritis	81.0	4.7
7	All accidents[a]	72.3	4.2
8	Malignant neoplasms (cancer)	64.0	3.7
9	Certain diseases of early infancy	62.5	3.6
10	Diphtheria	40.3	2.3
	Total		64.0
	1960		
	All causes	955.0	100.0
1	Diseases of the heart	366.4	38.7
2	Malignant neoplasms (cancer)	147.4	15.6
3	Vascular lesions affecting the central nervous system	107.3	11.3
4	All accidents[b]	51.9	5.5
5	Certain diseases of early infancy	37.0	3.9
6	Pneumonia and influenza	36.0	3.5
7	General arteriosclerosis	20.3	2.1
8	Diabetes mellitus	17.1	1.8
9	Congenital malformations	12.0	1.3
10	Cirrhosis of the liver	11.2	1.2
	Total		85.0
	1970		
	All causes	945.3	100.0
1	Diseases of the heart	362.0	38.3
2	Malignant neoplasms (cancer)	162.8	17.2
3	Cerebrovascular diseases	101.9	10.8
4	Accidents	56.4	6.0
5	Influenza and pneumonia	30.9	3.3
6	Certain causes of mortality in early infancy[e]	21.3	2.2
7	Diabetes mellitus	18.9	2.0
8	Arteriosclerosis	15.6	1.6
9	Cirrhosis of the liver	15.5	1.6
10	Bronchitis, emphysema, and asthma	15.2	1.6
	Total		85.0

Source: President's Science Advisory Committee Panel on Chemicals, *Chemicals and Health* (Washington, D.C., Government Printing Office, 1973) p. 152; U.S. Department of Health, Education and Welfare, Public Health Service, *Facts of Life and Death*, DHEW Pub. No. (HRA) 74–1222 (Washington, D.C., Government Printing Office, 1974) p. 31.

a Violence would add 1.4 percent; horse, vehicle, and railroad accidents provide 0.8 percent.

b Violence would add 1.5 percent; motor vehicle accidents provide 2.3 percent; railroad accidents provide less than 0.1 percent.

e Birth injuries, asphyxia, infections of newborn, ill-defined diseases, immaturity, etc.

mortality rates in U.S. counties have been found to be correlated with the location of petroleum refineries, as well.[5]

Moreover, the incidence of cancer within a single metropolitan area has been found to vary significantly with the source of municipal drinking water. That is, *even after filtration,* the drinking water of certain New Orleans residents that originates in the Mississippi River and the drinking water of certain Cincinnati residents that originates in the Ohio River have been linked to several types of cancer.[6] In fact, the Environmental Protection Agency (EPA) has proposed that all systems serving more than 75,000 people use carbon filtration.

Of the 2 million known chemical compounds, 30,000 of which are in substantial use, a growing number have been identified as carcinogens and as many as 1,000 others are suspected of being so. The former include such familiar compounds as asbestos, arsenic, benzene, chlorine, chloroform, vinyl chloride, and coal tar. In addition, the flame retardant Tris (2,3-dibromopropyl) phosphate, used to treat children's sleepwear, was recently banned by the Consumer Product Safety Commission and the garments ordered recalled from retail outlets because Tris was found to induce cancer in laboratory test animals. On still another front, the Food and Drug Administration is seeking to limit the concentrations of PCBs (polychlorinated biphenyls) found in dairy products, poultry, eggs, and fish. The FDA ban on saccharin was proposed because of that additive's carcinogenic effect on laboratory animals in Canadian experiments.

In addition to the dangers posed by these and many other substances, certain modern technologies carry with them great health risks. For example, the dispersal of freon and other aerosol propellants by spray cans of deodorant, paint, hair conditioners, and disinfectants has been shown to deplete the ozone layer of our atmosphere. If the depletion is sufficiently severe, climatological changes could cause crop and vegetation loss and increased incidences of skin cancer brought about by more direct exposure to solar radiation. High altitude flight resulting in emissions of oxides of nitrogen can also cause ozone depletion.

[5] See the report of a study by William J. Blot, Louise A. Brinton, Joseph F. Fraumeni, Jr., and B. J. Stone of the Environmental Epidemiology Branch of the National Cancer Institute in "Cancer Mortality in U.S. Counties with Petroleum Industries," *Science* vol. 198 (October 7, 1977) pp. 51–53.

[6] Talbot Page, Robert Harris, and Samuel Epstein, "Drinking Water and Cancer Mortality in Louisiana," *Science* vol. 193 (July 2, 1976) pp. 55–57; R. C. Buncher, "Cincinnati Drinking Water—An Epidemiologic Study of Cancer Rates," University of Cincinnati Medical Center, 1975.

TABLE 4-2   Observed Latency Period in Seventy-Eight Workers Exposed to Aromatic Amines

Length of latent period in years	Percentage of workers with tumors, by length of exposure in years					
	Up to 1	1	2	3	4	5 and over
Up to 5	0	0	0	0	0	0
10	0	0	0	0	0	11
15	0	17	22	0	10	45
20	4	17	22	40	30	69
25	9	17	22	70	70	88
30	9	17	48	70	80	94

Note: For example, of those workers who were exposed for two years 30 years ago, 48 percent had tumors.
Source: Wilhelm Hueper, "Medicolegal Considerations of Occupational and Nonoccupational Environmental Cancers," chapter 7 in Charles Frankel, ed., *Lawyers' Cyclopedia: and the Land* (forthcoming).

The substances and technologies to which we have referred might indeed represent a serious threat to human health and well-being. To understand why the formulation of policy regarding their control is so difficult, consider certain of their vexing characteristics.[7]

The single most troublesome characteristic of most toxic substances is the latency of their effect. These latency periods generally are fifteen to forty years in length but have been as long as seventy-five years.[8] The latent period varies with the length of exposure and with the presence of other factors or co-carcinogens—for example, cigarette smoking can shorten the latency period associated with radiation exposure by as much as 33 percent. Table 4-2 shows the relationship between length of exposure to toxic substances of persons who work with aromatic amines and the length of their latency periods.

These long latencies make the control of toxic substances extremely difficult. Clearly, it is too late to aid those exposed to a toxic substance during the latency period even if the cause of the disease is recognized upon its eventual appearance. Seldom is the cause obvious, however. This is because long latency periods almost guarantee that the affected individuals will have worked at a variety of jobs, lived in a number of different places, and altered their dietary and other habits since the time of their exposures. This makes it difficult to isolate the effect of exposure to a partic-

[7] For a much more thorough discussion of the characteristics of toxic substance and related problems, see Talbot Page, "Environmental Risk," *Ecology Law Quarterly*, in press.
[8] Council on Environmental Quality, *Environmental Quality—1975* (CEQ, Washington, D.C., 1975) p. 27.

ular substance some twenty to forty years earlier. Moreover, population mobility, which is often desirable for economic reasons, greatly complicates toxic substance identification and control.

In addition, the general public is easily misled by long latency periods to believe that no substance to which they were so long ago exposed could cause a current disease. Typical is the viewpoint expressed in the following excerpt from a letter to a newspaper editor protesting asbestos control in Montgomery County, Maryland:

> For a goodly part of my life I have been hammering, breaking, sawing, chopping, sniffing, licking and otherwise analyzing rocks including lots of serpentine and related materials. . . . For weeks I dumped bags of ground-up asbestos into a hopper and probably inhaled thousands of times more asbestos than the average Montgomery County resident would see in a lifetime. Now, more than 30 years and several hundred-thousand cigarettes later, lo, I am still living and healthy.[9]

This view is especially alarming in the face of clear evidence that latency periods can easily exceed thirty years.

Uncertainty further complicates toxic substance policy. Consider, for example, the adverse side effects that might attend the use of aerosol propellants. The realization of these effects—the process of environmental transfer, as it is called—depends upon very complicated physical, chemical, and meterological interactions about which there is often sharp disagreement among scientists. It is difficult to legislate that which even scientists appear to understand imperfectly. Similar problems arise with respect to the physiological mechanisms involved. The process by which exposures to toxic substances results in tumors or other physical problems is still not understood by biochemists, geneticists, or physicians. Here, too, uncertainty hampers our ability to formulate sound policy.

The Spectrum of Appropriate Policy

Given the gravity and scope of toxic substance problems, our primary interest lies in examining current policies designed to cope with them. Before doing so, however, it will prove useful to consider the merits of two hypothetical, contrasting, and, as we will see, unrealistic approaches to toxic substance control. This will enable us to understand better the strengths and weaknesses of current policy.

[9] *The Washington Post,* June 23, 1977.

The Market Solution

Under very special conditions, the transactions that take place in what economists call the free market can be shown to "solve" the problems that arise from dangerous working conditions, environmental disamenities, or unsafe consumer products. That is, economic forces can sometimes obviate or at least reduce the need for corrective governmental policy. Might the markets for labor, land, or certain products operate in such a way that *no* federal toxic substance policy is required?

This will be the case *if* the wage rates of workers exposed to toxics exactly compensate them for risks they both understand and voluntarily accept and *if* the prices of land and certain commodities reflect the risks borne by those who purchase them. We will examine these "ifs" in some detail, since they will determine the usefulness of what we have called the market solution as a response to toxic substance problems.

Consider first a product, the production of which must necessarily expose workers to a toxic substance that will increase their chances of contracting cancer. Suppose that there are many workers and a wide variety of jobs for which they compete and that these workers are aware of these other employment opportunities and can change jobs at little or no cost. Suppose also that workers are fully informed as to the risks inherent in each and every job. In such a situation, wage premiums would have to be offered to workers to induce them to voluntarily accept hazardous jobs. Wages will be bid up above the rate in the safe occupations to that point at which enough workers are found who are willing to accept the higher cancer risk at the prevailing wage.

The size of this wage premium depends upon the risk preferences of the labor force. If many workers are willing to risk exposure to the toxicant for very little extra pay, the wage premium need not be large. If most workers are "risk avoiders," however, the wage differential required to attract the required workers may be quite large.

Employers have other possibilities open to them, however. Namely, they can elect to install equipment designed to eliminate the toxic substance hazard altogether or they can supply workers with protective equipment or clothing that eliminates or lessens the risk from exposure. Employers will elect the latter course as long as the additional cost of eliminating the toxic hazard (or protecting workers from it) is less than the amount they would have to pay workers to accept the risk. In other words, employers will balance the marginal cost of hazard elimination with the marginal benefits it generates (a reduced wage bill).

In this simple example, no government intervention would be required. Wages will rise in risky occupations just enough to compensate workers to voluntarily accept those risks. The fact that workers elect to do so is evidence of their preference for a risky but higher paying job as opposed to some other less risky, lower paying job. Moreover, employers need not be coerced into making safety improvements since they have an economic incentive to do so on their own, at least up to a point.

A further advantage bears mention. In this example, the risks that must be borne if the product is to be produced will be borne as cheaply as possible. This follows from the fact that the most risk-preferring workers are those who will take the risky jobs; since these workers are the ones requiring a small premium to do so, the total risk premium will be minimized. Also, those employers that can inexpensively eliminate occupational hazards will do so in order to avoid the wage premium they would have to pay if they did not do so. Thus, allowing the market to account for riskiness minimizes its cost.

In this example, if government were to intervene, it would do so unwisely. Suppose the government outlawed any exposure to the toxic in question. If employers could not prevent such exposures, the product could not be produced at all. If elimination of the exposure were highly costly, the price of the product would go up even though it could be produced much less expensively if workers were allowed to accept *on a purely voluntary basis* the risks that its production entails.

What about voluntary, nonoccupational exposures that arise because of environmental factors—proximity to a chemical plant, for example—or from the consumption of a product that contains a potentially toxic ingredient? Here, too, market forces could conceivably obviate the need for regulation. In the former case, land or housing prices near the site of a facility generating a risk of exposure to toxic substances could reflect the risks if they were widely understood, if a wide variety of other dwellings were available, and if households were aware of the opportunities and able to take advantage of them easily. In such a case, purchasers of "imperiled" dwellings would pay less for them than they would for otherwise identical but "safe" dwellings. Those most willing to occupy dwellings near the toxic facility would require the smallest premium (in the form of a reduced house price) to do so. In this way, the cost of bearing the risk would be minimized.[10] In a similar fashion, fully informed buyers of foodstuffs or

[10] However, if the pollution began *after* people had purchased housing surrounding the facility, these individuals would suffer capital losses. Action to redress these losses might be called for in such a case.

clothing containing toxic additives would require lower prices (relative to identical, but safe substitutes) to induce them to buy. Producers would have incentives to eliminate risky additives up to that point at which it is more expensive to do so than it is to accept lower prices for the products they sell.

These two examples illustrate the process by which toxic risks are said to be "capitalized" into house or product prices. They further illustrate the inadvisability of government intervention when risks are voluntarily borne by informed individuals and where profit-conscious firms have an economic incentive to eliminate certain risks. In such cases, the market for labor, land, or a particular product produces the "optimal" amount of risk. If the government were then to intervene and mandate more or less risk, this balance would be upset. Given the potential for competitive markets to balance benefits and costs through individual decisions, it is no wonder that economists favor reliance on market mechanisms.

Whether or not government *should* stay out of toxic substance regulation, however, is quite another matter. It depends upon the degree to which conditions in the real world conform to those in our idealized examples. As one might suspect, there are several respects in which this conformity is quite poor. In other words, we will see that there is indeed a role for some sort of government intervention to protect against the risks posed by toxic substances. First, however, let us examine the role of the market in accounting for job-related and other kinds of risks.

Certain occupational accident risks (as opposed to health risks) do appear to be reflected adequately in market wages. For example, it has been shown that the wages of certain construction workers vary directly with the risks they face on the job.[11] Actuarial data indicate that these workers are willing to accept an additional $260 per year in exchange for an increased chance of .001 (one in one thousand) in the probability of suffering a fatal accident. Moreover, in most manufacturing jobs, hourly wages for a specific job depend upon "job rating." This in turn depends upon the skills the job requires, its strenuousness, as well as any accident risks it might entail that cannot be eliminated economically. Of 1,724 major collective bargaining agreements recently surveyed by the U.S. Department of

---

[11] Sherwin Rosen and Richard Thaler, "The Value of Saving a Life: Evidence from the Labor Market," in Nester Terleckyj, ed., *Household Production and Consumption,* (New York, National Bureau of Economic Research, 1976). See also Robert S. Smith, *The Occupational Safety and Health Act* (Washington, D.C., American Enterprise Institute, 1976). Smith argues that the accident provisions of the act were unnecessary given the ability of wage rates to reflect accident risks.

Labor, 260 made reference to hazardous duty wage differentials. The majority of these occurred in the nonmanufacturing sector, primarily in the construction industry, and the hourly premiums varied from 25 cents to more than one dollar.

There is fragmentary evidence of market adjustments for occupational exposures to long-term health hazards but this is deceiving. For example, a recent collective bargaining agreement governing carpenters' wages states:

> All carpenters working with creosoted or other toxic materials shall receive 25 cents per hour more than the scale of wages. Toxic materials shall be interpreted as materials which contain any treatment to preserve same and which will cause irritation of the skin or other parts of the human system and defined as toxic by the Ohio State Industrial Commission.[12]

However, note that the express concern of this contract is with acute rather than chronic effects in spite of the longer term hazards of creosote exposure. That is, eye or skin irritation, rather than the increased likelihood of cancer in later years, is being traded for higher present wages. Even such provisions as this are rare. As table 4-3 indicates, of the 260 contracts making provision for hazard pay differentials, 109 arose because of exposure to acids, fumes, or chemicals, but even these agreements were prompted by acute rather than chronic toxicity.

This should not be too surprising. Indeed, there is little reason to believe that wage rates will perfectly adjust for exposures to chronic toxics. First, workers are very far from being informed about the physically debilitating effects of the substances to which they are exposed. In fact, it is only recently that epidemiologists have become aware of the carcinogenic properties of many of these substances, vinyl chloride gas being but one example.

Unionization might be expected to facilitate the spread of knowledge about toxics. However, only 213 of the 1,724 collective bargaining agreements sampled by the Department of Labor contain any reference to disseminating accident, mortality, and morbidity information (see table 4-3). While unions are more effective than individuals in securing information on job hazards, less than a sixth of the workers in the Labor Department sample are covered by agreements which would provide them with the information they would need to bargain for compensating wage

[12] U.S. Department of Labor, Bureau of Labor Statistics, *Major Collective Bargaining Agreements: Safety and Health Provisions,* Bulletin 1425-16 (1976) pp. 47–48.

TABLE 4-3   Conditions to Which Hazard Differentials Apply in Major
Collective Bargaining Agreements, 1974–1975

(workers in thousands)

Condition	Agreements	Workers
All agreements	1,724	7,868.0
Total providing hazard pay	260	1,005.3
Falling	161	575.3
Excessive heat or fire	21	76.7
Radiation	12	30.6
Electrical work	13	25.0
Acids, fumes or chemicals	109	372.9
Explosives	42	249.7
Compressed air	80	293.9
Unable to determine	4	31.3
No reference to hazard pay	1,464	6,862.8

Note: Nonadditive.
Source: U.S. Department of Labor, "Major Collective Bargaining Agreements: Safety and Health Provisions," *Bureau of Labor Statistics Bulletin*, 1425–16 (1976) p. 64.

premiums. Moreover, only 20 percent of all workers are unionized, and we must assume that unorganized workers would find it more difficult to obtain information about health risks.

It is interesting to note that unions have shifted their focus away from wage differentials and toward strict government regulation of the workplace. No doubt this is due to their recognition that health risks are infinitely more difficult to identify and, hence, bargain over than accident risks.

Even the government has difficulty obtaining information about potentially toxic substances. For example, the director of the National Institute of Occupational Safety and Health (NIOSH) recently testified to a House subcommittee that of the 86,000 trade name products located in the workplace, NIOSH had been able to identify the chemical ingredients in but half. Of those, about 20,000 contained substances subject to Labor Department regulation, yet manufacturers refused to identify the ingredients in a third of those products, claiming that this information is protected by trade secrecy laws.[13] In view of NIOSH's inability to discover the identity of substances in the workplace, both toxic and otherwise, workers cannot possibly be informed as to the presence and gravity of the threats posed by toxic substances.

[13] *The Wall Street Journal*, April 28, 1977, p. 8.

Even more unsettling is the inclination of workers to disregard or even scoff at evidence of the potential toxicity of substances encountered in the workplace. This is due in part to the rash of counterclaims that often follows evidence of toxicity. Since workers have no way of knowing whose information is best, inertia, as much as anything, keeps them working at their potentially hazardous occupations. Even in the absence of counterclaims, however, workers often pay little attention to evidence of chronic toxicity. This seems to have two causes: first, they fail to believe that a substance is harmful if its supposedly adverse effects are not immediate and obvious; and second, workers appear to care little about illnessess that will not manifest themselves for twenty or more years.

Even if workers possessed and understood such information, it is highly unlikely that wage settlements would perfectly reflect long-term health threats. This is due to the narrow range of job opportunities workers often have—especially during periods of high unemployment. In other words, we cannot assume that there is a wide variety of jobs available to workers, as we did in our example.

In fact, job scarcity sometimes leads to bizarre confrontations between workers or local residents exposed to toxic substances and those attempting to intervene in their behalf. This was the case in the dispute between the Environmental Protection Agency and the Reserve Mining Company of Duluth, Minnesota.[14] There, the United Steel Workers local union fought to keep the Reserve Mining plant open; the neighboring towns of Silver Bay and Two Harbors joined Reserve as defendants in the case; and the city of Duluth had to be forced to join EPA as a plaintiff. This occurred in spite of clear evidence that the firm's discharges of taconite tailings into Lake Superior were responsible for what may have been dangerously high levels of asbestos fibers in the drinking water of Silver Bay, Two Harbors, and Duluth.

Similarly, Ojibway Indians in Grassy Narrows, Ontario, are currently resisting efforts by the Canadian Department of Health and Welfare to prevent them from eating fish taken from the Wabigoon River. They also opposed the ban on the commercial sale of fish which went into effect six years ago. The sales were banned because the fish are contaminated with mercury dumped into the river until recently by the Dryden Paper Company upstream from Grassy Narrows. The Indians' resistance has come in the face of evidence that mercury levels in their bloodstreams are as much

14 380 *F. Supp.* 11 (D. Minnesota, 1974).

as seventeen times greater than the maximum safe level. Their refusal to cooperate is explained by the very high rate of unemployment that resulted from the collapse of commercial and sport fishing when the ban on fish sales went into effect.

Lack of information also impairs the ability of housing and product markets to compensate for the risks posed by toxic substances. Clearly, most purchasers of Tris-treated garments had no knowledge whatsoever of its potential carcinogenicity and could not be presumed to be weighing those risks against the price of those products. Nor have food dye or saccharin users or those purchasing products with other toxic substances been aware of their risks. In fact, only in the case of cigarette smoking can we assume that consumers are sufficiently aware of the risks that inhere in the use of a product. In a similar fashion, the prices of houses do not accurately reflect the toxic risks to which their inhabitants might be exposed. Again, this is most often because households are unaware of these risks although it may sometimes be due to the scarcity of alternative housing. This is especially true of low income dwellings, those that are most frequently located near industrial sites.

In short, the necessary conditions for labor, land, or product markets to balance automatically the benefits and costs of exposures to toxic substances are not descriptive of the real world. Exposures that are voluntarily borne in our simple example are too often involuntarily borne in the real world. Workers generally have no knowledge of the very serious health hazards they face on the job; therefore, they are not consciously balancing current wages against future health risks. Few purchasers of products containing toxic additives are aware of their presence. Information about these toxic substances may not be generated and disseminated until long after many individuals have been exposed. These exposures, too, cannot be construed as representing voluntary tradeoffs between dollars and risk. This opens the door for a governmental role in the regulation of toxic substances. Before discussing current policy, we consider a hypothetical approach to the control of these substances.

Regulating Away Toxic Substances

What if the federal government simply were to ban all voluntary or involuntary exposures to potentially toxic substances arbitrarily defined as those that induce cancer or other serious disease in laboratory test animals? If successful, this policy would certainly eliminate any known risk of death or illness from exposure to the substances in question.

In general, such a policy would *not* be wise. As we have argued above, certain kinds of risks or risk-taking may be desirable; moreover, both the benefits and costs of risk-bearing must be considered in deciding the amount of risk society should be willing to take. A ban on all risk-bearing implies that the benefits that might arise from, say, limited exposures to toxic substances will always fall short of the costs of those exposures. This will no doubt be true in certain cases. For example, it seems safe to assert that the added convenience of aerosol sprays, as opposed to pump sprays, is not worth running the risk of ozone depletion and its possible consequences. Similarly, the benefits of food colorings, which, among other things, make hot dogs red rather than grey, hardly seem worth the cancer risks these additives apparently pose.

However, the hypothetical ban we are considering would eliminate all other known risks as well, ones that might be worth taking. Consider the case of Tris. An outright ban on the use of Tris eliminates the risk of its carcinogenicity, a risk that is apparently considerable. Such a ban also forces society to forego the benefits associated with its use, however. If other, nonhazardous flame retardants exist, these benefits will be small. But if no substitutes exist, and if Tris-treated garments would significantly reduce suffering and loss of life from fire-related accidents, these foregone benefits might be considerable. Depending on the additional lives that may be expected to be lost in fire accidents, as well as the number of additional cancers that would result if Tris were allowed to be used, it may or may not be a sensible policy to prohibit it.

The same is true for other toxic substances, of course. The nature of the benefits they generate may differ—some may be very useful, others not—as may the risks incurred through their use. We do ourselves a disservice when we introduce policy based on the risks but not the benefits of exposures to toxic substances.

Current Policy Regulating Toxic Substances[15]

Human exposures to toxic substances are controlled in the main under a wide variety of more or less equally important federal legislation. First, the quality of the media in which toxic pollutants appear is regulated by EPA through specific sections of the 1970 Amendments to the Clean Air Act, the Federal Water Pollution Control Act (FWPCA), and the Re-

[15] This section draws largely on the comprehensive review of federal cancer policy provided by Marion P. Suter and Warren Muir, "The Federal Role in Cancer Prevention," in Samuel Epstein, ed., *Environmental and Occupational Determinants of Human Cancer* (Springfield, Ill., Charles C. Thomas, 1977).

source Conservation and Recovery Act (RCRA), and by the Labor Department's Occupational Safety and Health Administration (OSHA), as well. Second, individual exposures arising from use or ingestion of products are regulated by the Food and Drug Administration (FDA), the Consumer Product Safety Commission (CPSC), and by EPA through federal pesticide laws and amendments, the Toxic Substances Control Act (TSCA), and the Safe Drinking Water Act. A necessarily brief review follows of the legislation under which each of these agencies regulates toxic exposures.

THE CLEAN AIR ACT That part of the Clean Air Act Amendments most relevant to the control of chronically toxic substances is Section 112, which provides for national emission standards for hazardous air pollutants for which no ambient air quality standard (Section 109) is applicable. (See chapters 2 and 3 for a discussion of these standards.)

Under Section 112, the administrator of EPA is directed to issue a list containing each hazardous pollutant for which he intends to publish standards; he is then to publish the proposed emission standards for each pollutant and hold hearings about them within 180 days from the time they are put on the list. The final standard is to be published within another 180 days unless the hearings provide information that convinces the administrator that the pollutant is not hazardous.

To date, EPA has issued standards for four pollutants under Section 112 of the Clean Air Act. In April of 1973, EPA put into effect standards that limit visible emissions of asbestos, designate equipment to control it, and prohibit certain uses of materials and operations that result in exposures to it. Next, standards were established for beryllium and mercury. Standards regulating emissions of vinyl chloride to the ambient atmospheric environment were proposed in 1975 and became final in 1976. The emissions standards called for reductions in ambient annual average vinyl chloride concentrations of 95 percent, with the maximum permissible concentration being set at 10 parts per million (ppm) at vinyl chloride manufacturing installations. This standard was designed to bring emissions to the level attainable with best available control technology (see chapter 2). EPA hopes to propose standards regulating benzene under Section 112 of the Clean Air Act by the summer of 1978.

THE FEDERAL WATER POLLUTION CONTROL ACT Like the Clean Air Act, the Federal Water Pollution Control Act contains a section specifically about the control of toxic pollutants. Under Section 307 the administrator is directed to compile a list of "toxic pollutants or combination(s) of such pollutants," to publish proposed effluent standards for the pollutants within 180 days, and to publish final standards within another 180 days of the proposed standards and the hearings that follow them.

While EPA has issued no final effluent standards for hazardous pollutants as defined in Section 307, they will be regulating on a phased schedule taking some time about 125 toxic chemicals currently polluting surface waters.[16] These standards will be based on best available technology to be determined on an industry-by-industry basis. However, discharge standards have been proposed for the pesticides aldrin, dieldrin, and DDT and for endrin, toxaphene, benzidine and PCBs.

THE OCCUPATIONAL SAFETY AND HEALTH ACT This act, which in 1970 established the Occupational Safety and Health Administration (OSHA) in the Labor Department and created an assistant secretary to head it, has as its avowed purpose ". . . to provide for the general welfare, to assure so far as possible every working man and woman in the nation safe and healthful working conditions and to preserve our human resources" [Section 2(b)].

OSHA was directed under the act to adopt as interim standards existing standards that had been recommended by private organizations (the National Fire Protection Association or the American National Standards Institute, for example), industry, or government. OSHA was then to establish under Section 6(b) permanent standards regulating occupational health and safety hazards which "most adequately assure, to the extent feasible, on the basis of the best available evidence, that no employee will suffer material impairment of health or functional capacity even if such employee has regular exposure to the hazard dealt with by such standard for the period of his working life" [Section 6(b)(4)].

OSHA may also promulgate short-term emergency standards when the secretary of labor determines "(A) that employees are exposed to grave danger from exposure to substances or agents determined to be toxic or physically harmful or from new hazards, and (B) that such emergency standard is necessary to protect employees from such danger" [Section 6(c)(1)]. Immediately following the promulgation of an emergency standard, however, the secretary of labor must begin the procedure by

16 Suter and Muir, "The Federal Role," p. 62.

which the more conventional standards described in Section 6(b) are established.

While OSHA has promulgated only four permanent Section 6(b) standards (for asbestos, vinyl chloride, coke oven emissions, and for a group of fourteen carcinogens), it has issued proposed standards for a number of other substances including arsenic, beryllium, and trichloroethylene. Recently OSHA issued a temporary, emergency standard limiting occupational exposures to benzene, which is believed to cause leukemia and other blood diseases and is used in the production of chemicals as well as in the printing, rubber, detergent, pesticide, and varnish industries. Even those pumping gasoline are exposed to benzene and may be covered by the standard.

According to OSHA's emergency standard, occupational exposures to benzene are not to exceed one part of benzene per million parts of air averaged over an eight-hour work day, a 90 percent reduction from the current 10 ppm standard. Moreover, workers are not to be exposed to more than 5 ppm over any quarter-hour period, an upgrading from the current standard of 25 ppm. Gasoline station operators are exempted from the temporary standard as well as from the Section 6(b) standard which OSHA proposed in May of 1977. At that time, OSHA did express its intention to limit exposures of gasoline handlers to benzene. In May, however, these benzene standards were suspended by the Fifth Circuit Court of Appeals on the grounds that they were improperly issued. OSHA has appealed this stay and the matter is currently pending in an appeals court.

In October, 1977, OSHA proposed a dramatic change in the way they would regulate occupational exposures to toxic substances. Specifically, OSHA proposed to develop three kinds of generic or model standards which would define the agency's response to substances of various kinds. For example, if a substance was a "confirmed carcinogen"—proof of this would require evidence from a test involving humans or a single species of mammals—a temporary emergency standard would be issued that would limit employee exposure; this would be followed by a permanent standard after six months. For "suspected carcinogens," a permanent standard less stringent than that for confirmed carcinogens would be proposed and the workplaces in which the substance appeared would be checked to see whether or not a more or less strict standard might eventually be appropriate. Other proposed standards are to cover substances about which too little is known to speculate about carcinogenicity and substances that may be carcinogens but are not found in occupational environments.

OSHA feels that the establishment of these generic standards will speed up the process by which occupational exposures to toxic substances are regulated. Under the proposed system, as soon as OSHA determines the category to which a substance belongs (that is, confirmed carcinogen, suspected carcinogen, and the like), the appropriate action would be specified. The agency would still have to determine the category to which specific substances belong, and the exposure limits to be established under the proposed or temporary standard. However, OSHA would no longer be working on a one-at-a-time basis but rather with groups of related substances simultaneously. This might also reduce the time the agency spends in litigation over the actions they have taken on individual substances. It will be important to see what comes of the OSHA proposal because it is being considered as a model for the other government agencies charged with regulating exposures to toxic substances.

THE FEDERAL FOOD, DRUG, AND COSMETIC ACT Not all human exposure to toxic substances comes from the air people breathe in their ambient or occupational environments or from toxic pollutants in water. The Food and Drug Administration regulates exposures arising from the ingestion of food or drugs or the application of cosmetic products. The nature of the regulations that FDA may impose, as well as the findings necessary to trigger action, vary according to whether the substance is a food, drug, or cosmetic, however.

Food and food additives are regulated under the original Food, Drug, and Cosmetic Act of 1938 and under the Food Additives Amendment of 1958. A part of the 1958 amendment has come to be known as the Delaney clause, and it states in part, "*provided,* that no additive shall be deemed safe if it is found to induce cancer when ingested in man or animal, or if it is found, after tests which are appropriate for the evaluation of the safety of food additives, to induce cancer in man or animal . . ." [Section 409(c)(3)(A)]. It is around this section of the Food, Drug, and Cosmetic Act that much controversy has revolved, and we will discuss the Delaney clause at some length later in this chapter. For now it is sufficient to say that the clause requires FDA to ban any carcinogenic food additive.

The Food, Drug, and Cosmetic Act also contains general safety provisions that allow FDA to prohibit the sale of food that "contains any poisonous or deleterious substance which may render it injurious to health" [Section 402(a)(2)(A)]. This general provision has been used to ban other artificial sweeteners (even before the Food Additives Amendment), safrole and related products, and cyclamates. These general safety provisions were also used to terminate the provisional listings of the food dyes red number 2, red number 4, and carbon black. FDA pointed out when issuing the recent proposed saccharin ban that they would have acted under the general safety provisions had they not been forced to take action under the Delaney clause.[17]

Regulations regarding a particular food additive may be proposed at any time by FDA. They must then make final the regulation within ninety days unless they are requested to hold a public hearing on the proposed regulation at which time evidence may be presented supporting or opposing it.

FDA's regulation of the substances found in drugs and cosmetics differs from the food additive regulations. While those wishing to introduce new drugs or food additives must demonstrate the safety of their products, cosmetic manufacturers need not do so. It is up to FDA to demonstrate that an ingredient is unsafe before action can be taken. That is, no premarket testing or registration is required of cosmetic manufacturers. If FDA wishes to ban a cosmetic ingredient, it can sue in federal court or initiate a proceeding that will lead to a ban by listing the product it wishes to prohibit. Recently, for example, FDA joined EPA and the Consumer Product Safety Commission in jointly proposing a ban on aerosol sprays, to become effective in April 1979. According to FDA head Donald Kennedy, this ban will have the effect of preventing 12,000 skin cancer cases annually.[18] FDA has also issued proposed and then final regulations prohibiting the use of vinyl chloride as an aerosol propellant. Similarly, prohibitions on the use of chloroform in cosmetics were issued in 1976.

THE CONSUMER PRODUCT SAFETY COMMISSION   The CPSC was created in 1972 to oversee the safety of a multitude of consumer products, many of which were regulated under preexisting legislation including the Flammable Fabrics Act, the Federal Hazardous Substances Act, and the Poison Prevention Packaging Act.

As in the case of cosmetic regulation by FDA, the Consumer Product Safety Act does not require the registration or testing of products (or both) prior to marketing. Rather, the burden of proof of toxicity for a product or component rests with CPSC. When a product is thought to be

---

[17] U.S. Department of Health, Education and Welfare, Food and Drug Administration, *The Saccharin Ban,* DHEW Publication (FDA) 77-2079 (May 1977).
[18] See "The Aerosol Ban Has Lost Its Sting," *Business Week,* May 30, 1977, pp. 30–31.

unsafe by the commission, they may require that warning labels be affixed or that the product be packaged differently. If these measures are not adequate to protect public health and safety, the CPSC can issue outright bans. Administrative proceedings may also be initiated by citizens or citizen groups through petition to the commission which must then decide whether the hazard poses "an unreasonable risk of injury."

In fact, the CPSC's recent ban on the use of Tris in sleepwear and the recall of Tris-treated garments was initiated by the Environmental Defense Fund, a private, nonprofit public interest group, which had earlier petitioned the CPSC to require warning labels on fabrics treated with Tris. The basis of their petitions were bioassays conducted by the National Cancer Institute that established Tris as a potent animal carcinogen in several species and at several sites in the body. One estimate put at 50,000 the additional annual cancers that could result from exposures to Tris by infants between birth and their first year.[19]

Earlier the CPSC had banned vinyl chloride in certain aerosol propellants over which they had jurisdiction—those not covered by FDA. More recently, the commission voted to ban the use of asbestos in wall-patching compounds and in the imitation logs used in home fireplaces; moreover, they have initiated studies considering bans on asbestos in brake linings, floor tiles, paints, and modeling clay. This, too, came in response to petitions initiated by public interest groups.

THE FEDERAL INSECTICIDE, FUNGICIDE, AND RODENTICIDE ACT AND AMENDMENTS Pesticide laws initially were designed to ensure honesty in packaging and safety in use, but have evolved to enhance environmental quality and protect public health as well. The Federal Insecticide, Fungicide, and Rodenticide Act (FIFRA) and the Federal Environmental Pesticide Control Act (FEPCA) that amended it now provide among other things for the registration of all pesticides and the uses to which they are put, the certification of individuals who apply certain restricted pesticides, and premarket testing of all new pesticides.

EPA will permit the registration of a product which "... will perform its intended function without unreasonable adverse effects on the environment" [Section 3(c)(5)(c)]. All pesticide registrations expire every five years and must be renewed. If the registration of a particular pesticide or pesticide use is denied, the administrator of EPA must publish reasons for

[19] See Morton Mintz, *The Washington Post*, April 8, 1977, pp. A1, A4.

denial in the *Federal Register*. If the administrator wishes to cancel a pesticide use for any reason, he must notify the registrant who then has thirty-one days to request a hearing on the cancellation. When the administrator feels that the use of a pesticide constitutes an "imminent hazard"—defined in Section 2(1) as a "situation which exists when the continued use of a pesticide during the time required for cancellation proceeding would be likely to result in unreasonable adverse effects on the environment or will involve unreasonable hazard to the survival of a species declared by the secretary of the interior to be endangered"—he can immediately suspend that use. At the same time, a notice to permanently cancel that use must also be issued [Section 6(c)(1)].

EPA has suspended the registration of all crop uses of DDT, aldrin, and dieldrin and most uses of heptachlor and chlordane because of evidence of their carcinogenicity as well as their persistence in the environment. It is important to note that these suspensions rested on the demonstration that the risks inherent in the use of the pesticides outweighed the benefits they generated. Registrants attempted to show otherwise, as they are permitted to do under regulations published by EPA. Recently, EPA has also moved against pesticides containing Kepone, chloroform, endrin, and chlorobenzilate.

THE TOXIC SUBSTANCES CONTROL ACT   The Toxic Substances Control Act (TSCA) was enacted in 1976, five years after it was first introduced in Congress. Generally speaking, it is intended to fill the gap between the regulation of pesticides by EPA under FIFRA (as amended) and the regulation of food, drugs, and cosmetics by FDA. It is expected to play a major role in federal toxic substance policy.[20]

The Toxic Substance Control Act gives EPA the following wide authority: to require testing of any new chemical or new use of an existing chemical when it "may present an unreasonable risk of injury to health or the environment" (Section 4), where the cost of the tests are borne by the manufacturer; to control the manufacturing, distribution, and sale of chemical substances ranging from relatively mild labeling requirements through strict prohibitions and extending to seizure or recall of "imminently hazardous" substances (Section 6); and to require the provision by

[20] "From Microbes to Men: The New Toxic Substances Control Act and Bacterial Mutagenicity/Carcinogenicity Tests," *Environmental Law Reporter* vol. 6 (November 1976) pp. 10248–10252.

proponents of a new chemical of information on that chemical's name, properties, structure, intended levels of production and use, and by-products created. This information is to be provided at least ninety days in advance of the intended date of marketing of a new chemical and is to include information on occupational exposures and the health effects of such exposures [Section 8(a)(2)(E) and (F)]. Under Section 10 of TSCA, EPA is directed to carry out research, testing, and monitoring necessary to implement the provisions of the act; this is to include the development of a system by which data on toxic substances is collected and can be retrieved and under which government research and information on toxics—from whatever source—is coordinated.

The act requires the administrator of EPA to take action to regulate polychlorinated biphenyls (PCBs). Labeling and disposal regulations for this group of chemicals were issued in July 1977, their restriction to closed systems is to be ordered by January 1978, and prohibitions on their production and distribution are to be issued by July 1979. In May of 1977 EPA issued proposed regulations on chlorofluorocarbons. The first effective date of their regulation is to be October 15, 1978 at which time a proposed ban on manufacturing is to go into effect. Hearings on these proposed regulations began in August of 1977. EPA is about to consider proposed regulations on polybrominated biphenyls (PBBs), the accidental use of which recently led to the contamination of and consequent slaughter of cattle in Michigan. As 1977 drew to a close, EPA ordered the chemical and petroleum industry to begin to supply the information on production and composition that the Toxic Substance Control Act authorized them to collect.

THE SAFE DRINKING WATER ACT The Safe Drinking Water Act was passed in 1974. Under its provisions, the administrator of EPA is directed to establish national interim primary drinking water regulations which ". . . shall protect health to the extent feasible, using technology, treatment techniques, and other means, which the Administrator determines are generally available (taking costs into consideration) . . ." [Section 1412(a)(2)]. The administrator is also directed to establish recommended—rather than mandatory—maximum contaminant levels for each toxic substance that ". . . may have an adverse effect on the health of persons. Each such recommended maximum contaminant level shall . . . allow an adequate margin of safety" [Section 1412(b)(1)(B)]. When these recommended maximum contaminant levels are converted to final national primary drinking water standards, the final standards are to be as close to the recommended standards "as is feasible" [Section 1412(b)(1)(B)(3)].

In promulgating the interim standards in 1975, EPA recommended maximum contaminant levels for arsenic, other inorganic substances, and the pesticides endrin, lindane, methoxychlor, toxaphene, (2,4-D), (2,4,5-TP), and Silvex.[21] No standards have been promulgated for the other organic compounds found in drinking water although the carcinogenicity of some of these compounds has been known for twenty years.[22] These are primarily chlorinated hydrocarbons—chloroform, bromodichloromethane, and bromoform, for example—which result from the chlorination of water already containing organic chemicals. EPA is expected to issue standards for these organics as part of a revised interim primary drinking water regulation. EPA's delay in regulating organic compounds is said by the agency to be based on the lack of information on their health effects, although a number of studies have linked these organics and other carcinogens to abnormally high incidences of cancer in the general population.

THE RESOURCE CONSERVATION AND RECOVERY ACT Subtitle C of the Resource Conservation and Recovery Act (RCRA) of 1976 deals with "Hazardous Waste Management." Because this act is so new, we have had little experience with toxic substance control under this subsection of the law. Nevertheless, many feel that the act may play an important role in toxic substance policy.

Section 1004(5) of the act defines hazardous waste as ". . . a solid waste, or combination of solid wastes, which because of its quantity, concentration, or physical, chemical, or infectious characteristics may (a) cause, or significantly contribute to an increase in mortality or an increase in serious irreversible, or incapacitating reversible, illness; or (b) pose a substantial present or potential hazard to human health or the environment when improperly treated, stored, transported, or disposed of, or otherwise managed."

Within eighteen months of the passage of the act, the administrator of EPA is to have established standards governing the generation, transportation and treatment, storage, and disposal of hazardous wastes. In addition he must establish regulations requiring persons who own or operate

[21] Suter and Muir, "The Federal Role," p. 106.
[22] Nicholas Wade, "Drinking Water: Health Hazards Still Not Resolved," *Science* vol. 196 (June 24, 1977) pp. 1421–1422.

hazardous waste treatment, storage, or disposal facilities to have permits to operate these facilities. The specification that the act deal with "solid wastes" will restrict the number of toxics regulated under it. For example, emissions of vinyl chloride or benzene apparently cannot be controlled under the Resource Conservation and Recovery Act. Nor will the act prove useful in limiting exposure to spent uranium or other radioactive materials since these are specifically exempted from its coverage [Section 1004(27)].

Policy Problems and Recommendations

Regulatory Inconsistency

Even the brief review presented above gives some indication of the unevenness or inconsistency of current federal toxic substance policy. This inconsistency begins with the various definitions of toxic or hazardous substances, continues through the regulatory options available to agencies, and extends to conflicting mandates about the extent to which the agencies should consider the economic costs of proposed regulations. Under one piece of legislation, the government must prove the toxicity of a substance while under another it is left to proponents to demonstrate its safety. Furthermore, the mandated margin of safety to be achieved varies from act to act. In table 4-4 we present for purposes of contrast several of the features of the federal legislation regulating toxic substances.

There are subtle differences in the definition of toxics among the major pieces of legislation, the most important of which concerns the likelihood of harm. In the Clean Air Act, the Safe Drinking Water Act, and the Resource Conservation and Recovery Act, toxic or hazardous substances are defined as those which "may" cause various kinds of adverse effects. This indicates that the substance need only have the *potential* to do harm to be subject to the provisions of the legislation. However, the Federal Water Pollution Control Act, parts of the Toxic Substances Control Act, and the Federal Insecticide, Fungicide, and Rodenticide Act as amended all define toxics as those which "will" produce adverse effects. This is clearly a more restrictive definition, requiring prior proof of toxicity. One could imagine a substance qualifying as a hazardous air pollutant under the Clean Air Act but not under the water pollution amendments because its toxicity is suspected but not yet demonstrated.

TABLE 4-4 Federal Legislation Regulating Toxic Substances

Legislation	Definition of toxic or hazard	Type of regulation	Degree of protection	Burden of proof	Balancing of costs
1970 Clean Air Act Amendments	"an air pollutant . . . which . . . may cause, or contribute to, an increase in mortality or an increase in serious irreversible, or incapacitating reversible, illness" Section 112(a)(1)	Emission standards	". . . an ample margin of safety to protect the public health . . ." Sec. 112(b)(1)(B)	EPA	No
Federal Water Pollution Control Act	". . . pollutants which will . . . cause death, disease, behavioral abnormalities, cancer, genetic mutations, physiological malfunctions, physiological deformation . . . or physical deformations." Sec. 502(13)	Effluent standards, ambient standards	". . . ample margin of safety." Sec. 307(a)(4)	EPA	No
Occupational Safety and Health Act	Not defined	Exposure standards	"adequately assures to the extent feasible that no employee will suffer material impairment of health or functional capacity . . ." Sec. 6(b)(5)	OSHA	Yes. Sec. 6(b)(5)
Toxic Substances Control Act	those substances ". . . presenting an unreasonable risk of injury to health or the environment . . ." Sec. 6(a)	Premarket notification and testing; prohibitions on manufacturing, processing, and distribution; information on chemical	Not specified	Proponent	Yes. Sec. 2(b)(3)

	Definition	Regulation	Standard	Proponent	Burden of proof/components must be supplied to EPA
Food and Drug Administration	Not defined	Labeling; bans on products deemed "unsafe"	"... necessary for the protection of public health ..." Sec. 406[346]	Proponent for drugs and food additives; FDA for cosmetic ingredients	No, in case of food additives; yes, for drugs and cosmetics
Federal Insecticide, Fungicide, and Rodenticide Act and the Federal Environmental Pesticide Control Act	One which results in "... unreasonable adverse effects on the environment or will involve unreasonable hazard to the survival of a species declared endangered ..." (imminent hazard). Sec. 2(l)	Registration of all pesticides and uses; permits for applicators; cancellation or suspension of specific pesticides or uses	Not specified	Proponent	Yes. Sec. 6(b)(2)
Safe Drinking Water Act	"... contaminant(s) which ... may have an adverse effect on the health of persons." Sec. 1401(1)(B)	Maximum contaminant standards	"... to the extent feasible ... (taking costs into consideration) ..." Sec. 1412(a)(2)	EPA	Yes. Sec. 1412(a)2
Resource Conservation and Recovery Act	one which "may cause, or significantly contribute to an increase in mortality or an increase in serious irreversible, or incapacitating reversible, illness; or, pose a ... hazard to human health or the environment ..." Sec. 1004(5)(A)(B)	Standards for generators, transporters of hazardous waste; permits for treatment, storage or disposal of hazardous waste	"that necessary to protect human health and the environment ..." Sec. 3002-3004	EPA	No

This inconsistency is also manifested in the degree to which the required standards are to protect the public and its environment. Under the Clean Air Act and the Federal Water Pollution Act, the standards are to provide an "ample margin of safety." OSHA regulations should "adequately assure . . ." safety, while the Safe Drinking Water Act calls for standards which protect the public ". . . to the extent feasible. . . ." This wording would seem to indicate that a substance should be strictly regulated if it is transmitted through air or water, less strictly regulated if workers are exposed to it on the job, and regulated only if economical when it occurs in drinking water. A number of toxic chemicals, vinyl chloride being but one example, can occur in all these media. There is little reason why permissible public exposure to them should depend upon their location alone.

What if these different margins of safety eventually come to define the lengths to which we will go to protect the public from toxic exposures? For example, suppose that the administrator of EPA interprets the "ample margin of safety" in the Clean Air Act or the Federal Water Pollution Control Act as meaning that $3 million worth of economic benefits may be foregone to prevent an additional cancer death that would result from exposure to a toxic. Suppose, also, that the administrator only deems it "feasible" under the Safe Drinking Water Act to forego $1 million in benefits to prevent the same death from occurring. Then, an additional cancer death that would cost $2 million to prevent (in terms of foregone benefits) would be averted if it were to result from exposure to a hazardous air or water pollutant but not if it were to be caused by a drinking water contaminant! In other words, if different margins of safety in different acts come to define the effort to be expended in defense of human health, a life may be worth saving under one act but not under another. Rational policy generally requires that human lives be valued identically by the government regardless of the way they are to be saved, in much the same way that private firms must impute equal value to the outputs they expect from various kinds of investment.

Subtle differences in definition are important for another reason. Current court battles over toxic substance policy revolve around proving that risk is present. This issue will eventually be resolved when testing procedures are developed and accepted that will indicate the presence or absence of risk. When this happens, however, the battle will no doubt shift to revolve around *how* risky a substance is. At this point, the difference between "ample," "adequate," and "feasible" margins of safety will become important because these margins may determine which substances may be permitted under particular legislation.

An equally important inconsistency between the various pieces of toxic legislation involves benefit and cost comparisons. As we pointed out in chapter 2, such comparisons are essential if the government is to make the best use of those resources they receive from taxpayers. Yet much of the important toxic legislation makes no provision whatsoever for such comparisons. Both the Clean Air Act and the Water Pollution Control Act are silent on the importance of costs in establishing toxic standards. Since Congress has been specific about the role of costs in establishing other ambient standards, some have taken this silence to mean that cost considerations are irrelevant to toxic substance control under the air and water pollution laws.[23] No mention is made of policy costs under the Resource Conservation and Recovery Act, either. However, the phrase, "... taking costs under consideration ...," is an explicit and obvious feature of the Safe Drinking Water Act. Why costs should be important there, but not elsewhere, is unexplained.

Note that Congress has been inconsistent not only between separate pieces of legislation but also within a single act. The Federal Food, Drug, and Cosmetic Act mandates FDA to weigh the benefits of proposed new drugs against the risks they generate. This mandate accounts for FDA's delay in approving a number of new drugs, called "beta-blockers," designed to treat heart disease. However, if food or color additives or new animal drugs are carcinogenic in animal tests, they are not permitted regardless of their beneficial effects. Such inconsistencies make little sense. Note that the burden of proof differs within the Food, Drug, and Cosmetic Act, as well; the government must prove the dangerousness of cosmetic ingredients, while drug manufacturers must demonstrate the safety of their products.

Ethical Dilemmas

One stark fact emerges from the discussion so far. Although both the FDA and the CPSC regulate products that may contain potentially toxic components, under no federal law is cigarette smoking regulated.[24] This is in spite of the incontrovertible evidence linking smoking with lung cancer, emphysema, heart disease, and other serious illnesses.

There are a number of reasons for the favored regulatory treatment that tobacco products have received, some of which are no doubt political. One of the reasons is not political, however, but has to do with paternalism and

[23] Suter and Muir, "The Federal Role," pp. 51–52.
[24] Tobacco companies have been required to affix warning labels to cigarette packs and are prohibited from advertising on radio and television.

individual responsibility. As such, it is relevant to federal policy toward other toxics. Individuals, the argument goes, should be able to decide for themselves whether the risks of cigarette smoking are worth the pleasure they derive. As long as they are cognizant of the risks, and as long as non-smokers are not harmed by others' smoking, it is argued that the government should not prohibit smoking. In other words, since the risks are *internal* to the act of smoking, individuals must decide for themselves whether or not to bear them. But if this is so, why do we not regulate by information campaigns and similar warnings those other toxic substances that are internal to product use or food consumption? Why prohibit the use of saccharin in diet sodas and toothpaste rather than merely warn consumers of the risks they run in using these products?

There are at least two reasons why society might opt for some paternalism in the form of stricter control of toxic substances. At least one of these reasons—and perhaps both—points toward more stringent regulation of tobacco products, as well. First, it might appear that individuals can observe the effects of the prolonged use of tobacco or other voluntarily consumed toxics and decide about using them in the same way they can observe the accident risks associated with a particular job and decide upon accepting or rejecting it. This analogy is not perfect, however. In the latter case, a worker temporarily can accept occupational accident risks but later decide to refuse them and rid himself of the risk if he acquires additional information about the risks or if his preferences change. In other words, the "gamble" is continually repeated, information is continuously generated, and acceptance need not be once and for all.

This is not true of voluntary exposures to toxic substances, however. There the gamble often takes the form of prolonged exposure on the job or through product use of a "once and for all" nature. That is, the individual must accept the consequence of the gamble even if new information or a change in tastes later makes him wish he had chosen not to accept it. Thus, one might justify government intervention on the grounds that individuals, while willing to accept toxic exposures at one point in their lives, will feel very differently later and, therefore, benefit from regulation.

Another case for government regulation rests on the significant effects on later generations of current levels of exposure to toxic substances. For example, saccharin has been shown to lead not only to higher levels of bladder cancers in the laboratory animals consuming it but also to abnormally high numbers of tumors in their offspring, even when the offspring were not exposed to saccharin. If these second-generation effects also occur in humans,[25] a coercive policy may be justified on the grounds that the risks of toxic substance exposures are borne by other than those who voluntarily accept them. Such a policy is made more defensible as health effects are transmitted through generation after generation to individuals for whose welfare those initially exposed cannot be presumed to be responsible.

What about the argument that current regulations on toxic exposures will prevent higher medical and insurance costs for all individuals in the future? Does this justify a federal toxic substance policy? The answer here is not unequivocal. If private insurers can determine the likelihood of individual exposures to toxic substances, they will adjust their rates accordingly. Chemical workers, for example, could be expected to pay higher rates than those less likely to be exposed to toxic substances. Similarly, smokers or saccharin users would pay higher health and life insurance rates than nonusers. If such information about likelihood of exposure were available, there would be no need for federal intervention to correct for this "externality."

If, however, this information were unavailable to private insurers or if some form of national health insurance scheme eventually covers everyone's medical costs, a government role appears possible. For in such a case, it might be worthwhile (efficient) to prevent exposures now and avoid costly medical treatment of the victims of these exposures at a later date.

Finally, in those many instances in which exposures to toxic substances are either involuntary or inadvertent, government intervention clearly is justified not on grounds of paternalism but because of an external effect that cannot be priced in an economic market.

Testing Problems

A major set of problems with current toxic substance policy centers around testing. These problems are ones of extrapolation, expense, delay, and incentive; they often appear formidable enough to undermine our entire toxic substance regulatory effort.

Consider first the sheer number of tests necessitated by federal regulation of suspected toxic substances. Under provisions of the Toxic Substances Control Act, EPA has compiled an initial list of chemicals which

[25] There is evidence that pregnant women exposed to lead can give birth to children who suffer from lead poisoning. See James C. Hyatt, *Wall Street Journal,* August 2, 1977, p. 1.

numbers 30,000. However, this list will be expanded manyfold since individual companies can use or manufacture as many as 100,000 different chemicals.[26] At least a thousand new chemicals are introduced each year and new uses of existing chemicals far exceed that number. As we have seen above, the burden of the premarket testing required under the Toxic Substance Act, the Insecticide, Fungicide, and Rodenticide Act, and the Food, Drug, and Cosmetic Act falls on proponents. Hence, the acts do not impose an immediate burden on scarce federal resources. This situation changes, however, as soon as an agency becomes suspicious of or wishes to challenge the testing procedures or results presented by proponents. The agency must then undertake its own tests and can easily become swamped in the process, able only to fight the most pressing battles at any one time.

The expense of such tests poses another problem. Standard laboratory animal tests to determine the toxicity of a single chemical can take as long as three years and cost as much as $750,000. Even at a more conservative $200,000 per test, only thirty-seven new chemicals could have been tested by EPA under TSCA during fiscal year 1977 and only if the entire appropriation of $7.4 million had gone into testing, which it clearly could not have. The need for less expensive but still reliable tests is obvious.

Preliminary results indicate that certain *in vitro* tests—those that take place not in human or animal bodies but in test tubes—may fill this need. These tests involve introducing substances suspected of toxicity to cultures of bacteria that have lost the ability to grow. If the substance is a mutagen, and therefore a likely carcinogen, the bacteria begin to grow again and, conveniently, at a rate indicative of the potency of the toxic substance. The allure of such tests lies in their brevity and cost—two weeks and $500 respectively. There is still some question about whether *in vitro* tests are as reliable in identifying carcinogens as animal tests. However, one such test developed by biochemist Bruce Ames of the University of California has identified 90 percent of a group of known carcinogens while pointing a finger at very few noncarcinogens; it has even identified a carcinogen that had initially "slipped through" animal testing.[27]

Industry has lead the government in support of *in vitro* tests in certain cases. This should not be surprising since the private sector has a strong incentive to help develop tests that will allow them to determine quickly

---

[26] Rachel Scott, "Toxic Chemicals," *The Washington Post,* May 29, 1977, p. B5.
[27] Gina Kolata, "Chemical Carcinogens: Industry Adopts Controversial 'Quick' Tests," *Science* vol. 192 (June 18, 1976) pp. 1215–1217.

and inexpensively the acceptability of potentially profitable new products.[28] Because the government stands to benefit from the development of such tests as well, it should be supporting research on them wherever possible. If *in vitro* methods do prove the equal of animal tests, EPA could test 1,500 chemicals for every one currently analyzed.

Even quick and inexpensive test procedures will be of little use to a public that does not understand or accept them. This is clearly a problem with current animal tests. The proposed saccharin ban was criticized on the grounds that no human would ever consume saccharin in amounts comparable to those fed the test animals (the "800-diet-sodas-a-day" argument). In fact, test dosages are high because we want to be able to observe a toxic effect if it exists. Since this would be statistically impossible at actual dose levels *given the relatively few test animals we can afford to use,* dosages are increased manyfold. This leads to the complaint cited above and to the assertion that "any substance will cause cancer at such high levels" (shown to be false for sugar, aspirin, salt, and many other common substances).

It would be very useful for the government to undertake one or two more large-scale, well-publicized tests of suspected toxics (called "megamouse" tests) using dose levels comparable to human exposures.[29] While undoubtedly expensive, these tests would have the effect of demonstrating to a skeptical public that toxicity is not merely a function of high doses.[30] At the same time, we should do all we can to improve our ability to extrapolate from high to low doses without the use of expensive mega-mouse tests.[31]

It is of course also imperative that we investigate mouse-to-man extrapolations. Suppose that prolonged exposure to a substance increases the chance of cancer in mice by 20 percent. Does this mean that human risk will likewise increase by 20 percent from exposure to the substance? While animal tests can indicate which substances are potentially toxic to humans,

[28] This same incentive has led private concerns to experiment with food additives that exist in such large molecules that they cannot be absorbed by the body. If such additives can be developed, food dyes and artificial sweeteners might be allowed back on the market. See Jerry E. Bishop, *The Wall Street Journal,* April 26, 1977.

[29] A mega-mouse test using the suspected carcinogen beta-naphthalimine is underway at the National Center for Toxicological Research.

[30] Recent Canadian epidemiological studies have linked saccharin use to increased incidence of human cancer.

[31] See Marvin Schneiderman, Nathan Mantel, and Charles Brown, "From Mouse to Man—or How to Get from the Laboratory to Park Avenue and 59th Street" *Annals of the New York Academy of Sciences* vol. 246 (January 31, 1975) pp. 237–248.

these tests cannot tell us much about the degree of risk. Further research is needed here.

A final problem with the testing of toxics has to do with the economic incentives facing manufacturers or other proponents. If firms discover in premarket tests that a chemical has toxic properties and reports these results, they are likely to be prohibited from using the chemical at all, or at least in some desired uses. Since there are no well-defined protocols specifying testing procedures, firms may be tempted to choose those procedures most likely to shed favorable light on the substances they wish to introduce. In some instances, these firms may even have an incentive to falsify their tests or pressure private testing companies to falsify or withhold unfavorable results.[32]

To remove this incentive three steps are necessary. First, well-defined testing procedures must be established and applied throughout all agencies regulating toxic substances. Next, federal verification of controversial test data submitted by proponents must be quickened. This will require much larger budgets for the testing divisions of the agencies. President Carter has taken a step in this direction by increasing the appropriation for toxic substance control from $7.4 million to $29.0 million in his fiscal year 1979 budget. Finally, extremely stiff penalties must be assessed those who violate established protocols or falsify results.[33] Until and unless these steps are taken, we must expect premarket testing to be much less effective a screen against toxic substances than it is intended to be.

The Delaney Clause

The recent ban on saccharin proposed by FDA has generated considerable criticism of the Delaney clause in the Food Additives Amendment to the Food, Drug, and Cosmetic Act. So great has been the public outcry that Congress is now considering legislation to regulate saccharin individually, apart from the statutes of the FFDCA relevant to it. In fact, legislation has been introduced in the House of Representatives to repeal the Delaney clause and has attracted nearly 200 cosponsors.[34]

[32] There is some evidence that falsification has already occurred. See *The Washington Post,* March 12, 1977, p. 3.

[33] On December 12, 1977, the Velsicol Chemical Corporation was indicted on charges that it conspired to conceal the results of pesticide test data.

[34] HR 5166, 95 Cong. 2 sess. (1978). There is also a movement to weaken the clause by modifying it to allow carcinogenic additives to animal feed as long as the residues of the additive are undetectable. See the *Federal Register,* February 22, 1977.

On its face, the clause would not appear controversial, providing, as it does, an absolute and automatic prohibition on the addition of carcinogenic substances to food. This hardly seems unreasonable until one realizes that this prohibition is in force *regardless of the desirable properties an additive may have.* As we pointed out above, the desirable features (benefits, in other words) of food colorings or some other additive may be insignificant. In such a case, the Delaney clause "costs" us very little if used to prohibit such additives. But users of saccharin, primarily diet soda consumers, claim that it is a valuable, even invaluable, aid in weight control. In other words, the benefits we will be forced to forego if saccharin is banned under the Delaney clause might be great. Under these circumstances, the total prohibition on risky additives looks less good.

It might be tempting to dismiss the anti-FDA sentiment by saying that a few extra pounds per consumer are not worth the added risk of cancer. But since heart disease is related to obesity, saccharin may have life-extending properties to the extent it prevents obesity. Thus, in formulating a saccharin policy, we should properly weigh the added cancer deaths which might result from its widespread use against the lives which might be saved because of its weight-reducing effects. This is simply another application of the rule, advanced in chapter 2 and employed in chapter 3, that sound policy making depends upon careful consideration of *both* benefits and costs. *Since the Delaney clause expressly prohibits such a comparison, it should be replaced with a rule that allows for benefit–cost or benefit–risk comparisons.*

In saying this, however, we wish to make several observations. First, the Delaney clause has not been the obstacle to sound policy making its critics have suggested. In fact, the recent proposed saccharin ban represents only the third time in nearly twenty years the clause has been used to ban a food additive.[35] Moreover, its use is narrowly circumscribed. It does *not* apply to pesticides and pesticide residues (in spite of their potential carcinogenicity) nor to substances like the polychlorinated biphenols found in fish, poultry, and eggs that are unintentionally added to foods. Moreover, some argue that ambiguities in the wording of the Delaney clause make it unclear whether a substance must be *ingested,* as opposed to inhaled or absorbed through the skin, to be prohibited under the clause.[36]

---

[35] The other two substances were little known additives occurring in food packaging containers.

[36] Suter and Muir, "The Federal Role," p. 90.

The Delaney clause also looks less bad when we consider the current state of risk–benefit analysis. By this we mean that it is currently far more difficult to identify and measure the risks that will arise from toxic exposures than it is to measure the costs of other, more conventional government projects. In fact, it is more difficult in many cases to determine even the benefits which will result if a substance is not regulated. For example, although doctors have testified to saccharin's usefulness in weight control, there is no scientific evidence to corroborate their assertions.

Clearly, we need to concentrate research efforts on improving risk–benefit analysis so that we may weigh benefits and costs of toxic exposures.[37] Until we can, however, the Delaney clause makes some sense as a safety-first criterion. That is, given the large number of people likely to be exposed to a toxic food additive, as well as their probable ignorance of its potential toxicity, it makes some sense to prohibit exposure until methods are developed that will allow a more accurate determination of the "optimal" amount of risk. This the Delaney clause does. At the same time, it protects FDA from the political pressure to which it would no doubt be subjected if the ban were discretionary rather than automatic.

The Use of Economic Incentives

In the preceding chapters we pointed out that economic incentives can often be used in place of direct regulation. Might such incentives, which usually take the form of taxes or subsidies, be used to limit exposures to toxic substances without at the same time limiting individual choice or involving government in very difficult and expensive day-to-day monitoring activities? This final section discusses briefly one way that government policy might be used to limit toxic exposures without doing so by fiat.

This approach would involve the use of "toxic taxes" on products containing harmful substances. For example, lunchmeats, hot dogs, bacon, and pork sausage are all known to be high in nitrite content, food preservatives which when ingested can form potent carcinogens called nitrosamines. Rather than ban altogether products containing nitrites, or limit its involvement to the dissemination of information about the risks inherent in these products, the government could levy a tax on them not unlike the special excise taxes currently levied on a wide variety of products (some of which—cigarettes and liquor, for example—are taxed for the very rea-

---

[37] See U.S. Environmental Protection Agency, Office of Health and Ecological Effects, "Hazardous Wastes: A Risk–Benefit Framework Applied to Cadmium and Asbestos," EPA-600/5-77-002 (February 1977).

son that they are a "nuisance"). The proceeds of a toxic tax, which might be considerable given the number of products containing potentially harmful substances, might then be used to fund cancer research and treatment, or research on possible substitutes for the toxic additives. Cigarettes, diet sodas, sun tan lotion, and other products, the usage of which is demonstrated to be dangerous, would be candidates for this tax.

The tax would have the effect of raising the price of the products in question and thereby discouraging their consumption. It would have another advantage, too. That is, it would allow individuals to choose freely among the many products in the market. If the tax were coupled with a vigorous campaign to inform consumers about the risks associated with certain products, it might be an effective way to limit individual exposures. As individuals become more informed about product risks and (we would hope) voluntarily reduce their consumption of dangerous products, the tax could be lowered gradually.

This tax would do nothing about occupational exposures, however, which account for a large share of total human exposure to toxic substances. Occupational exposures might be reduced if workmen's compensation claims forced firms to bear at least part of the costs of their employees' job-related illnesses. For reasons discussed above, however, it would be very difficult to link illnesses to specific employers during workers' occupational histories. Hence, workmen's compensation may not be an entirely successful mechanism by which to eliminate occupational exposures. On a related front, more than 400 asbestos workers recently sued both the federal government and PPG Industries and Corning Glass Works for allowing the workers to handle asbestos without informing them of the risks of so doing.[38] The defendants settled out of court for $20 million. If this example induces other workers who have contracted occupational illnesses (like cancer or mercury poisoning) to sue for damages, we can expect industries to clean up their workplaces to some extent *even in the absence of OSHA or similar regulations.*[39]

Moreover, the government can be expected to provide more and better information to workers, and be more vigilant about enforcing the regulations they have established, if they, too, are liable for damages.

---

[38] See "Living and Dying with Asbestos," *The New York Times,* December 25, 1977, section 4, p. 6.

[39] In fact, other suits have been filed against a number of pesticide-producing companies whose employees have developed serious diseases or disorders. See Richard D. Lyons, "Pesticide: Boon and Possible Bane," *The New York Times,* December 11, 1977, p. 1.

In other words, this apparent reassignation of the liability for occupational illness from employees to employers and the government will act as an economic incentive to the latter: employers will eliminate exposures to toxic substances up to the point at which the cost of doing so exceeds the benefits to be gained (in the form of lower expected court and out-of-court damages). In addition, if employers are more informed about occupational risks than employees, or can obtain this information at a lower cost, this shift in liability may be economically efficient as well as effective in eliminating occupational exposures. The use of such suits in the courts in no way guarantees that the right amount of exposure reduction will take place, however. Excessive damage awards may lead firms to expend *more* than the socially optimal amount on protective equipment, for example.

Conclusions

Designing policies to respond to the threat posed by toxic substances is not easy. In fact, it may be the single most difficult environmental problem we have yet faced. This is so not only because of the considerable uncertainty about the identity of toxic substances and the ways in which they do their great damage or because of the long latency periods often associated with exposures to them. These problems are also difficult because their solution may require alterations—occasionally drastic—in the conditions in which people work, the products they consume, and the technologies they employ in their daily lives. Changes like these are not easily made.

We have seen that economic forces sometimes have the potential to alleviate the need for corrective policy when occupations or products are risky. However, the conditions necessary for a market solution to the toxic substance problem cannot be presumed to describe the world as we know it. The governmental role which is thus necessitated has taken a familiar form—the establishment of standards that in some cases limit and in other cases prohibit exposures to toxic substances. These standards and the other regulatory options available appear in a number of pieces of legislation that together form an umbrella of protection against toxic substances.

One problem with this umbrella is its irregular construction. That which it is to protect us against is defined differently in different legislation. Moreover, the protection that the umbrella is designed to offer—what legislators have chosen to call the margin of safety—varies from act to act. Finally, as we have seen, certain sections of the umbrella are to be designed with costs in mind while other sections are to protect us regardless of the expense. Toxic substance policy could be improved if the legislation forming this protective umbrella were amended to provide for protection that depends uniformly on costs as well as benefits.

Testing for the identity and potency of toxic substances poses additional problems. Here we can do little more than recognize the seriousness of the problem and work to commit more funds to testing programs. Equally as important is the dissemination of the information obtained in these tests and its translation into terms readily understandable to those who could benefit from it. It is also important to create proper incentives for private firms to use acceptable test methods and to divulge quickly and completely the results of their tests.

Finally, while we cannot expect free markets to solve on their own the problems associated with toxic substances, we should not rule out the use of economic incentives to help do so. One such incentive, a toxics tax, might reduce individual exposures to toxic substances while information is being generated and disseminated that might induce individuals to minimize their exposures, even in the absence of such incentives.

CHAPTER 5

Environmental Policy and the Distribution of Benefits and Costs

HENRY M. PESKIN

IT IS HARD to conceive of any federal environmental policy—or, indeed, any federal policy—that does not affect various people differently. If a policy were designed in such a way that all affected parties were made better off and none worse off, then the fact that some gained more than others would probably not be of great concern to the designers of policy. At least, this is what one might surmise from the policy designer's frequent emphasis on total benefits and costs. The fact that policies with benefit–cost ratios greater than unity have the *potential* of making everyone better off has apparently eased the conscience of many a policy maker. In the real world, however, such potential outcomes are rarely realized. Regardless of the total of benefits and costs, the usual state of affairs is that some parties gain while others lose.

Federal environmental policy is not exceptional in this respect. What may be exceptional about it is that there seems to be widespread political acceptance for the environmental policies we have adopted even though there is evidence that the number of losers may exceed the number of gainers. In this chapter we will first discuss why this disparity between gainers and losers is an expected consequence of the design of the policy. Then, using data from a study of the distributional consequences of the Clean Air Amendments of 1970, we provide evidence that substantiates these expectations. Finally, we speculate on the political implications of the observed and expected distributional effects. In particular, we shall discuss those aspects of air pollution policy that have made it politically acceptable even though a minority of the population seem to enjoy benefits in excess of the costs they are forced to bear as a result of the policy. We shall also speculate on certain existing aspects of the Clean Air Amendments and certain suggested changes in them that may, in fact, make the law less politically acceptable in the future.

While one may quarrel with our methods and even more so with our quantitative estimates, we feel that such analyses are crucial to a full understanding of the political and economic implications of alternative environmental policies.

Uneven Benefits and Uneven Burdens

Our task of identifying who will benefit from and who will bear the costs of pollution control is difficult because there is no general agreement as to who are the actual beneficiaries. This lack of agreement is due to conflicting perceptions of the nature of pollution and environmental quality.

There are those who believe that environmental quality is a commodity provided equally to everyone and enjoyed by all members of society. According to this view, no individual member would be able to purchase more environmental quality than his neighbor even if he wished.[1] If this view were adopted, one might conclude that environmental quality improvements would benefit everyone equally. Yet this conclusion does not necessarily follow. For, even if the *physical* quality of the environment had improved identically for all citizens, these physical improvements might not be valued equally by all of them. As Baumol has argued, it is likely that those with more money might place a higher value on environmental quality improvements if only by virtue of the fact that they can pay more for them.[2] For this reason, if one accepted the view that environmental quality is a purely public commodity, then it could be argued that the rich would benefit the most from environmental cleanup.

On the other hand, there is another view that emphasizes the variability of pollution across geographical locations. According to this view, house-

---

[1] Economists call such commodities "purely public." National defense is most often used as an example of such a pure public commodity.

[2] William J. Baumol, "Environmental Protection and Income Distribution" in Harold M. Hochman and George E. Peterson, eds., *Redistribution Through Public Choice* (New York, Columbia University Press, 1974).

holds can determine the pollution to which they are exposed by choosing their residence. Households can thus, "purchase" environmental quality like any other private commodity by buying a home in an unpolluted neighborhood. However, since poorer households often have very little choice of residential location, they often end up in polluted neighborhoods where rents or property values are depressed. Therefore, under this latter view, while environmental quality is perceived to be more nearly a private commodity, adjusting the consumption of this commodity is difficult for many individuals, especially for those with low incomes.

Consequently, while the rich would appear to benefit most under the former, public-commodity view of environmental quality, the urban poor would clearly benefit most if environmental quality were viewed as "purchasable" through location. Therefore, conclusions regarding the distribution of environmental quality improvement depend critically on which view of environmental quality is adopted.

When one considers the costs of cleaning up pollution as well as the benefits, it becomes even more difficult to theorize about the distributional consequences. There are many ways to finance a pollution reduction program and each way can present its own pattern of financial burdens to members of society. A federal program financed with the federal income tax structure is likely to place a heavier burden on the rich (that is, be more progressive) than if the program were administered and financed by the states and local governments with their generally less progressive tax structures.[3]

Actually, the more prominent environmental programs—those discussed in chapters 2 and 3, for example—are characterized by a combination of control strategies, with the initial financial burdens shared by several layers of government, industrial sectors, and households. The ultimate distributional consequences of these complex programs, however, depend on the way in which their initial financial burdens are shifted to the general population. In principle, this shifting depends on the tax structures of the various levels of government, the structure of the markets within

[3] A tax structure is said to be progressive if the share of a taxpayer's income paid in taxes increases with his or her income. In a similar vein, we say that the cost structure of a policy is progressive if the share of income allocated to the costs rises with income, and that the benefit structure of a policy is progressive if benefits as a fraction of income *decline* with higher incomes. Finally, we say that the net benefit structure of a policy is progressive if benefits minus costs as a fraction of income decline with higher incomes. Note that if benefits minus costs are negative, this definition means that a progressive net benefit structure requires that the net-benefit-to-income ratio be less negative for poorer income classes.

which the industrial sectors operate, and the ownership of governmental debt and private capital.

One clear implication of these observations is that no realistic environmental policy is likely to have *uniform* distributional effects—that is, no policy will affect each and every person, family, or household in the same way. Moreover, the ultimate impact may be very difficult to predict. As a result, while a particular policy approach may at first appear equitable to the general public, its final distributional consequences might not be judged fair at all. For example, while it may seem fair (and it may make good economic sense) to require the steel industry to pay for its own cleanup, it is likely that these costs can easily be shifted to steel customers and ultimately to final consumers. To the extent that such a shifting is possible, the financing of the cleanup will take on the aspects of a general sales tax because steel is a major component of a large number of products destined for final consumption. What at first seemed fair ultimately may appear regressive and unfair, since the poor will bear a proportionately greater burden of the cost than the rich.

Of course, if it were also the case that the poor were the primary victims of the steel industry's pollution, they might receive proportionately larger benefits from the policy. Thus, when *net* benefits are considered, the total impact of the policy could be progressive and, again, judged fair.

To make final assessments of the distribution of benefits and costs requires a difficult type of empirical analysis. There are perhaps two unsatisfactory characteristics of such analysis. First, it will be almost impossible to draw general conclusions about all environmental policies since the analysis must be tailored to specific approaches, and the distributional effects of one pollution control strategy may easily differ from those of another. Second, the factors that determine the policy's ultimate effect on families are so complex that it is impossible to undertake the analysis without making a number of strong assumptions, many of which are disputable. Our analysis of the Clean Air Amendments, discussed in the next section, evidences both these characteristics.

Analysis of the Clean Air Amendments[4]

The Clean Air Amendments of 1970 seem typical of current environmental legislation in approach and complexity. As chapters 2 and 3 point

[4] This section is based on Leonard P. Gianessi, Henry M. Peskin, and Edward Wolff, "The Distributional Effects of the Uniform Air Pollution Policy in the United States," unpublished RFF Discussion Paper D-5, April 12, 1977.

TABLE 5-1   Annual Air Pollution Benefits and Annual Costs to Attain Benefits, 1968

(millions of 1970 dollars)

Standard industrial code	Sector	Benefits	Industry cost to meet EPA standards[a]
01	Agriculture	201	1,137[b]
07	Agricultural services	214	107
08	Forestry	864	160[b]
10	Metal mining	14	19[b]
11–12	Coal mining	72	161
13	Oil and gas drilling	27	8
14	Nonmetal mining	13	7
15–17	Construction	98	169[c]
19	Ordnance	4	3
20	Food products	138	55
21	Tobacco products	4	2
22	Textiles	49	19
23	Apparel	10	2
24	Wood products	36	63
25	Furniture	11	3
26	Pulp and paper	265	90
27	Printing, publishing	8	2
28	Chemicals	865	199
29	Petroleum products	1,316	207
30	Rubber products	97	11
31	Leather products	14	6
32	Stone, clay, glass	1,164	254
33	Primary metals	2,712	858
34	Fabricated metals	69	32
35	Machinery except electrical	63	16
36	Electrical machinery	48	10
37	Transportation equipment	117	27
38	Instruments	17	3
39	Miscellaneous manufacturing	23	3
40	Railroads	156	66[b]
41	Local and suburban transit	139	165[b]
42	Motor freight	120	133[c]
44	Water transportation	180	49[b]
45	Air transportation	46	274[b]
46	Pipelines	15	34
49	Utilities	4,760	1,634
55	Gas stations	87	540[b]
50–81	Trades and services	942	1,405[c]
82	Education	18	67[c]
88	Households	3,981	12,157[d]
91–93	Governments	153	2,303[c]
Total		19,130	22,460

Note: Estimates revised May 15, 1976.

Source: Adapted from L. P. Gianessi, H. M. Peskin, and E. Wolff, "The Distributional Effects of the Uniform Air Pollution Policy in the United States," unpublished Discussion Paper D-5 (Washington, D.C., Resources for the Future, 1977) table 1.

[a] The primary data source was U.S. Environmental Protection Agency, *The Economics of Clean Air,* Annual Report of the Administrator (March 1972). Many EPA cost numbers have since been revised

out, the law attempts to attack air pollution from two sides. First, acceptable standards of ambient air quality are established. Second, there is an effort to mandate acceptable levels of emissions for particular classes of emitters—certain major stationary sources, new facilities, facilities that emit hazardous pollutants, and mobile sources. States and localities are left in the unenviable position of making both these approaches "mesh." That is, given the mandated emissions policies, states and localities are expected to devise plans to achieve the mandated ambient standards.

Because of the complexities of the legislation, an analysis of likely distributional consequences makes it necessary to estimate what will, in fact, be done (that is, what particular strategies will be adopted), as well as the costs and benefits of so doing. Fortunately this speculative exercise was largely accomplished by the Environmental Protection Agency (EPA) in their 1970 report to Congress.[5] This report assumes that in addition to mobile-source emissions requirements, the ambient standards in the act will be attained by certain technological responses on the part of industry. EPA has estimated the costs of these responses as well as the dollar value of the likely benefits from air pollution control at the national level.

We have made a variety of adjustments to these data, the most important being the attribution of these costs and benefits to Standard Industrial Classification (SIC) sectors, an operation that, in turn, required filling in data gaps using other published sources.[6] The results of these adjustments as well as the national totals are shown in table 5-1.

The next step in the analysis was to distribute these costs and benefits to individuals in the population. Actually, we distributed these totals to families rather than individuals since the family is more often the usual focus of

---

[5] U.S. Environmental Protection Agency, *The Economics of Clean Air,* Annual Report of the Administrator (March 1972).

[6] The biggest gap was the neglect of benefits due to automobile pollution control. This adjustment was based on the work of L. R. Babcock and M. L. Nagda, "Cost Effectiveness of Emission Control," *Journal of the Air Pollution Control Association* vol. 18 (1973) pp. 1973–1979.

---

upward. Many other sources (e.g., journal articles, contractors' reports, industry studies, and the like) were used to obtain the two-digit SIC breakdowns. Complete documentation on these sources and estimating methods is available from the project investigators. EPA does not provide estimates of the costs to meet standards for fuel combustion from stationary sources broken down by sector. Therefore, aggregate EPA cost estimates are distributed by estimated fuel usage. EPA cost estimates reflecting emission levels in 1977–78 were adjusted to the 1968 base year by assuming a fixed proportion between a sector's activity level and its emissions.

[b] EPA standards not established. Cost estimates are based on industry estimates of clean-up costs and EPA contractors' reports.

[c] Estimate assumes all gasoline vehicles are fitted with pollution control equipment necessary to meet 1977 standards.

[d] Estimate based on 1970 automobile pollution.

distributional analyses, and certain of the data needed for this step are only available by family units.[7]

Before discussing the details of our distribution techniques, we should point out the basic methodological approach. It is impossible to observe the actual impacts on millions of people of a policy that has yet to be fully implemented. Therefore, instead we "observe" the impacts on a random sample of the population of a policy that is *assumed* to be fully implemented. The random sample is the one-in-a-thousand 1970 Census Public Use File, a self-weighting sample of household and person records of the 1970 population census. Our approach is an example of a class of approaches known as microsimulation techniques.[8] These techniques have become feasible only because of the ability of the modern computer to process rapidly extremely large data sets. In our case, we have had to process over 60,000 household and 500,000 individual records.

Benefit Estimates

National benefit totals were first distributed to regions known as Census County Groups and to subportions of these groups, known as Standard Metropolitan Statistical Areas (SMSAs). Each individual within these regions was assumed to receive an even share of a region's estimated benefit total. Thus, within a region, a family's benefit was determined solely by the number of its members.

The procedure for distributing the national benefit totals to regions, the assumptions behind the procedure, and its weaknesses are fully discussed in two recent studies.[9] Here, we make only the following observations about our procedure. We basically assume that pollution damage (and, hence, the benefits from alleviating such damage) is proportional to local physical air quality or pollution concentrations.[10] Hence, we reject the pure public-commodity view of environmental quality. Two factors that

[7] Families in our analysis are defined as U.S. Census primary families and unrelated individuals over fourteen years old.

[8] See Guy Orcutt, Martin Greenberger, John Korbel, and Alice Rivlin, *Microanalysis of Socioeconomic Systems: A Simulation Study* (Harper and Row, 1961).

[9] Gianessi, Peskin, and Wolff, "Distributional Effects;" and Leonard P. Gianessi, Henry M. Peskin, and Edward Wolff, "The Distributional Implications of National Air Pollution Damage Estimates," in F. T. Juster, ed., *Distribution of Economic Well-Being* (Cambridge, Mass., Ballinger for the National Bureau of Economic Research, 1977).

[10] In turn, the relative air quality of two regions is assumed to be proportionate to the relative rate of emissions in the two regions. County groups are assumed to be large enough that spillovers can be neglected but small enough to permit an assumption of homogeneous air quality within the region.

may have nonproportional influences on damage are also neglected. The first is the income of the damaged party. As we pointed out above, Baumol and others have argued that the dollar valuation a person places on physical environmental damage can vary with the person's income; furthermore, there is reason to believe that the valuation increases as the individual becomes wealthier. Our analysis does not account for this. The second neglected factor is the possibility of "increasing returns" to bad health from pollution concentrations. There is reason to believe that when the air is rather clean, small increments in pollution concentrations will have small detrimental effects. However, increments of the same size can have very large detrimental effects when the air is very dirty.

Since we distributed a fixed national benefit total, neglect of these two factors may work in opposite directions. Ignoring income differences may imply that we underestimate the policy benefits to wealthier people relative to poor people. However, to the extent that the poor live in more highly polluted areas, and would benefit the most from improvements in very polluted air, the opposite is the case. Thus, the proportionality assumption may provide a good approximation of relative damages in spite of the neglect of the nonproportional influences of income and the potentially cumulative health–pollution concentration relationships.

Table 5-2 lists the ten areas where the average benefits per family of controlling air pollution are the highest and lowest.[11] While it is not surprising that the residents of the heavily industrialized northeastern areas have the most to gain from pollution control, it is perhaps surprising that these benefits are concentrated in so few regions. Our analysis suggests that over 30 percent of total national benefits go to the residents of the five dirtiest SMSAs, although they account for but 8 percent of the U.S. population. As we shall see, costs appear to be much more widely distributed. Therefore, the concentration of benefits in a very few areas is the major determinant of all our subsequent results concerning the ultimate distributional consequences of the 1970 Clean Air Amendments on income classes and racial groups.

Cost Estimates

The costs of air pollution abatement in table 5-1 were distributed to families in one of three ways, depending on whether the initial incidence of

---

[11] The failure of Los Angeles to appear in the list of the ten highest benefit areas is a consequence of the fact that the national damage estimates do not give a heavy weight to automotive pollutants.

TABLE 5-2   Areas with Highest and Lowest Per-Family Gross Benefits Under the 1970 Clean Air Amendments

Rank	County group or SMSA	Dollars per family
	Ten Highest	
1	Jersey City SMSA	2,547.29
2	New York, N.Y. SMSA	1,169.94
3	Erie SMSA	1,040.37
4	Newark SMSA	864.41
5	Paterson SMSA	782.99
6	Detroit SMSA	762.77
7	Chicago SMSA	660.71
8	Cleveland SMSA	652.12
9	Providence SMSA	631.39
10	Gary SMSA	622.94
	Ten Lowest	
1	Alaska	0.32
2	Nevada, S. Utah	1.42
3	Montana	2.53
4	S. New Mexico, W. Texas	2.98
5	Wyoming, W. Nebraska	2.98
6	N. New Mexico	3.79
7	Arizona	3.85
8	S.W. Texas	4.09
9	N.W. Texas	4.15
10	C. Texas	4.63

costs fell on industries, governments, or households. Industrial costs—which we assume to be passed on in the form of higher product prices—were apportioned to families according to an estimate of their total consumption (which, in turn, was based on their income). The apportionment of governmental costs—assumed to be paid for by tax increases rather than reductions in other expenditures—was based on estimates of family tax burden. Household costs, which for the most part, are automobile pollution control costs, were apportioned on a per-vehicle-owned basis, one of the many household characteristics reported in the Public Use Sample.[12]

No region of the United States can claim an overwhelming preponderance of vehicle ownership or families residing in a given income class. Therefore, average per-family costs are spread much more narrowly be-

---

[12] This description oversimplifies the actual task. In addition to the need for data on consumption levels and tax rates by income class, a procedure had to be devised for assigning cars to families. The Public Use File only reports vehicle ownership by household, and a household may contain several families and unrelated individuals or both. Details of the procedure are reported in Gianessi, Peskin, and Wolff, "Distributional Effects."

TABLE 5-3   Areas with Highest and Lowest Per-Family Costs Under the 1970 Clean Air Amendments

Rank	Area	Dollars per family
	Ten Highest	
1	Oxnard-Ventura SMSA	438.96
2	Bridgeport SMSA	422.86
3	Anaheim SMSA	416.95
4	Paterson SMSA	405.04
5	San Jose SMSA	401.18
6	S.W. Texas	400.22
7	Columbia SMSA	396.73
8	Alaska	396.11
9	Lansing SMSA	395.76
10	Dayton SMSA	395.30
	Ten Lowest	
1	S. Arkansas, W.C. Mississippi	254.56
2	Jersey City SMSA	263.18
3	M.W. Mississippi	270.16
4	N. West Virginia	274.14
5	N.W. Florida	279.63
6	Central S. Carolina	279.63
7	N.C. Missouri	282.08
8	New York, N.Y. SMSA	284.11
9	N. Mississippi, W. Tennessee, E. Arkansas	286.77
10	C. Tennessee	289.23

tween the ten highest cost areas and the ten lowest cost areas than are the per-family benefits. These high and low cost areas are shown in table 5-3. What differences do exist are explained by the fact that the high cost areas have relatively fewer low income families and high per-family automobile ownership.

Net Benefits

Net benefits are defined as the difference between per-family benefits and costs. When one calculates average net benefits per family for all 274 county groups and SMSAs, it appears that these average net benefits are positive for only a minority of these areas. For the air pollution policy as a whole, there appear to be only twenty-four areas (accounting for about 28 percent of the U.S. population) where average net benefits per family are positive. If the automobile policy is considered in isolation, only four areas (the Jersey City, New York, Paterson, and Newark SMSAs) show positive net benefits.

These results should not be surprising since we have seen that costs seem to be spread, geographically, far more evenly than benefits. The areas enjoying positive net benefits are those that suffer from a disproportionately large share of the nation's air pollution.

These results also imply that only a minority of the nation's population—principally those who live in the highly polluted areas—gain on net from the 1970 Clean Air Amendments. A more exact estimate of gainers and losers can be obtained by inspecting estimated benefits and costs for each family in the Public Use Sample. By this procedure, it is estimated that about 19 million families—or 29 percent of all families—enjoy positive net benefits. When the automobile policy is considered in isolation, only about 16 million families gain on net. It should be noted, however, that while net gainers appear to be in the minority, their gains on average greatly exceed the loss of net losers even though, as table 5-1 shows, total losses (costs) exceed total gains (benefits) by about $3 billion.

The rankings of net benefits shown in table 5-4 reflect both the wide dispersion in gross benefits and the relatively narrow dispersion in costs. The order of the areas with the highest net benefit is nearly the same as the order of highest gross benefits shown in table 5-2. The areas with the lowest net benefits differ insignificantly in their rankings and are representative of a large number of areas which have per-family costs in the $300–400 range, and which enjoy the very low per-family benefits common to areas with low levels of urbanization.

Income Relationships

Table 5-5 shows average benefits, costs, and net benefits by family income classes and by race. These data provide another view of the relative benefits and burdens of the air pollution control policy.

It is apparent that the industrial air pollution control policy and the household (primarily atuomobile) policy have markedly different impacts when viewed in relation to income. Nearly all income and racial groups enjoy, on average,[13] positive net benefits from the control of industrial air pollution. In contrast, no racial group or income class appears to gain from the control of automobile emissions. Except for those in the highest income class, non-whites appear to be the only net gainers from the 1970 Clean Air Amendments as a whole—a consequence of their lower average vehicle ownership (which lowers automobile control costs), their larger

---

[13] This qualifier is important because there are individual families that gain or lose in all income and racial classes.

TABLE 5-4   Areas with Highest and Lowest Per-Family Net Benefits
Under the 1970 Clean Air Amendments

Rank	County group or SMSA	Net benefit (dollars per family)
	Ten highest	
1	Jersey City SMSA	2,284.11
2	New York SMSA	885.83
3	Erie SMSA	700.85
4	Newark SMSA	509.59
5	Detroit SMSA	385.15
6	Paterson SMSA	377.95
7	Chicago SMSA	317.87
8	Providence SMSA	283.91
9	Cleveland SMSA	278.80
10	Gary SMSA	264.09
	Ten lowest	
1	S.W. Texas	−396.13
2	Alaska	−395.79
3	Nevada, S.W. Utah	−379.42
4	Santa Barbara SMSA	−362.08
5	Wyoming, W. Nebraska	−350.35
6	S. New Mexico, W. Texas	−349.71
7	Tucson SMSA	−347.52
8	C. Nebraska	−345.12
9	E.C. California	−343.57
10	N.E. Colorado	−342.23

average family size (which increases per-family benefits), and their tendency to reside in more urbanized locations (areas that receive the greatest pollution reductions).

Total benefits appear to increase as income rises, implying that higher income groups suffer (prior to the policy implementation) greater absolute damage than the poor. This finding, which is counter to those of Freeman and of Zupan,[14] may appear strange to those who picture the poor living in highly polluted urban slums. Although this characterization is no doubt valid, it must be kept in mind that the poorest of the poor actually live in relatively clean rural areas. Since both the Freeman and the Zupan studies dealt with specific SMSAs, and not with the entire nation, they did not observe the pollution to which the rural poor are exposed.

[14] A. Myrick Freeman III, "Distribution of Environmental Quality," in Allen V. Kneese and Blair T. Bower, eds., *Environmental Quality: Theory and Method in the Social Sciences* (Baltimore, Md., Johns Hopkins University Press for Resources for the Future, 1972); and Jeffrey M. Zupan, *The Distribution of Air Quality in the New York Region* (Washington, D.C., Resources for the Future, 1973).

TABLE 5-5   Annual U.S. Per-Family Air Pollution Control Costs and Benefits by Income Class and Race
(dollars)

					Income class					
Costs and benefits	Less than 3,000	3,000 to 3,999	4,000 to 5,999	6,000 to 7,999	8,000 to 9,999	10,000 to 11,999	12,000 to 14,999	15,000 to 19,999	20,000 to 24,999	25,000+
Industry and govt. costs										
Whites	59.79	81.90	102.63	130.47	155.90	177.56	210.49	248.17	299.87	457.29
Non-whites	59.79	81.90	102.63	130.47	155.90	177.56	210.49	248.17	299.87	457.29
Total	59.79	81.90	102.63	130.47	155.90	177.56	210.49	248.17	299.87	457.29
Industry and govt. benefits										
Whites	100.27	123.49	138.94	177.39	228.40	258.04	294.59	334.85	377.25	392.57
Non-whites	166.13	216.42	286.31	337.07	391.29	399.25	490.57	491.77	500.95	495.76
Total	112.57	138.76	160.33	195.48	242.19	267.16	306.99	343.27	382.75	395.22
Industry and govt. net benefits										
Whites	40.48	41.59	36.32	46.92	72.50	80.48	84.10	86.68	77.38	−64.72
Non-whites	106.34	134.52	183.68	206.60	235.39	221.69	280.08	243.60	201.08	38.47
Total	52.78	56.86	57.70	65.01	86.29	89.60	96.50	95.10	82.88	−62.07

Household costs (automobile)										
Whites	92.87	131.01	153.75	179.69	204.27	225.04	245.92	274.29	299.99	303.78
Non-whites	52.75	82.33	100.81	138.89	152.96	175.16	197.35	228.70	250.82	287.24
Total	85.25	123.01	146.03	175.04	199.91	221.82	242.83	271.83	297.81	303.35
Household benefits										
Whites	27.00	33.34	36.21	44.66	58.59	65.61	76.00	88.40	102.58	112.91
Non-whites	44.11	59.07	84.69	89.78	100.49	113.26	129.67	138.16	128.63	146.28
Total	30.25	37.56	43.28	49.79	62.14	68.69	79.41	91.08	103.74	113.77
Household net benefits										
Whites	−65.87	−97.67	−117.54	−135.03	−145.68	−159.43	−169.92	−185.89	−197.41	−190.87
Non-whites	−8.64	−23.26	−16.12	−49.11	−52.47	−61.90	−67.68	−90.54	−122.19	−140.96
Total	−55.00	−85.45	−102.75	−125.25	−137.77	−153.13	−163.42	−180.75	−194.07	−189.58
Total costs										
Whites	152.66	212.91	256.38	310.16	360.17	402.60	456.41	522.46	599.86	761.07
Non-whites	112.54	164.33	203.44	269.36	308.86	352.72	407.84	476.87	550.69	744.53
Total	145.04	204.91	248.66	305.51	355.81	399.38	453.32	520.00	597.68	760.64
Total benefits										
Whites	127.27	156.83	175.15	222.05	286.99	323.65	370.59	423.25	479.83	505.48
Non-whites	210.24	275.49	371.00	426.85	491.78	512.51	620.24	629.93	629.58	642.04
Total	142.82	176.32	203.61	245.27	304.33	335.85	386.40	434.35	486.49	508.99
Total net benefits										
Whites	−25.39	−56.08	−81.23	−88.11	−73.18	−78.95	−85.82	−99.21	−120.03	−255.59
Non-whites	97.70	111.16	167.56	157.49	182.92	159.79	212.40	153.06	78.89	−102.49
Total	−2.22	−28.59	−45.05	−60.24	−51.48	−63.53	−66.92	−85.65	−111.19	−251.65

TABLE 5-6 *Average Incidence of Air Pollution Control Costs and Benefits by Income Class and Source for the United States*

(percentage of income)

					Income class					
	Less than $3,000	$3,000 to $3,999	$4,000 to $5,999	$6,000 to $7,999	$8,000 to $9,999	$10,000 to $11,999	$12,000 to $14,999	$15,000 to $19,999	$20,000 to $24,999	$25,000 +
Costs										
Industry and govt.	3.4	2.4	2.1	1.9	1.7	1.6	1.6	1.4	1.4	1.1
Household	4.8	3.6	3.0	2.5	2.2	2.0	1.8	1.6	1.3	0.7
Total	8.2	6.0	5.1	4.4	3.9	3.6	3.4	3.0	2.7	1.8
Benefits										
Industry and govt.	6.3	4.0	3.2	2.8	2.7	2.4	2.3	2.0	1.7	1.0
Household	1.7	1.1	0.9	0.7	0.7	0.6	0.6	0.5	0.5	0.3
Total	8.0	5.1	4.1	3.5	3.4	3.0	2.9	2.5	2.2	1.3
Net benefits										
Industry and govt.	2.9	1.6	1.1	0.9	1.0	0.8	0.7	0.6	0.3	−0.1
Household	−3.1	−2.5	−2.1	−1.8	−1.5	−1.4	−1.2	−1.1	−0.8	−0.4
Total	−0.2	−0.9	−1.0	−0.9	−0.5	−0.6	−0.5	−0.5	−0.5	−0.5

If a family's share of pollution control costs is viewed as a tax, while the family's benefit is viewed as a subsidy, then the "progressivity" of this tax-subsidy package can be analyzed by dividing the cost and benefit totals of table 5-5 by the average incomes of the various income classes. These results are displayed in table 5-6.

Since average per-family cost as a percentage of income declines with income, the relative burden of the air pollution control policy clearly falls more heavily on the poor. In other words, the cost structure is "regressive."[15] On the other hand, the benefits are "progressive"—the rich enjoy fewer benefits per dollar of income than the poor.

Overall, net benefits, although negative for all classes, appear neither progressive nor regressive (indeed, they are proportionally distributed for incomes above $10,000). However, there is obviously a big difference between the burdens of the policy with respect to its industrial component as opposed to its household (primarily automobile) component. The net benefits of industrial air pollution control appear not only to be positive for almost all income groups but also progressively distributed. The net benefits of the household component, on the other hand, because of its large costs relative to benefits for all income classes, are both negative and regressive.

Alternative Strategies for Air Quality Improvement

As noted earlier, final assessment of the likely distribution of benefits and costs for any specific environmental policy is quite difficult without thorough empirical analysis. Nevertheless, we can hazard a few educated guesses about the distributional effects of certain alternative air pollution control policies.

Consider, for example, the two-car strategy discussed in chapter 3. Such a policy would not only be less expensive (with little effect on benefits), but, as Harrison argues, it would also be less regressive since large SMSAs

---

[15] Although percentages differ, this regressive pattern was also observed by Freeman, "Distribution of Environmental Quality"; Nancy S. Dorfman and Arthur Snow, "Who Will Pay for Pollution Control?" *National Tax Journal* vol. 28, no. 1 (March 1975) pp. 101–115; and Robert Dorfman, *Incidence of the Benefits and Costs of Environmental Programs,* Discussion Paper No. 510 (Harvard Institute of Economic Research, October 1976). The pattern was also shown for automobile policy only by A. Myrick Freeman III, "The Incidence of the Cost of Controlling Automotive Air Pollution," in F. T. Juster, ed., *Distribution of Economic Well-Being* (Cambridge, Mass., Ballinger for the National Bureau of Economic Research, 1977); and David Harrison, Jr., *Who Pays for Clean Air?* (Cambridge, Mass., Ballinger, 1975).

tend to have wealthier car-owning populations than smaller SMSAs and rural areas.[16] These smaller SMSAs and rural areas would be relieved of the costs of controlling automobile emissions.

However, estimating the distributional consequences of changes in industrial air or water pollution control policies is more difficult. Suppose, for example, we abandon a national air pollution control policy for one that allows regions of the country freedom of choice with respect to environmental policy. Because, unlike automotive control costs, the final "location" of industrial control costs is not necessarily the location where they are initially incurred, the distributional results will depend on complex trade and market patterns.

Thus, while certain suggested policy alternatives—effluent charge systems, for example—may be attractive on grounds of economic efficiency, they may be no better or no worse in terms of their distributional equity. Much depends on how the charge system is administered, especially with respect to the purpose of the charges, their levels, and the disposition of collected revenues.

If the purpose of an effluent charge is to bring about approximately the same emission reductions that are presently the targets of current regulations, then the distributional patterns will not be very different from what they are now. However, since charges are thought to be more efficient than mandated controls,[17] total pollution control costs can be expected to be somewhat lower, thereby resulting in a larger number of net gainers. On the other hand, the distributional pattern may be greatly different if the charges are to be set in accordance with local (rather than national) preferences. It is quite possible that very clean rural areas, desirous of industrial growth, would choose to set very low charges. If so, the current high-cost, low-benefit pattern typical of these areas could change to a low-cost, low-benefit pattern, depending again on the way industrial commodities flow.

It is also difficult to predict what effect the collected revenues will have. Under many charge schemes these revenues could be substantial even if the desired level of air quality is attained.[18] If, for example, these revenues

---

[16] Harrison, *Who Pays?*

[17] See chapter 2 for a discussion of this proposition.

[18] While some schemes suggest a zero charge when a target level of water quality is attained, an ideally efficient policy requires the charge to equal the marginal social damage of a small increase in the target level and the marginal social opportunity cost of a small decrease in the target level. Generally, these marginal social damages and costs, and hence the charge, are non-zero, even when an ideally efficient pollution level obtains.

were to be used for general tax relief, the policy would tend to be more regressive, since the wealthy bear larger proportional tax burdens. An opposite result would obtain if these revenues were used for the construction of publicly owned pollution control facilities designed to substitute for private industrial facilities. Such a policy would relieve the regressive burden of the costs of the replaced industrial facilities. An even more progressive outcome would be assured if these revenues were targeted for low income populations.

However, our analysis indicates that "poor aim" is a likely feature of such policy targeting. The difficulty of determining the actual distributional pattern of the burden of policy costs makes it difficult to use the policy's revenues (or even general revenues) as a means of subsidizing or offsetting these costs. This problem is not confined to pollution control policies but to any tax or subsidy proposal such as the recent suggestions to use subsidies to offset the cost of various aspects of the president's energy policy.

Political Acceptability

Both our qualitative discussions and our empirical analysis of the 1970 Clean Air Amendments support the conclusion that the burdens and benefits of environmental policy are likely to be unevenly distributed across regions, income classes, and races. Indeed, our estimates suggest that net gainers are in the minority and are confined to a few presently highly polluted regions.

Regardless of these characteristics, Congress and the public have generally supported environmental programs, although enthusiasm may be waning. If citizens vote in their own self-interest, as many believe them to do, one might wonder why U.S. environmental policy enjoys the support it has. There are several possible explanations and we shall focus on three of them.

The Analysis Understates the Benefits

Any apparent inconsistency between public support for environmental programs and the relatively small number of net gainers may be entirely illusory. If the true benefits are greatly understated, then net gainers may, in fact, be in the majority. Indeed, a critic of EPA's benefit estimates may cite the public support of the programs as evidence that the benefits are underestimated. However, since the public might well support such a program even if the benefit estimates are accurate (as will be argued below), such "evidence" is rather weak.

Nevertheless, it is impossible to prove that all the benefits of a clean environment have been quantified or are even capable of being quantified. In particular, there may be overriding social benefits generated by cleaning up the environment that are of a public commodity nature and that are independent of any private or regional gains. Those who assert that a clean environment is a national birthright to which all are entitled are implicitly asserting the existence of such a benefit.

Lack of Knowledge of Actual Costs and Benefits

Of course, in explaining the political support, the actual existence of possibly unquantified benefits is not as important as the *perception* of their existence. It is entirely possible that our analysis has accurately pictured all the costs and benefits but that these true "facts" were not available to congressmen or the public during the mid-1960s when support for environmental legislation was most enthusiastic.

Although one may question whether there was a full understanding of the level and distribution of benefits (especially in view of the uncertainties surrounding benefit estimation), there is some evidence that policy costs and their distribution were not fully appreciated by supporters of environmental regulation. Often expressed was the view that pollution control was a problem of corporate power—that the costs of environmental quality improvements would be drawn solely from corporate profits[19] (and this was the source of corporate opposition).[20] The fact that the final cost burdens were likely to be regressive was not emphasized—at least publicly.

Certainly the early widespread support for environmental policy and the more recent and cautious attitudes could be explained by the fact that perception of the true costs and benefits is only beginning to be realized. Yet, as we shall see, there is still another plausible explanation.

Consistency with Distributive Goals

The analysis of the distributive impacts of the 1970 Clean Air Amendments indicates that those who gain when both benefits and costs are taken

[19] For example, see John C. Esposito, *Vanishing Air* (New York, Grossman Publishers, 1970).

[20] The inconsistency between the assumption of no shifting of control costs to consumers and the implicit assumption of corporate monopolies facing inelastic demands was not appreciated.

into account are more likely to be non-white, low income, inner-city residents. The law apparently serves to shift welfare toward a population group that is also a focus of a large body of explicit redistributive policy.[21] It is quite likely that certain pro-environment congressmen were influenced by the image of the inner-city resident living with both the burdens of poverty and dirty air. To these congressmen, the redistributive character of the environmental policy is simply another point in its favor.

If this conjecture is correct, it does not bode well for certain aspects of water quality legislation or for certain suggested amendments to the Clean Air Act. That is, it has been estimated that 70 percent of the benefits of improved water quality will be in the nature of improved recreational opportunities.[22] These benefits will be biased toward the wealthy since those in the higher income classes are the major users of water-based recreation.[23] In a similar fashion, suggested policies to limit air quality degradation in already clean areas cannot help but dampen economic growth, and, regardless of how noble the objectives may be, such growth-limiting policies, unless accompanied by substantial redistribution efforts, will almost certainly harm the poor who have yet to attain high levels of wealth far more than the rich who already have. To the extent that these and other aspects of environmental policy are perceived as primarily benefiting the wealthy, they may lose the support of welfare-oriented congressmen.

Conclusion

None or all of the above three explanations may account for congressional attitudes toward current environmental policy. It is difficult to prove or disprove any of these conjectures. What we can say with certainty is that environmental policy has potentially profound distributional implications. These policies are inherently biased with respect to their impact on different families and different geographical regions. This chapter has suggested that this lack of neutrality can have and may have had an impact on the political acceptability of the legislation. It is a possibility that should not be ignored when considering future legislation.

[21] It is obviously not the sole focus. Most welfare recipients are white and many live in rural areas.
[22] Fred H. Abel, Dennis P. Tihansky, and Richard G. Walsh, "National Benefits of Water Pollution Control" (Washington, D.C., Office of Research and Development, U.S. Environmental Protection Agency, n.d.).
[23] C. J. Cicchetti, J. J. Seneca, and P. Davidson, *The Demand and Supply for Outdoor Recreation* (New Brunswick, N.J., Bureau of Economic Research, Rutgers University, 1969).

CHAPTER 6

Investment, Inflation, Unemployment, and the Environment

ROBERT H. HAVEMAN and V. KERRY SMITH

(IN RECENT YEARS we have been bombarded with conflicting assertions about the incompatibility of environmental quality with other important goals. On the one hand, opponents of the environmental movement argue that stiff controls will be inflationary, will impede economic
growth, will deprive firms of needed productive investment, will lead to
plant closures, and will cause a loss of jobs. On the other hand, increasing numbers of environmentalists have argued that it is possible simultaneously to create jobs, conserve energy and nonrenewable resources,
and protect the environment.[1]

---

[1] One such group Environmentalists for Full Employment publishes a newsletter
in an effort to form a coalition between workers and environmentalists to attain
these goals. In their first newsletter, which appeared in November 1975, they state
their goals as:
  A. Modern technologies that are excessively capital intensive and energy
     wasteful simultaneously destroy the environment, deplete resources, and
     cause structural unemployment. These problems must be attacked con-
     currently, and such technologies must be rejected.
  B. U.S. economic history is a parade of innovations using more and more
     capital, energy, and resources. In a world of increasing population and
     diminishing resources, it is more efficient to fully employ human resources
     while conserving capital and natural resources. But most economic an-
     alysts have not yet grasped this new reality.
  C. U.S. policy makers have consistently failed to internalize all the costs of
     our economic system—including pollution, unemployment, and other
     social costs—in their economic procedures. We must follow the principles

The policy prescriptions which emanate from each viewpoint are quite disjointed. In one view it is suggested that policy makers should tend to the job of guiding the economy toward full employment and stable prices rather than seek the more elusive and less important goal of an improved environment. Alternatively, environmentalists contend that the potential exists for "millions more jobs in labor-intensive, environmentally benign industries."[2] In order to create jobs, environmentalists assert that we must abandon our labor-saving technologies in favor of those that are both labor intensive and based on renewable resources.

The claims of both sides deserve serious consideration—especially when the unemployment rate continues to hover above 6 percent and inflation proves resistant to our conventional policy tools. Because of both the potency and inconsistency of these claims, we will use this chapter to explore what is known of the extent to which the kinds of environmental policies discussed in chapters 2 through 4 do conflict with full employment policy and with efforts to control inflation. More generally, we will attempt to appraise the effect of environmental policy on a variety of economic variables—prices, employment, and regional output patterns.

Questions regarding the macroeconomic impact of actual or proposed public policies are among the first to be posed by the media, the public, and policy analysts. As an example, witness the response to President Jimmy Carter's energy proposals. Yet, in spite of the interest in these matters, there have been few comprehensive and reliable analyses of the economic impacts of environmental policy.

The reasons for this are not difficult to perceive. First of all, the channels by which environmental policies affect the economy are muddy and meandering. As we emphasized in earlier chapters, both air and water quality laws are regulatory in nature. These legislative mandates involve specific standards, and often subsidies to help defray the costs of meeting them. In the process, Congress seeks to alter the behavior of individ-

---

of ecology that state that nothing is "free," nothing is "throw away" and that everything must be accounted for on a closed-loop basis.

D. National leaders have naively assumed that material satisfaction for everyone can be obtained through a policy of undifferentiated growth. Since this policy has clearly failed both the environmentalist and the worker, we must strive for a fairer redistribution of the nation's resources rather than a continued expansion of resource intensive production, the fruits of which are inequitably shared.

[2] See "Who We Are," *Environmentalists for Full Employment*, no. 1, November 1975, p. 1.

uals, municipalities, and business firms. And it is this change in behavior which generates the impacts on the economy. But seeking to alter behavior is not the same as altering it. Environmental quality legislation is administered by a number of agencies, some of which are quite effective while others are less so. And, in some cases, courts are involved in determining the change in behavior that will be induced by the legislation.

A fair amount of economic analysis has considered the response of individual firms and municipalities to various kinds of incentives, regulations, and administrative arrangements. Because these responses deal with individual economic units, we say that they are microeconomic in nature, yet they add up to full-blown impacts on the economy. In part because of the uncertain nature of the individual responses to the existing regulatory framework, an effort to consider them as a whole has not often been attempted. At best, the translation of a regime of subsidies, regulations, and enforcement mechanisms into estimates of new capital equipment purchases and new labor requirements will involve some guesswork and some simplifying assumptions.

There is a second reason that reliable estimates of the economic impact of environmental policy are hard to come by: the initial recipient of a mandate to change behavior—say, a polluting firm—is often able to shift the real cost of the mandate away from himself and onto others. For example, we saw in chapter 5 how, by raising prices to cover the costs of newly required pollution control equipment, firms can shift the financial burden of that pollution control onto consumers. Such policy-induced price changes, in turn, make it difficult to discover the full economic impact of certain policies. One must trace the long series of resulting price, demand, and output effects through the economy. If we stop before these effects have fully worked themselves out, we will have considered only the preliminary economic impacts of the policy change.

As we will see in this chapter, analyses of the economic impacts of environmental policy usually begin by identifying the two primary channels by which a policy triggers changes in the economy. The first of these channels is that of direct public expenditures for the construction, installation, and operation of pollution control equipment. The federal construction grants for municipal waste treatment plant construction discussed in chapter 2 are an example. The second primary channel is the private spending necessitated by the legislated standards and enforcement efforts. The installation of smokestack scrubbers by an air polluter in order to meet air quality standards is an example. In both cases, increased demands for certain goods and services are imposed on the economy, and in both cases, the allocation of the nation's resources will be affected. Because these increases in demand can be significant, especially when a new environmental policy forces dramatic changes in manufacturing processes, it is to be expected that the size and composition of the nation's gross national product (GNP) will be affected by the policy.

It is at this point that environmental policy may be perceived as being in conflict with other objectives. Production costs in some key industries may increase faster than in others, causing both price effects and economic dislocations. Moreover, for those individual businessmen who must increase their prices to cover the increased costs, environmental policies will generally be viewed as depressing sales and therefore considered undesirable. The effects of such environmental policies are translated into further economic impacts in a variety of ways. Marginal plants in some regions may have to close down earlier than they otherwise would, while plants in other regions may experience increased sales. If the regions experiencing cutbacks are already growing slowly, environmental policy may well hasten their competitive disadvantage with respect to other regions of the country and their populations.

Yet as we have pointed out, we cannot have more of everything. Tradeoffs are necessary between environmental quality objectives and the range of other social objectives—full employment, price stability, energy conservation, and economic growth to name but a few. Only if the aggregate economic impact of environmental policy and its regional, industrial, and occupational composition is known in quantitative terms will decision makers be able to make rational choices about these tradeoffs.

In addition to these aggregate impacts and their sectoral composition, their timing is important to policy makers. Stabilization policy is a difficult and treacherous enterprise in its own right. It is even more treacherous if it has to be undertaken simultaneously with other policies that also shock the economy. Thus, stabilization policy will be more successful if decision makers have some idea of when and where (in what sectors and regions) environmental policy will affect the economy.

It is to these issues that this chapter is addressed. In the next section, we will describe the various approaches that have been used to estimate the aggregate and sectoral economic effects of environmental policy. Following this, we summarize the results of several major studies from the United States and other countries and attempt to appraise their reliability. Later, estimates from these studies are used to evaluate a number of assertions regarding the effect of environmental policy on the overall health of our economy. Then, after appraising the available models and techniques, we conclude by drawing a few implications for environmental policy from the evidence so far available.

Techniques for Estimating the Economic Impacts of Environmental Policy

Public policies, or any other outside "shock" to the economic system, initiate a set of changes which work their way through the economy, leaving in their wake a set of altered prices, outputs, and resource allocations. Environmental policy is no exception. It is this set of altered economic variables which we will call the economic impact of a policy. While some of these impacts are *direct* and easy to perceive—for example, the increased output in the pollution control equipment industry—others are *indirect* and hidden. An example of the latter impact would be the decrease in employment in the steel industry resulting from reduced sales that follow the increased steel costs and prices required to cover the installation of pollution abatement equipment.

Two broad types of modeling techniques have been developed to estimate these direct and indirect impacts. They are distinguished by the way in which they "track" the economic changes imposed on the economy by changes in environmental policy. One is a "bottom-up" approach in the sense that it attempts first to measure the impact of a policy change on individual households and businesses in the economy and then to trace in a very detailed way the changes in demands, outputs, and prices which this change induces. The numerous individual responses and impacts are then added up to yield the aggregate impact of the policy. Appropriately, this approach is often referred to as a microsimulation technique.

The second type of approach is a "top-down," or macroeconometric approach. The strategy here is first to specify a system of aggregate relationships in the economy, then to identify how the policy change will affect one or a few of the key aggregate economic variables in the system—for example, the demand for investment goods—and finally to predict the performance of the economy in both the presence and the absence of the policy change in question. Only after measuring the impact of the policy on aggregate variables is there an effort to delve deeper and estimate the effects on individual sectors of the economy. This latter approach has been conducted with a class of models referred to as macroeconometric models, generally the same ones used to forecast the level of overall economic activity.

This brief discussion does not do justice to either class of models. Some microsimulation models, for example, have a number of aggregative relationships built into them. In a similar fashion, some of the macroeconometric models incorporate rather detailed descriptions of specific sectors of the economy—the financial sector, the foreign sector, and the like. In this section, we will first define these models more specifically and show how they are used for estimating the impacts of environmental policy. It should be noted that these techniques and our discussion of them imply nothing about the wisdom of existing environmental policies, or the benefits and costs of alternatives to those policies. The purpose of these techniques—and our discussion—is simply to describe the economic effects of the policies. However, because the discussion of the models is somewhat technical, the reader interested in a summary of the results and policy issues may skip to page 175.

Microsimulation Models

In recent years, the microsimulation technique[3] has been used widely by researchers to evaluate policy measures in a number of areas, especially in the tax and income transfer fields. The first step in such a technique is to identify a population of individual firms or households that will be affected by the policy in question. Each unit in this population is described in some detail. For example, each household is characterized by income level; family size and composition; region; and age, sex, educational, and racial characteristics. Similarly, firms might be classified by sector, size, age of equipment, and the like. Then, the impact of the policy on each unit is estimated, and this will of course depend on the characteristics of each. For instance, a firm with an effluent load might experience a need to install control equipment, with the extent of the required investment depending on the volume and composition of the effluent. The next step is to evaluate

---

[3] For further description of the microsimulation methodology, see the discussion in Barbara R. Bergmann, "A Microsimulation of the Macroeconomy With Explicitly Represented Money Flows," *Annals of Economic and Social Measurement* vol. 3 (July 1974); and Harold W. Guthrie, Guy H. Orcutt, Steven Caldwell, Gerald E. Peabody, and George Sadowsky, "Microanalytic Simulation of Household Behavior," *Annals of Economic and Social Measurement* vol. 1 (April 1972).

how this policy impact will affect other decisions the firm or household makes. Will the required additional investment cause prices to increase and by how much? Or the demand for labor to decrease and by how much? Finally, these induced decisions will affect still other households or firms, inducing still other responses, and so forth. When all of these effects have worked themselves out according to the rules of the economic model, the various impacts on households and firms of the policy being considered can be added up and described by classes of units—for example, income groups for households, industries for firms, and regions for both firms and households.

Clearly, the larger the number of discrete micro-units, the more complex the modeling task. To make the effort manageable, some researchers have grouped units into classes—for example, by income, industry, occupation, or region. Within each group, then, each individual unit is treated in the same manner, so that some detail is lost in order to achieve a more workable model. In such cases, the effect of environmental policy on a group of firms is estimated, and the induced response on unit production costs, prices, and input demands for the group is simulated. In turn, these changes are passed on through the economy, thereby altering relevant economic variables—prices, costs, sales, incomes—of other groups. Ultimately, such changes will result in an altered mix of goods and services produced in the economy, different relative prices, and new input allocations, as each of the affected markets reaches a new equilibrium.

To clarify the nature of this technique, we will use as an example one of the most comprehensive microsimulation models for evaluating the economic impacts of environmental policy—that developed by Kevin Hollenbeck in 1976. Hollenbeck applied his model to the stationary source regulations of the 1970 Amendments to the Clean Air Act.

In this technique, Hollenbeck merges a microsimulation model of household decisions with a seventeen sector, input–output model of industry behavior. The structure of the combined model incorporates several fundamental economic relationships that are necessary for estimating the full economic effects of the policy. These relationships include, among others:

1. the effect of pollution control investment induced by a policy on the final demand for goods in each sector of the economy

2. the effect of the policy on the price level of the goods produced by polluting industries

FIGURE 6-1   *The Hollenbeck Microsimulation Model*

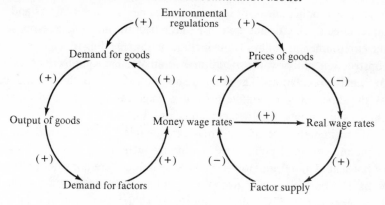

(+) and (−) indicate direction of induced responses

➤s indicate direction of causation

Source: Kevin Hollenbeck, "The Employment and Earnings Incidence of the Regulation of Air Pollution: A Policy Evaluation" (Ph.D. dissertation, University of Wisconsin, 1976). Reprinted with permission of the author.

3. the effect of relative price changes on the composition of consumer demand

4. the effect of price changes on wage rates and, in turn, the effect of changes in wage rates on the quantity of labor supplied

5. the effect of changes in the demand for goods on the outputs of industries which directly supply these goods and on industries which are second, third, and later round suppliers of the directly affected industries

6. the effect of industrial output changes in the demand for labor, employment, the wage rate, earnings, and household incomes

7. the effect of household income changes on the level and composition of household consumption.

In figure 6-1, the pattern of interactions in the Hollenbeck model is depicted. The positive (+) and negative (−) signs indicate the direction of the induced response and the arrows show the direction of causation. For example, if the money wage rates increase, the prices of goods will increase, holding all other things constant. But if the supply of labor increases, then the model assumes that the money wage rate will drop.

As mentioned previously, conceptually it is possible to divide the total impact of a policy measure into two components—direct effects and indirect effects. The former are those that reflect the immediate response to the environmental policy. These include public spending for equipment or construction, and private expenditures for abatement equipment necessary to meet the regulations. The latter are all of the responses that are induced by the direct effect—relative price and wage rate changes and induced changes in outputs, employment, and earnings.

Microsimulation techniques make it possible to analyze in detail the economic effects of policies by identifying such effects by each category of household and firm. However, these techniques are not without limitations. For one thing, they give no indication of the timing of the impacts. In a sense the microsimulation approach is "timeless" in that it offers a snapshot of the structure of the economy with the environmental policy in effect that can be compared with another snapshot without the policy. For another thing, the elaborate detail contained in some of these models sometimes impedes their reliability and reduces one's confidence in the estimates they yield. After one is finished cumulating several rounds of induced impact, each of which is based on uncertain estimates of other induced impact, how much faith can be placed in the ultimate results?

Macroeconometric Models

The second approach to estimating the impact of environmental policy addresses more successfully the problems of timing and reliability of the aggregate estimates. It does so, however, at the cost of sectoral detail. When the macroeconometric approach is applied to environmental policy, the basic tool of the analysis is an operating, conventional macroeconometric model, like those of Data Resources Inc., Wharton Economic Forecasting Associates, or Chase Econometrics Inc. One first selects a specific model to represent the aggregate economy. Then, whichever model one begins with, the next step is to alter the model to reflect the special nature of the policy measures, the effects of which are to be estimated.

Most of the successful macroeconometric models are based on some variant of standard Keynesian economic theory. Accordingly, a number of aggregate variables are estimated, including GNP and total employment. In addition, these variables are decomposed into subcategories. In the case of GNP, for example, such subcategories would include consumption, investment, imports, exports, and government spending. Consumption and investment spending, in turn, are related to variables such as income, interest rates, and the stock of inventories. Within most of these models, the interrelationships between industries are described by an input–output matrix, and the amount of employment is jointly determined by the labor demands of producing sectors and the labor supply of various types of workers. Typically, a financial sector is included in the model, as well as a system of equations (sometimes called markup relations) designed to reflect the impact on prices of changes in production costs and the utilization of capacity.

In figure 6-2, the structure of one such macroeconometric model—the Wharton Economic Forecasting Associates (WEFA) annual model—is shown. By starting with the box at the bottom labeled "exogenous factors" and following the arrows, one can see how the several components of the model interact with each other to determine GNP and its components (designated by the final demand box in the upper left-hand corner of the figure), as well as the level of employment, prices, and income flows.

To evaluate the economic effects of environmental policy using such a framework, one must first decide how the policy will alter one or more of the exogenous factors so as to set the model in motion. Second, the internal structure of the model must be altered if the structure of the policy is such as to change some fundamental relationship that is a part of the model.

In the analyses we discuss later in this chapter, the primary exogenous factors which were altered included the level of investment (representing the purchase of abatement equipment by business firms) and the level of government spending for pollution abatement. The level of these expenditures in various years was first specified and then entered into the model as a pattern of changes in exogenous investment. The analyses discussed later also assumed that the environmental policy altered some of the basic relationships that are a part of the model. For example, new pollution control investment was presumed to have no positive effect on output; as a result, the value of industrial assets against which returns are measured increased, with no concomitant increase in total productive capacity. Moreover, it was assumed that the required maintenance of the equipment would add to the production costs of the affected industries and to the prices which they would charge for their output. Both of these adjustments to the model were difficult to specify in advance with precision, and as a

FIGURE 6-2   Structure of the Wharton Annual and Industry Forecast-ing Model

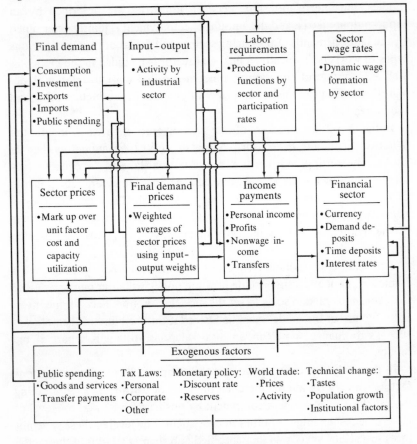

Note: Investments in pollution abatement equipment are given exogenously to the model and not de-termined as a part of the final demand block in the upper left box of the flow chart.

Source: Ross Preston, "The Wharton Long Term Model: Input Output Within the Context of a Macro Forecasting Model," *International Economic Review* vol. 16 (February 1975) p. 4. Copyright © 1975 by the Wharton School of Finance and Commerce, University of Pennsylvania, and the Osaka University Institute of Social and Economic Research Association. Reprinted with permission.

result a good deal of judgment and ad hoc estimation had to go into the alteration.

The accuracy of the exogenous impacts and the alteration of the model are crucial to the reliability of the final results. For example, con-sider a case in which the adjustment of production costs, and hence prices, in individual industry sectors is inaccurate. As a result, the estimated direct impacts on these industries are faulty. Perhaps more seriously, these errors will spread because the output of these industries may enter as an intermediate input to other industries and an impact on the production costs of these industries will be recorded. And in turn the prices these industries charge—the indirect price impacts—will be biased.

In both the microsimulation models and the macroeconometric models, then, judgment plays a crucial role. In the former, the judgment revolves around determining how individuals—businesses and households—are affected by pollution control policy. In the latter, the primary judgments involve the aggregate impacts resulting from underlying sectoral changes in response to the policy initiatives.

Estimated Economic Impacts

The last decade has seen numerous estimates of the effect of environmental policy on the economy. These have ranged from ad hoc, back-of-the-envelope calculations to estimates derived from elaborate computer models. Most studies have traced the impact of policy only through what we have called the direct effects—the impacts that result in immediate and readily observable demands for output (for example, pollution abatement equipment) and for labor (for example, that used in construction of municipal waste treatment plants). Few have followed the trail of impacts through the economy to estimate the indirect effects as well.

The first comprehensive evaluations of the macroeconomic implications of environmental regulations were conducted by Chase Econometric Associates with EPA support. Since this first effort, the Chase analysis has been replicated several times and included in the Council on Environmental Quality's (CEQ's) annual report. In this section we first discuss the results of the most recent of these evaluations and compare them with both a recent microsimulation analysis of the employment effects of the Clean Air Act and similar macroeconometric studies conducted for the Netherlands and Japan.[4]

---

[4] Our treatment of the comparative macroeconomic effects in the analyses from different countries draws on the earlier review in Robert H. Haveman, "Employment and Environmental Policy: A State-of-the-Art Review and a Suggested Approach" OECD working paper (Paris, Organisation for Economic Co-operation and Development, February 1977).

The Chase Analysis

The Chase analysis follows the basic outlines described above, including several additional adjustments to the structure of the original model.[5] These additional adjustments were the following:

A.   the index of industrial production was increased to reflect manufacture of automobile emissions control devices

B.   the consumption estimates for transportation services were also increased to reflect higher operating costs imposed by pollution control devices

C.   corporate profits were reduced to reflect the added costs of pollution control.

First, the amended model is run as if current environmental regulations did not exist. The current and future levels of such aggregate variables as GNP, the price level, the unemployment rate, private investment and consumption, the trade balance, and interest rates are estimated. Then, the model is again run—this time assuming that the current regulations are in effect. Again, the level and time path of the macroeconomic variables are estimated. The difference between the two runs of the model is interpreted to be the economic impact of federal environmental policy. In other words, the model gives us a view of the economy with and without our major environmental policies so that we can appraise their effects.

The basic data inputs to the Chase model are the CEQ estimates of: (1) the increments to annual pollution abatement investments for 1976–1983

[5] In simulating the Chase model the pattern of industry expenditures on pollution abatement equipment is assumed to be known over time. These increased investments are entered into the model by displacing the prior relationships that describe the determinants of investment in plant and equipment to reflect the aggregate annual increase. Both the interest costs and the maintenance and depreciation costs associated with the equipment affect prices through sectoral price markup equations.

By introducing the cost increases associated with pollution abatement expenditures on an industry-by-industry basis it is possible to take explicit account of both the "first round" or initial effects (i.e. price increases associated with the cost increases noted earlier) and the effects of these changes on industries that buy the directly impacted commodities as inputs.

One final aspect of the incorporation of environmental policies is the treatment of abatement capital. It is assumed that the earned rate of return on productive capital (that which is not associated with pollution abatement) must increase to maintain the level of overall rate of return on all capital. This behavior follows from the assumption that abatement equipment is assumed to be unproductive, hence increasing the total return required per unit of output.

and (2) the increases in annual operating and maintenance costs by industries which are required to comply with federal legislation. In order to understand CEQ's estimates so that they might be used in the analysis, it is important to distinguish them from the pollution abatement expenditures as estimated by the Bureau of Economic Analysis (BEA) or the Census Bureau. Based on specific surveys, BEA attempted to estimate the *actual* expenditures for pollution abatement equipment made by specific industry groups. The CEQ attempted to estimate the *portion* of total pollution control investments that was directly attributable to federally mandated pollution abatement and control requirements.

The CEQ projections were made over an eight-year period on an industry-by-industry basis (see table 6-1). All of the results of the Chase model must be conditioned by the validity of these projections—both their levels and the timing of the investments by industry. It should be noted at the outset that the CEQ figures must be largely judgmental, since all available data on actual investment expenditures reflect individual firms' perceptions of the impact of pollution control regulations.

Clearly, an appraisal of the Chase model's predictions should be considered concomitantly with an evaluation of CEQ's incremental investment estimates since the former depend on the latter. Unfortunately, we do not have a standard against which to compare the CEQ estimates. In order to offer some perspective on them, we compare in table 6-2 the average annual investments they envisage as necessary to meet the federal standards with the actual investment increments in 1974 through 1975 as reported by business enterprises and other industrial and commercial establishments.[6]

Several sources of data on estimated actual abatement expenditures are available. Those based on an enterprise survey by BEA and a second set based on an establishment survey of the Census Bureau are reported in table 6-2. For many industries, the actual increment in investment expen-

---

[6] It is important to recognize this distinction between the enterprise and the establishment level of analysis. The former may represent a composite of quite different production technologies, all with different requirements for pollution abatement equipment. These estimates are reported under the industrial classification considered to be the primary activity of the enterprise. Accordingly these figures, as reported by BEA, may include manufacturing and nonmanufacturing establishments within companies classified in manufacturing. It also excludes manufacturing establishments in companies classified as nonmanufacturing. For further attempts to reconcile these estimates, see William B. Sullivan, "An Analysis and Reconciliation of Universe Estimates of Pollution Abatement and Pollution Abatement and Control Expenditures," draft manuscript, Office of Regulatory Economics and Policy, U.S. Department of Commerce, July 1, 1977.

TABLE 6-1 *Estimated Incremental Pollution Control Expenditures, 1970–1983*[a]

(billions of 1974 dollars)

	Air pollution abatement costs 1970–75		Water pollution abatement costs 1970–75		Air pollution abatement costs 1976–83		Water pollution abatement costs 1976–83	
	Investment	Annual operating & maintenance	Investment	Annual operating & maintenance	Investment	Annual operating & maintenance	Investment	Annual operating & maintenance
Food & beverages[b]	0.19	0.15	0.54	0.55	0.33	0.89	0.54	1.77
Textiles	0.0	0.0	0.08	0.10	0.0	0.0	0.23	0.38
Pulp and paper products	0.87	0.45	0.59	0.46	1.11	4.25	4.10	3.48
Chemicals	0.84	0.79	0.84	0.85	1.27	3.54	7.61	10.74
Petroleum[c]	1.43	0.86	1.21	1.77	0.57	3.29	2.36	4.51
Rubber & misc. plastic products	0.10	0.09	0.0	0.0	0.25	0.64	0.0	0.0
Other nondurables	0.09	0.04	0.11	0.09	0.24	0.55	0.54	0.73
Stone, clay & glass	0.65	0.62	0.06	0.21	1.37	3.32	0.03	0.53
Iron & steel	1.19	1.25	0.35	0.32	1.88	6.17	1.81	1.80
Primary nonferrous metals	1.83	1.42	0.17	0.12	1.25	6.67	-0.02	0.39
Machinery	0.42	0.53	0.69	0.21	0.69	2.20	8.19	4.59
Motor vehicles	0.08	0.08	0.0	0.0	0.01	0.29	0.0	0.0
Other transportation equipment	0.06	0.09	0.31	0.25	0.06	0.28	0.80	1.57
Other durables	0.72	0.81	0.35	0.28	1.08	3.27	1.20	1.97
Total industrial	8.50	7.17	5.29	5.21	10.11	35.34	27.40	32.46
Electricity	4.75	3.35	2.20	1.00	11.03	28.95	2.53	7.49
Utilities	0.10	0.07	0.0	0.0	0.26	0.61	0.0	0.0
Other nonmanufacturing	0.18	0.20	0.41	0.13	0.17	1.73	0.75	1.63
Total fixed source	13.53	10.79	7.91	6.35	21.56	66.63	30.69	41.58
Mobile-source emission controls	5.59	22.93	0.0	0.0	32.02	56.81	0.0	0.0

Source: Chase Econometric Associates, Inc., *The Macroeconomic Impacts of Federal Pollution Control Programs: 1976 Assessment,* prepared for the Council on Environmental Quality and the U.S. Environmental Protection Agency (New York, 1976) p. 5.   [a] The cost estimates used in this analysis are consistent with the most recent CEQ estimates of "incremental abatement costs" published in its 1975 annual report. The CEQ defines "incremental" abatement costs as expenditures made to satisfy the requirements of federal environmental legislation beyond what would have been spent for pollution control in the absence of this legislation.   [b] Includes feedlots.   [c] Includes mining.

TABLE 6-2 *Annual Pollution Abatement Investment Increments as a Percentage of Total New Investment, Actual versus Required, 1974–1975*

(percentage)

| Industry group | Annual Increase 1974–1975 | | | | | | CEQ[a] Required Increase | | | | | |
| | BEA | | | Census | | | BEA | | | Census | | |
	Air	Water	Total	Air	Water	Total	Air	Water	Total	Air	Water	Total
Durable goods	00.20	00.40	00.60	00.30	00.31	00.61	n.a.	n.a.	n.a.	n.a.	n.a.	n.a.
Primary metals	02.70	01.62	04.32	03.70	01.46	05.16	10.4[b]	05.9	16.3	08.14	04.65	12.79
Electrical machinery	−01.11	−01.14	−02.25	−00.08	−00.08	−00.16	01.5[c]	17.8	19.3	01.17	13.97	15.14
Machinery (except elect.)	00.07	00.23	00.30	−00.12	00.09	−00.03	n.a.	n.a.	n.a.	n.a.	n.a.	n.a.
Transport. equipment	−00.41	00.00	−00.41	−00.66	−00.18	−00.84	00.28[d]	03.15	03.43	00.2	02.6	02.8
Stone, clay & glass	−00.67	01.14	00.47	−02.08	00.25	−01.83	10.8	00.2	11.0	11.5	00.2	11.7
Other durables	−00.53	00.40	−00.13	−00.41	00.12	−00.29	02.78[e]	03.1	05.88	02.58	02.86	05.44
Nondurable goods	01.27	01.70	02.97	01.42	01.30	02.72	n.a.	n.a.	n.a.	n.a.	n.a.	n.a.
Food incl. beverages	00.46	00.21	00.67	00.09	−00.59	−00.50	01.37	02.25	03.62	01.3	02.1	03.4
Textiles	00.58	00.00	00.58	00.59	00.34	00.93	00.00	02.5	02.5	00.00	03.4	03.4
Paper	−01.37	01.21	−00.16	02.35	03.30	05.65	06.3[f]	23.2	29.5	05.4	20.1	25.5
Chemicals	01.03	02.62	03.65	02.19	02.46	04.65	03.2	19.2	22.4	02.8	16.9	19.7
Petroleum	03.40	02.37	05.77	03.08	01.95	05.03	03.9	16.0	19.9	00.9	03.74	04.64
Rubber	−00.54	00.20	−00.34	00.00	−00.48	−00.48	02.1[g]	00.0	02.1	02.1	00.00	02.1
Other nondurables	−00.45	01.15	00.70	00.07	00.00	00.70	02.1[h]	04.8	06.9	01.9	04.3	06.2
Manufacturing Total	00.74	01.05	01.79	00.81	00.77	01.58	03.6[i]	09.7	13.3	02.75	07.47	10.22

Note: n.a. = not available.

a CEQ data on air and water pollution abatement costs are from 1976–1983; therefore all data were divided by eight years to find the average annual investments.

b CEQ data for primary metals are broken down into "iron and steel" and "primary nonferrous metals."

c CEQ data for machinery are not broken down into components.

d CEQ data are composed of "motor vehicles" and "other transportation" equipment.

e The CEQ group "other durables" is not necessarily the same as "other durables" as used in BEA and Census data.

f CEQ data are for "pulp and paper products."

g CEQ data are for "rubber and miscellaneous plastic products."

h The CEQ group for "other nondurables" is not necessarily the same.

i CEQ data used were under the heading of "total industrial."

ditures for air and water abatement is less than 1 percent of the increase in total capital spending, and in no case does it exceed 6 percent. Notice that in several cases the change in abatement investments is actually negative (the numbers preceded by a minus sign in the table). Such reductions in *actual* investment expenditures should not be surprising. Given uncertainty about the future legislative mandates and levels of enforcement, it is not unreasonable to expect that private investments may be inhibited and perhaps even fluctuate in response to the "regulatory climate."

In the last six columns of table 6-2 are shown the average annual CEQ estimates of the *required* increase in abatement equipment spending as a percentage of new investment, using BEA and Census total pollution investment estimates. In nearly all cases, these required amounts are substantially larger than the actual amounts. In very few cases do they lie below 2 percent, and in a number of cases, they exceed 10 percent. For the manufacturing sector as a whole, required expenditures for air pollution control are about 4 percent of new capital spending, and expenditures for water pollution control are about 8 percent.

Current air and water pollution policies, then, do imply the need for either a net increase in investment spending for pollution abatement, or a diversion of other investment expenditures into those for pollution control. Clearly the economic effect of these amounts could be substantial. However, the actual effect that they have will depend on the conditions in the economy at the time they occur. If there is a good deal of slack in the economy, output and employment can be expanded with the likely inflationary effect small. However, if there is little unemployment and production capacity is rather fully utilized, major pollution control investments could have a substantial impact on the price level.

The Chase macroeconometric model provides an evaluation of these effects by adding the demands imposed by environmental policy on top of the baseline operation of the economy. In this way, the performance of the economy both *with* and *without* the effect of environmental policy can be observed. Table 6-3 reports the impact of a pollution control policy on several macroeconomic variables over the 1976–1983 period.

For each of the variables considered, we report the percentage difference between the baseline forecast (the economy without the regulations) and the economy as it would appear with the regulations in effect. Three alternative scenarios are displayed. The first, referred to as BASE-CEQ, compares the economy with regulations in effect with a long-term forecast that predicts relatively low unemployment rates until mid-1977, followed by a recession in 1978 and recovery in 1980. Unemployment remains in

TABLE 6-3   Impact of a Pollution Control Policy on Macroeconomic Variables, Expressed as the Percentage Difference Between the Economy Without the Policy (BASE or FULL) and with the Policy (CEQ or HC), 1976–1983

(percentage)

Macroeconomic variables	Years							
	1976	1977	1978	1979	1980	1981	1982	1983
Real GNP								
BASE-CEQ	0.09	−0.48	−1.03	−1.16	−1.42	−1.70	−1.97	−2.17
BASE-HC	0.14	−0.59	−1.28	−1.40	−1.73	−2.09	−2.44	−2.68
FULL-CEQ	0.11	−0.53	−0.93	−1.16	−1.41	−1.74	−1.95	−2.27
Consumer price index								
BASE-CEQ	1.56	2.26	2.72	3.17	3.64	4.05	4.47	4.71
BASE-HC	1.82	2.74	3.40	3.90	4.53	5.03	5.59	5.94
FULL-CEQ	1.54	2.32	2.78	3.39	3.84	4.41	4.77	5.34
Growth rate of consumer price index								
BASE-CEQ	0.7	1.1	1.0	0.8	0.8	0.8	0.7	0.7
BASE-HC	0.9	1.4	1.2	1.0	1.1	1.1	0.9	0.9
FULL-CEQ	0.8	1.2	0.9	0.9	0.9	0.8	0.8	0.8
Unemployment rate								
BASE-CEQ	−5.56	−7.35	−2.41	−2.02	−1.15	0.00	1.64	3.64
BASE-HC	−8.33	−10.29	−3.61	−3.03	−2.30	−1.43	0.00	1.82
FULL-CEQ	−5.48	−7.94	−3.64	−2.13	−2.27	0.00		4.55
Real fixed investment (Producers' durables)								
BASE-CEQ	6.04	4.96	3.62	4.05	3.19	1.87	0.84	0.35
BASE-HC	7.46	6.01	4.50	4.98	4.07	2.39	0.92	0.49
FULL-CEQ	5.70	5.01	2.76	2.56	2.07	1.35	0.52	0.22
Housing starts								
BASE-CEQ	−6.62	−19.15	−21.15	−13.29	−10.05	−12.57[a]	−13.14	−13.48
BASE-HC	−7.95	−23.40	−25.00	−15.38	−12.44	−14.66	−16.00	−16.85
FULL-CEQ	−6.33	−13.59	−11.79	−9.59	−10.67	−12.38	−14.74	−16.65
Aa corporate bond rate for new issues								
BASE-CEQ	8.43	10.84	11.71	13.90	15.05	13.88	12.82	12.01
BASE-HC	10.51	13.50	14.56	17.62	18.91	17.48	16.03	15.01
FULL-CEQ	8.48	11.56	12.42	12.65	12.90	12.90	12.54	13.40

Source: Chase Econometric Associates, *Macroeconomic Impacts* pp. 12–14, 19–20, 21–22.

[a] Estimate appears to be a printing error.

the 6-percent range in both recovery periods. The second scenario BASE-HC uses estimates of incremental pollution abatement investment and costs that are arbitrarily increased by 25 percent, and the same baseline economic forecast is used as in the BASE-CEQ evaluation. The final scenario FULL-CEQ uses the Congressional Budget Office (CBO) five-year projections as a baseline. These projections presume the economy will experience close to full employment conditions. The same incremental investment and cost estimates used in BASE-CEQ are employed in FULL-CEQ.

It should be noted that these results refer to the *percentage difference* in the relevant variables with and without the CEQ environmental investments and annual costs. The figures in table 6-3, then, should be interpreted as predicting the effect of the various pollution control scenarios. For example, considering the unemployment rate and the BASE-CEQ analysis, we find that environmental measures serve to *reduce* until 1981 the unemployment rate from the levels that would obtain in the absence of environmental policies. Beyond 1981, the Chase model predicts modest increases in the unemployment rate because of environmental legislation. Thus the employment-generating impacts outweigh those that would tend to reduce employment during periods when investments to protect the environment are large. These impacts taper off toward the end of the simulation—and, indeed, show some increased unemployment—when investment demands are offset by the loss in productivity and slowdown in the rate of growth of real GNP caused in part by the higher prices.

The predicted impact of environmental legislation on other variables is also quite interesting. Among the economic impacts considered, the environmental measures appear to have their greatest impacts on housing starts and financial markets (in addition to those already discussed for the unemployment rate).[7] The effect on housing starts is easily understood once one realizes that about 40¢ of each dollar spent on pollution control investments comes from reductions in other private investment. The bulk of this effect is felt in residential construction activity where credit availability, increases in construction costs, and a tightening of the labor market serve to constrain housing starts.

The timing of the macroeconomic effects of environmental policies is closely tied to the timing of the investment expenditures necessitated by these policies. Since the estimates of incremental environmental investment are judgmental, the estimates of full macroeconomic effects reflect these same judgments, and must be so interpreted. Therefore, given the significant role of such judgments, it seems reasonable to compare the Chase estimates with other available estimates of the impacts of environmental policies.

---

[7] It should be noted that the Chase model has a relatively simple monetary sector. These findings will be quite sensitive to the avenues present in the model for interaction between the "real" and monetary sectors.

Comparison of Chase Analysis with Other Analyses

Two types of comparisons will be made. The results of the Chase analysis will be compared first with the results of a microsimulation study and then with macroeconometric results from other countries.

These comparisons are presented in table 6-4.[8] In the first column, the impacts derived from the Chase BASE-CEQ scenario are summarized. The second column summarizes the findings from Hollenbeck's microsimulation study which evaluated the economic impact of the stationary source provisions of the Clean Air Act. In Hollenbeck's analysis, it is assumed that the direct impacts of the Clean Air Act are spread evenly over a nine-year period during which the policy is to be implemented. Seventeen industrial sectors, four occupations, and five income classes are also distinguished in the study, and relationships describing the transactions of one industry with another are incorporated into the model. Both demand and supply responses are built into the model, as well. When the economy receives the direct impacts of the policy, responses occur which

---

[8] There have been several other types of studies of the employment effects of environmental programs. One study which developed a methodology that gained acceptance in later studies was described by Bruce M. Hannon and Roger H. Bezdek in their article "Job Impacts of Alternatives to Corps of Engineers Projects," *Engineering Issues—Journal of Professional Activities* vol. 99 (October 1973). In it, they analyzed the following question: "what would be the effect on the net demand for labor in various occupations if the water resources investment budget in the U.S. federal government were reduced by X billions of dollars while spending on a range of alternative federal programs were [sic] increased by a comparable amount?"

Using the composition of final demands by industrial sector plus direct labor requirements per unit of investment in water resource projects and per unit of investment in waste treatment plant construction, they calculated gross output requirements for each sector resulting from alternative final demand assumptions. Labor demands implied by the gross output requirements were estimated by sector using industry-specific labor-output ratios. Their labor demands were further disaggregated by occupation.

Their results suggest that comparable investments in waste treatment plants were 30 percent more labor intensive than water resource investments after taking into account direct and on-site labor requirements and the indirect effects from the nature of inter-industry requirements.

The U.S. Bureau of Labor Statistics subsequently used this method to evaluate the entire set of federal pollution control abatement expenditures. (U.S. Department of Labor, Bureau of Labor Statistics, *Impact of Federal Pollution Control and Abatement Expenditures on Manpower Requirements*, Bulletin No. 1836, 1975.) Unlike Hannon and Bezdek, however, their study carefully distinguished worker-years of employment demand from "jobs" created, which mixes part- and full-time employment. For the whole program the BLS study estimated 67,000 jobs would be created per one billion dollars of federal pollution abatement expenditures.

TABLE 6-4 A Comparison of Effects of Selected Environmental Programs on Macroeconomic Variables

Economic Indicators	Chase Econometric	Hollenbeck Microsimulation	Netherlands study	Japanese study
Inflation	Over the 1970–1983 period, consumer price index rises 4.7% more with than without pollution control policy. The average annual rate of inflation due to the policy .6%.	For the steady-state investment profile, the consumer price index is .35% above what it would otherwise be.	Consumer price index increases by 1.2% after 7 years, due to the policy.	Average sectoral price increases range from 1.9 to 3.1 percent over the planning period with the result dependent on target level of abatement selected.
Economic growth	The policy causes a short-term increase in real GNP, but by 1983 GNP is 2.2% below the baseline.	There is a decline in real GNP, but the percentage cannot be calculated from reported data.	Total production declines by 3.6% after 7 years, due to the policy.	GNP rises during the first years of policy implementation, but then falls, with the net effect being slightly positive.
Unemployment	The unemployment rate is lower during periods of high investment caused by the policy, but by 1983 is 4% higher than baseline.	Employment is reduced by .21% with the greatest reduction falling on the low-skilled.	Employment declines by 1.3% after 7 years, due to the policy.	The employment pattern is similar to the output pattern, and over the period only a few extra jobs are created.
Investment	Approximately 40¢ of each dollar of abatement investment represents the diversion of alternative private investments. The greatest adverse impact is on residential construction.	Not considered in the model.	Investment (excluding housing and environment) declines by 7.1% after 7 years, due to the policy.	Not considered in the model.
Specific sectors	All industries show some price increases with the greatest impact in utilities, nonferrous metals, paper, autos, iron and steel, stone, clay and glass, chemicals and	Utilities; primary iron and steel; agriculture; mining and construction; and stone, clay and glass experience the largest price increases.	Biggest employment reductions felt in agriculture and services, with some increases in building construction.	Some employment increases recorded for the metals, machinery, and construction industries. Slight reductions are recorded for the food, pulp and paper, and other manufactured goods.

reflect these relationships and the economy adjusts until a new equilibrium is achieved.

The direction of all of the main economic effects is similar in the Chase and Hollenbeck analyses. However, while there is consistency in the estimated impacts on inflation, the finding of consistency should be interpreted quite carefully. The Chase analysis reflects both the air and water pollution abatement programs, while the Hollenbeck study estimates the impacts generated only by the stationary source air pollution program.

When one compares the detailed results from the two studies, some important differences are observed. For example, while the Chase analysis reports increases in *all* prices,[9] Hollenbeck's results suggest some price declines in the industrial machinery, furniture, and other nondurable and durable categories. These declines are somewhat difficult to interpret.[10]

To check the generality of its results, the Chase analysis can be compared with two other macroeconometric studies—one for the Netherlands and the other for Japan. Both of these studies estimate impacts on aggregate variables similar to those in the Chase study. However, the nature of the environmental policies that are evaluated differs from those of the United States since the Netherlands and Japan have different kinds of environmental policies. As a result, our comparison will be limited to the *direction* of the impacts.

Consider first the Dutch analysis, the results of which are summarized in the third column of table 6-4. This study is a regular part of the econometric modeling program at Holland's Central Planning Bureau. The policies evaluated in the study are: (1) construction and operation of waste treatment plants, (2) end-of-pipe controls on industrial water discharges, (3) the adaptation of automobiles for pollution abatement purposes, (4) the desulfurization of gas and fuel oil and (5) the removal of nonchemical wastes.

The estimated investment and annual costs necessitated by these policies were used as inputs in the Dutch model in much the same way as in the Chase analysis. The policy alternatives were differentiated according to the time period over which the expenditures were implemented. Both seven and twelve year variants were considered. The directions of the impacts on aggregate variables are similar in both variants. As one might ex-

---

[9] See table 6-5.

[10] On pp. 164–165 of his dissertation "The Employment and Earnings Incidence of the Regulation of Air Pollution" (University of Wisconsin, 1976), Hollenbeck explains decreases in the nominal prices of goods as resulting from decreases in unit labor costs that are associated with increases in unit investment costs.

pect, the magnitude of the impacts for most variables is greater when the policy is assumed to be implemented during a shorter period. As the third column of the table 6-4 indicates, the results are similar in direction to those of the Chase and Hollenbeck studies.

The impacts on specific sectors of the economy differ in the Dutch study and the two U.S. studies; this is to be expected, given the rather different kinds of policies that are evaluated. The increases in employment in building construction predicted in the Dutch study would seem to contradict directly the implications of the Chase analysis (where substantial private investment is foregone, because of the diversion of investment capital into pollution abatement equipment). In the Chase model, one expects and finds a decline in employment in the construction industry (see table 6-5).

The Dutch and U.S. studies also show contradictory effects for the agriculture and the service sectors where the Chase results forecast employment increases rather than decreases. The Dutch and U.S. results may be explained by differences in the policies, the composition of the sectors, or the structure of the economies themselves. They highlight a basic point, however, namely, that our understanding of the sectoral impacts of environmental policy is quite limited.

This uncertainty becomes even more troublesome when the Japanese results are considered. Like the Chase and the Netherlands studies, the Japanese results are also derived from simulations with a macroeconometric model. Their model, however, contains substantially more sectoral detail than the other two. Three direct impacts of environmental policy are accounted for in the Japanese analysis: (1) the expansionary effects of the required antipollution investment; (2) the contractionary effects of the cost and price increases necessitated by the pollution control investments; and (3) the structural changes in sectoral demand and output. These effects are assumed to be stimulated by government regulations designed to reduce air and water emissions to target levels in the period from 1972 to 1977. Both a high and low target were used in the analysis.[11]

This study estimated the required annual private investment to achieve both the air and water targets by using technical coefficients describing the "required investment per unit of pollution abatement" for sixty sectors. The cost and price effects were also estimated at this level; after interactions with a macroeconometric model of the Japanese economy, the

---

[11] Unfortunately, the results of these exercises were not, to our knowledge, subjected to evaluation after the fact, now that the actual effects of environmental policies over this period are known.

TABLE 6-5   *Estimated Impacts on Individual Industries*

(percentage change)

Industry	By 1978			By 1983		
	Prices	Output	Employ-ment	Prices	Output	Employ-ment
Agriculture	0.3	−0.8	+0.6	0.6	−1.3	+1.3
Mining	0.4	−1.2	−0.1	0.7	−2.5	−0.4
Construction	0.1	−2.1	−0.4	0.2	−3.5	−0.2
Food	0.7	−0.5	+0.7	1.2	−1.5	+1.2
Tobacco	0.2	−1.0	+0.6	0.4	−2.7	+0.9
Textiles	0.5	−1.4	−0.1	0.9	−2.5	−0.2
Apparel	0.3	−1.2	−0.2	0.5	−2.2	−0.6
Lumber	0.6	−4.4	−1.3	1.5	−4.4	−0.6
Furniture	0.3	−1.5	−0.7	0.5	−3.1	−1.3
Paper	3.0	−1.3	−0.2	6.2	−2.9	−1.0
Printing	0.2	−1.2	−0.1	0.3	−3.1	−1.3
Chemicals	1.7	−1.2	−0.3	4.8	−2.8	−1.1
Petroleum	1.6	−1.0	+0.4	2.3	−2.0	+0.7
Rubber	0.6	−1.6	−0.5	1.0	−4.2	−1.4
Leather	0.4	−0.8	0.0	0.9	−1.4	−0.3
Stone, clay & glass	2.0	−2.0	−0.7	3.2	−3.4	−1.0
Iron & steel	2.3	−1.4	−0.2	4.1	−2.9	−0.3
Nonferrous metals	5.4	−0.7	+0.4	8.1	−2.4	+0.3
Fabricated metals	0.4	−1.2	0.0	0.8	−3.1	−0.6
Nonelectrical machinery	1.0	+0.2	+1.1	2.8	−1.6	+0.3
Electrical machinery	0.5	−1.4	−0.3	1.2	−3.5	−1.0
Autos	2.5	−2.1	−0.5	5.5	−5.6	−2.4
Other trans. eqpt.	0.3	−1.0	+0.2	0.6	−0.9	+0.8
Instruments	0.2	−0.7	+0.4	0.4	−2.7	−0.4
Misc. manufacturing	0.2	−0.9	+0.3	0.4	−1.7	−0.7
Transportation services	0.3	−1.1	+0.4	0.5	−2.7	+0.5
Communications	0.2	−1.2	±0.1	0.4	−4.0	−1.5
Utilities	15.2	−0.7	+0.5	27.8	−1.8	+0.6
Trade	0.3	−1.0	+0.2	0.6	−2.7	−0.8
Finance, insurance & real estate	0.5	−0.8	+0.1	0.8	−2.4	−1.0
Other services	0.4	−1.1	+0.8	0.7	−2.6	+1.6

Source: Chase Econometric Associates, Inc., *Macroeconomic Impacts* p. 18.

macroeconomic effects were decomposed into the implications for each of twenty sectors for each of the years from 1972 to 1977.[12] The last column in table 6-4 summarizes some of the key conclusions of this study.

[12] The effects of this investment on costs and prices were estimated for the same sixty sectors through a dynamic response model that estimated the sectoral cost and price changes through time. This price effect was then used to adjust those equations in a macroeconometric model of the Japanese economy that included the relevant sectoral price deflators. Then, the effects estimated in the first two steps were incorporated in a 140-equation macroeconometric model of the Japanese economy. This resulted in estimates of the effects of policy change on macroeconomic

The Japanese analysis is a comprehensive one and does take into account many of the channels of impact. There are some limitations to the study, however. First, it ignores the possible demand-reducing effects from industrial financing of pollution control investments. This could account for the difference between the macroeconomic results of this study and those undertaken for the United States and the Netherlands. Second, the Japanese study does not undertake an analysis of the entire complex of environmental policy, but only a subset of the full policy. Third, the consumption demand effects and the transformation from macro- to microeconomic effects are based on arbitrary and unspecified behavioral assumptions. While not completely unreasonable, they could be improved by additional estimation. Finally, no explicit response in the labor market is incorporated into the estimates, nor are operating costs taken into account. These things notwithstanding, the study does trace numerous economic impacts of environmental policy back to rather detailed sectors of the economy. It also presents the estimates over time.

Limitations of Economic Impact Analyses

Like all empirical work, the analyses described in the previous section have numerous limitations. The available data have to be molded to fit the models; basic relationships are not known with reliability and some effects reflect judgment as much as analysis.

Before considering the implications such analyses have for several general policy debates, it is important to reemphasize a major shortcoming of each of the two kinds of models providing evidence for such debates. First, we must realize that the macroeconometric models are very aggregative and capable of misleading us about the effect of environmental policies on a particular sector, especially if that sector is small. This will be so even if the model correctly predicts the overall size of the change in which we are interested. On the other hand, the microsimulation models—while very good at providing us with sectoral detail—do not give us any idea of the *timing* of the changes. Yet this timing may be as important as the changes themselves.

Because of the limitations inherent in each approach, there is no single methodology for evaluating both the macroeconomic and the sectoral im-

---

variables (GNP, capacity, monetary variables, and balance of payments) for each of the years from 1972 through 1977. An input–output model was used to estimate the output and employment effects by sector from the macroeconomic outputs.

plications of environmental policies. Moreover, no future modeling effort—even one which consistently combines both macroeconometric and microsimulation methods in a dynamic way—will overcome what is perhaps the most important shortcoming of impact evaluation efforts. This involves the lack of appropriate data for modeling the economy, and the inability to estimate reliably the role of environmental variables in the basic behavioral relationships on which such models rest.

Some Assertions and the Evidence

As is true for other controversial policy issues, advocates and opponents of environmental policy have forecast differing economic effects of such policy. As often as not these assertions have little basis in fact. In this section we will deal briefly with three issues that have attracted attention in the environmental area. Each of the issues we consider has arisen because of the assertions of various advocacy groups on the basis of information that is far from complete.

The "Capital Crisis" and Environmental Policy

It has often been argued that the expenditures required for pollution control equipment will impose a substantial strain on financial markets. By mandating investments in pollution abatement equipment, it is suggested, federal policy will divert capital from more productive, growth-inducing investments in plant and equipment. When the capital needs for abatement equipment are added to the other projected capital requirements for the next decade, the strain will be too great. Private savings will be unable to meet the demand for funds, the argument proceeds, and the aggregate economy will suffer as a result.

While there are many implications which can be drawn from previous studies, this is not one of them. The argument does not seem to reflect an accurate appraisal of the process of capital formation in the United States. The macroeconomic studies discussed earlier—especially the Chase study—fail to support this assertion.[13] Even when the diversion of invest-

---

[13] It should be noted, however, that formal microsimulation models of a firm's behavior would lead one to conclude that environmental policies have the potential of affecting those decisions involving the level and timing of investments in productive capital, as well as replacement investments.

The macroeconomic effects do not appraise the empirical magnitudes of these effects. Rather they are conditional on prior estimates of investments in pollution abatement equipment and *assume* that environmental policies do not have a sufficiently strong impact at an aggregate level to change the structure of estimated investment equations.

ment unrelated to pollution but induced by federal environmental policy is taken into account and the investment in abatement equipment is treated as nonproductive, the macroeconomic estimates yielded by the model suggest that the impact of environmental policy on real GNP is negative but quite small. Over the full period considered, real GNP (in the BASE-CEQ scenario shown in table 6-3) continues to grow at a somewhat reduced rate. Thus, while the required pollution abatement investments serve to reduce real GNP, they are not sufficient to inhibit its growth.

This result is supported by two recent studies on the availability of private investment capital commissioned by the Joint Economic Committee. These studies concluded that the slow rate of U.S. capital formation in the recent past was the result of imbalances and inefficiencies caused by the persistent inflation and recession. Rather than readjusting our environmental targets to more "realistic" levels because of a capital shortage, the studies indicated that fiscal policy should aim for consistent, noninflationary expansion of aggregate demand to stabilize the setting within which investment decisions must be made.[14] In fact, a recent Department of Commerce evaluation of the business fixed investment required over the period from 1975 to 1980 estimates that total investment as a percentage of GNP, including both the requirements for pollution abatement and equipment changes necessary for reduced energy dependence, will be at about the level of past experience.[15] The ratio of the cumulative business fixed investment to cumulative GNP for this time span is about 12 percent, which is slightly below the mean for this ratio in the 1950s as well as in the pre-recession year of 1973.

Thus, some nonpollution investments will be foreclosed because of the investment necessitated by environmental policy. However, the results of the Chase econometric analysis suggest that this effect is sensitive both to

---

[14] See Barry Bosworth, "The Issue of Capital Shortages," in *U.S. Economic Growth From 1976 to 1986: Prospects, Problems and Patterns*, vol. 3 *Capital*, Congressional Joint Economic Committee, 94 Cong. 2 sess. (1976); and Robert Eisner, "The Corporate Role in Financing Future Investment Needs" in *U.S. Growth From 1976 to 1986: Prospects, Problems and Patterns*, vol. 3 *Capital*, Congressional Joint Economic Committee, 94 Cong. 2 sess. (1976).

[15] For discussion of the BEA estimates see Beatrice N. Vaccara, "Some Reflections on Capital Requirements for 1980," *American Economic Review Proceedings* vol. 67 (May 1973) p. 125. She notes:

> In order to assure a 1980 capital stock sufficient to provide for increasing productivity, full employment levels of output, pollution abatement and decreasing dependence on foreign sources of petroleum, during the period 1971–80, non-residential fixed investment (in 1972 prices) needs to total $1,473 billion or 11.4 percent of GNP.

the timing of the pollution control investments and to the condition of the economy. Therefore, rather than treating the goals of stabilization and environmental policies as in conflict, it may be useful to consider the avenues for complementarity. For example, if fiscal policy is to be expansive in nature—implying an increase in public spending—the possibility of subsidizing environmental investments should not be ignored. Such policies are not farfetched and might well be evaluated in terms of the Swedish experience with the coordination of environmental policies and macroeconomic stabilization.[16]

Jobs Versus the Environment

Industrial and union spokesmen often assert that stringent environmental regulations force plant closings and associated losses in employment. According to this view, the loss of jobs is a "natural" consequence of environmental policies.

As a result of these concerns, EPA has initiated the Economic Dislocation Early Warning System which reports the number and size of plants closed because of environmental standards, and the associated loss of jobs. The evidence from these reports suggests that the magnitude of these impacts is quite minimal from a national perspective. The most recent report of the system suggests that from January 1971 through December 1976, only 98 plants were closed because of environmental standards, causing a loss of 19,580 jobs.[17]

In effect, this view focuses only on the negative employment effects of environmental policy that result from reduced output effects associated with higher prices; it ignores the employment that is stimulated by the production of pollution control equipment as well as the beneficial effect of the pollution abatement. One of the basic contributions of the microsimulation and macroeconometric studies discussed earlier is that they permit consideration of all of the impacts simultaneously—both negative and positive. These models recognize that public expenditure and regulatory programs impose additional demands on the economy, in addition to diverting resources and increasing some costs. This occurs because there is *no* dollar-for-dollar substitution between investments in pollution abatement equipment and all other private investment. As we have indicated, the results discussed above suggest that during periods of unemployment comparable to those in most of the Western industrialized

---

[16] See Haveman, "Employment and Environmental Policy."
[17] See BLS Bulletin no. 1836.

nations in 1977, it is appropriate to consider the ways in which environmental programs can be designed to act as short-term economic stimuli coordinated with stabilization policy.

Regional Versus National Impacts

Finally, it is often suggested that the adverse localized effects of environmental policy will be severe despite the relatively modest impacts at a national level. While environmental policy may, on occasion, cause plants to shut down, it must be emphasized that this is not the only regional impact such a policy will have. In order to better understand the array of impacts that a particular environmental policy may have on a region, it is useful to distinguish the options available to a firm facing the regulations established by that policy. To begin with, we will assume that not complying with the regulations is not feasible, recognizing full well that for the short term, at least, it may well be a viable strategy (see chapter 2). For our purposes, we will assume that the firm has two options—it can acquire the equipment necessary to comply with the regulations, or it can shut down the plants involved. Clearly, those facilities that are closed will be those of marginal efficiency. Nevertheless, the bulk of popular attention has focused on the plant closings and employment losses.

Such adverse effects are only one side of the coin regarding regional impacts. What those who make much of these impacts fail to recognize is that the *net* stimulative effect of environmental policy at the national level must work to the advantage of individual regions and industries as well. Just as costs are concentrated regionally and industrially, so too are benefits. Some regions and industries are bound to benefit because of the jobs created in meeting the demands for pollution abatement equipment. Similarly, the construction industry will be benefited in whatever locality a new waste treatment plant is constructed. Some indication of the regional origin of these demands is given in figure 6-3, which is a map of the contiguous United States with the shaded areas identifying the level of air pollution abatement expenditures in 1975 by state. These expenditure levels would be higher and the pattern might be different, of course, if water pollution expenditures were included.

Table 6-6 presents the early warning job loss data cited above on a regional and industrial basis. Ten EPA regions are identified, along with seven industries. (Figure 6-4 shows the ten EPA regions.) This does show that the job losses are not spread evenly over the country when environmental regulations are established. For example, over one-fourth of actual job losses and 90 percent of the threatened job losses are concen-

FIGURE 6-3 *Manufacturers' Air Pollution Abatement Capital Expenditures, by State: 1975*

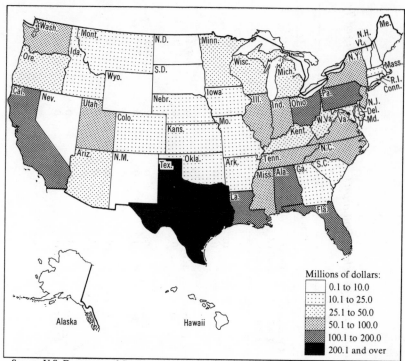

Millions of dollars:
	0.1 to 10.0
	10.1 to 25.0
	25.1 to 50.0
	50.1 to 100.0
	100.1 to 200.0
	200.1 and over

Source: U.S. Department of Commerce, *Pollution Abatement Costs and Expenditures 1975* (Washington, D.C., March 1977).

trated in region V. Indeed, if still more detailed categories were identified, the concentration of the losses and the local impacts would be even clearer. It was this sort of localized effect which caused the EPA to grant steel plants along a 24-mile stretch of the Mahoning River in Ohio an extension for meeting the Federal Water Pollution Control Act regulations. In effect, a rough-and-ready comparison of the benefits and the costs associated with improved water quality in the Youngstown-Warren region led to the judgment that this region should be given additional time to comply with the regulations.[18]

[18] Senator Edmund Muskie spoke precisely to this problem of the regional concentration of adverse employment effects in debate on the 1972 Amendments to the Clean Water Act. He stated:

The balancing test between total cost and effluent reduction benefits is intended to limit the application of technology only where the additional degree of effluent reduction is wholly out of proportion to the costs of achieving such marginal levels of reduction for any class or category of sources.

TABLE 6-6 *Jobs Affected: Actual and Threatened Closings Where Pollution Control Costs Were Alleged To Be a Factor, January 1971 Through December 1976*

Regions	Primary metal industries	Food & kindred prods.	Chemicals & allied prods.	Paper & allied prods.	Stone, clay, glass & concrete prods.	Fabricated metal prods.	Other industries[a]	Totals
I								
Actual	0	0	0	0	0	30	700	730
Threatened	0	0	0	0	0	0	74	74
II								
Actual	124	252	1,505	1,677	0	750	924	5,232
Threatened	0	0	0	0	0	0	0	0
III								
Actual	94	105	590	0	0	102	1,021	1,912
Threatened	0	204	38	0	0	0	533	775
IV								
Actual	942	0	0	217	0	0	0	1,159
Threatened	0	0	0	0	0	0	0	0
V								
Actual	670	165	2,230	500	210	0	1,778	5,553
Threatened	24,250	0	435	200	228	0	3,100	28,213

									Grand total
VI									
Actual	1,440	0	43	0	0	0	0	0	1,483
Threatened	0	0	400	0	0	0	0	0	400
VII									
Actual	70	272	0	0	0	0	0	0	342
Threatened	0	25	0	0	0	0	0	0	25
VIII									
Actual	0	0	0	0	0	0	0	0	0
Threatened	0	0	0	0	0	0	0	0	0
IX									
Actual	438	165	46	103	748	0	35	0	1,535
Threatened	1,810	0	0	0	0	0	0	0	1,810
X									
Actual	0	190	0	833	0	83	510	0	1,616
Threatened	0	0	0	0	0	0	0	0	0
Total									
Actual	3,778	1,149	4,414	3,330	958	965	4,968		19,562
Threatened	26,060	229	873	200	228	0	3,707		31,297
Grand total	29,938	1,378	5,287	3,530	1,186	965	8,675		50,859
Percentage	59	3	10	7	2	2	17		100

Notes: Economic dislocation information is compiled and reported by EPA regional offices. Dislocations involving fewer than 25 jobs are not reported.

Source: U.S. Environmental Protection Agency, *Quarterly Report to the Secretary of Labor on the Economic Dislocation Early Warning System* (1976, fourth quarter) attachment C, sheet 2 (as revised by EPA, February 14, 1978).

[a] Includes all dislocations where the combined "actual" and "threatened" plants amount to fewer than five.

FIGURE 6-4   Regional Offices of United States Environmental Protection Agency

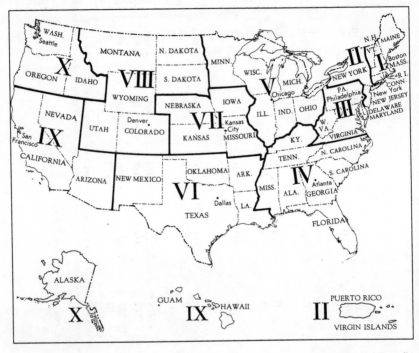

Source: U.S. Department of Commerce, Bureau of the Census, *Pollution Abatement Costs and Expenditures, 1975* (Washington, D.C., March 1977) p. 6.

Turning to the beneficial side of the ledger, it is important to note that the regional impact of the abatement expenditures does not necessarily correspond to the geographic pattern of the expenditures as given in figure 6-3, for example. It seems likely that the demands placed on a locally oriented industry, like the construction industry, will be met in the region creating the demand. However, the demands for products produced by an industry serving a national market—for example, the pollution abatement equipment industry—are likely to be concentrated in regions where the production capacity is located. Although both of these represent positive regional impacts, the foregone nonpollution investment also has a regional dimension. In any case all of these effects—job losses due to plant closings and foregone nonpollution investment and employment increases from expanded construction and the production of pollution abatement equipment—must be considered in appraising the effect of environmental policy on any particular region. These net impacts are, after all, what the models we described earlier sought to appraise for the economy as a whole. It is not fair to cite but one side of the coin and then "cry wolf." While all of these effects are, in principle, amenable to regional analysis, we know of no comprehensive estimates of net regional impact.

Implications for Policy Making

It may seem pretentious to suggest that the studies conducted to date offer information sufficient to improve the policy-making process. Detailed recommendations would certainly be unwise. Nonetheless, several broad guidelines do seem to emerge from our discussion of these studies. To begin with, we can state that the contrasting positions mentioned at the outset of this chapter are both inaccurate views of the relationship of environmental policy to the economy. The analyses conducted to date suggest that environmental policies will not cause sizable reductions in real GNP or employment, nor are they the boon to the economy claimed by some of their proponents. For the time being, and given the state of our knowledge of the role of environmental resources in the economic processes, it does seem that some tradeoffs will be necessary. On the one hand, existing environmental policies are not likely to be catastrophic. On the other hand, the assertions of Environmentalists for Full Employment regarding the complementarity of environmental policy and full employment are overly optimistic.

More concretely, we can identify four broad areas for improvement in environmental policies.

1. *Coordination of Environmental Measures with Stabilization Policies*

Pollution control decisions are the result of two sets of influences. The first arises from congressional mandates that offer the broad guidelines and objectives of policy in the area of environmental quality. Administrative agencies and the courts in turn translate these goals into specific policy measures through their individual actions. As a result of this process, primary attention has been focused on the effects of alternative specific policy mandates on households and firms—that is, the second stage of the process.

Thus we have often tended to neglect the fact that Congress mandates a wide array of goals, frequently failing to recognize that all cannot be achieved simultaneously. Inevitably some administrator is required to trade off one set of objectives for another. Or, worse yet, the compromises will arise indiscriminately from the conflicts between different administrative agencies. Such conflicts only serve to confuse and blunt all policy—both the objectives of stabilization and environmental programs. Often they foster waste of public resources.

Since all the analyses of the macroeconomic effects of environmental policies indicated that these effects depend in an important way on the conditions of the aggregate economy at the time they are implemented, increased coordination of environmental and stabilization policies should be an important goal in any revisions to the policy-making process. For example, some types of environmental policies provide a stimulus to certain classes of economic activity and hence offer a viable component for an expansionary fiscal policy. With such coordination, environmental objectives need not take a back seat to the goals of full employment and price stability. There are opportunities for cooperation rather than independent, mutually self-defeating actions, and these must be recognized.

2. Understanding the Sectoral Effects of Environmental Policy Measures

The formulation of sound environmental policies requires an understanding of the sectoral impacts that are generated. As we have emphasized, these policies will impose increased demands on a variety of economic sectors. Some sectors can respond faster than others to these demands. The more policies push the rate of response to its limits, the more likely it is that they will invite unwanted and, often, unanticipated side effects. The micro and macro models and their associated interindustry components suggest that in defining environmental programs we should strive to anticipate and plan for these unexpected contingencies. For example, offering substantial tax rebates to those installing solar panels (to reduce fossil fuel air pollution) invites difficulty if solar panel producers cannot respond quickly to dramatic increases in the demand for their products. In most cases firms forecast future demand based on past patterns. Such sudden increases in demand resulting from well-intentioned programs can result in rapid price increases and invite mediocrity in final products as firms struggle to meet these demand increases.

In formulating environmental policies, care should be exercised to ensure that the full range of sectoral effects of the policy are understood and that ameliorating measures are implemented when undesirable side effects can be anticipated.

3. *Adjustment Assistance*

It is often suggested that a program of compensation is necessary to cope with the employment losses associated with forced plant closings. While information on the magnitude of the direct effects (given in table 6-6) suggests that they are likely to be small, there is nonetheless concern over the potential for a severe total impact on a given region. On the other hand, it has often been argued that special adjustment assistance programs designed to cope with regional dislocations may induce undesirable responses from firms and individuals. For example, households may be enticed to remain in the area of a plant closing, if they are assured of support there. The resulting reduction in labor mobility is undesirable. In addition, firms recognizing that the threat of a plant closing will result in subsidization, postponement, or even a relaxation of compliance requirements may attempt to disguise the extent of the real impacts and the nature of their intentions. In both cases it will be difficult and costly to determine who a legitimate claimant is and what the extent of a reasonable claim is.

One solution is to designate such effects as transitory and ignore them. The complexity of the processes by which these impacts are spread over sectors, regions, and income classes—as the micro and macro models indicate—suggests that this strategy has some merit. However, because some environmental policies may involve substantial gains to some and losses to others, as chapter 5 points out, some recognition of these distributional impacts seems appropriate.

An alternative to adjustment assistance programs is the use of existing mechanisms for regional assistance through the Economic Development Administration (EDA). That is, one might envisage EDA offering special-purpose, regional assistance where it has been found that plant closings impose serious economic costs on a region. These programs would take effect *after* the closing and would be in conjunction with EDA's general program of promoting regional economic development.

4. *Improving Information*

Any policy or program is only as good as the information on which it is based. It seems remarkable that so little effort has been given to integrating environmental factors into formal economy-wide models. By and large, the appraisals of pollution control programs have had to proceed on an ad hoc basis through adjustments to an existing macro model with an interindustry component. While this process may offer a credible appraisal of the impacts for the short run, it is unlikely to be viable for long-run policy appraisal. One might well anticipate that environmental programs will shift the long-term patterns of consumption and production away from those activities responsible for generating the most emissions (in terms of volume and severity). Unfortunately, with the information available in the models we have discussed in this chapter, we cannot assess the magnitude of such changes. Thus the development of mechanisms for introducing "environmental variables" directly into behavioral models so that the underlying structural changes which may arise from environmental programs can be properly taken into account would seem to be of high priority.

Index

Index

Library of Congress Cataloging in Publication Data

Main entry under title:

Current issues in U.S. environmental policy.

Includes index.
1. Environmental policy—United States—Addresses,
essays, lectures.   2. Pollution—Economic aspects—
United States—Addresses, essays, lectures.   I. Portney,
Paul R.   II. Freeman, A. Myrick, 1936–
III. Resources for the Future.
HC110.E5C87   301.31′0973   78-4328
ISBN 0-8018-2118-5
ISBN 0-8018-2119-3 pbk.